Bush

NEW THEATRE VOICES OF THE SEVENTIES

sixteen interviews from
Theatre Quarterly
1970-1980

D1611950

in series with this book

NEW THEATRE VOICES OF THE FIFTIES AND SIXTIES
selections from Encore magazine 1956-1963

also by Simon Trussler

THEATRE AT WORK
with Charles Marowitz

BURLESQUE PLAYS OF THE EIGHTEENTH CENTURY

EIGHTEENTH CENTURY COMEDY

JOHN OSBORNE
Writers and Their Work

THE PLAYS OF JOHN OSBORNE: AN ASSESSMENT

THE PLAYS OF ARNOLD WESKER: AN ASSESSMENT
with Glenda Leeming

THE PLAYS OF JOHN WHITING: AN ASSESSMENT

THE PLAYS OF HAROLD PINTER: AN ASSESSMENT

JOHN ARDEN
Columbia Essays on Modern Writers

A CLASSIFICATION FOR THE PERFORMING ARTS

EDWARD BOND
Writers and Their Work

ROYAL SHAKESPEARE COMPANY 1978
and annually thereafter

New Theatre Voices of the Seventies

*sixteen interviews from
Theatre Quarterly
1970-1980*

edited by Simon Trussler

*from the original interviews conducted by
Clive Barker, Malcolm Hay, Roger Hudson,
Catherine Itzin, and Simon Trussler,
with a foreword by Martin Esslin*

London
EYRE METHUEN

First published 1981
in simultaneous hardback and paperback editions
by Eyre Methuen Limited
11 New Fetter Lane, London EC4P 4EE

This collection copyright © *1981 Simon Trussler*

ISBN
0 413 48920 5 (hardback)
0 413 48930 2 (paperback)

Acknowledgements

to Clive Barker, associate editor of *Theatre Quarterly* since
1978, for his participation in the interviews with David
Edgar and Snoo Wilson; to Malcolm Hay, assistant editor
of *Theatre Quarterly* since 1979, for his participation in the
interviews with Snoo Wilson and Howard Barker; to Roger
Hudson, co-founder and co-editor of *Theatre Quarterly*
from 1970 to 1974, for his participation in the interviews
with Edward Bond, Bill Gaskill, David Jones, David
Mercer, Tom Stoppard, and Kenneth Tynan; and to
Catherine Itzin, co-founder and co-editor of *Theatre
Quarterly* from 1970 to 1977, for her participation in the
interviews with Edward Bond, Howard Brenton, Bill
Gaskill, Trevor Griffiths, Peter Hall, David Hare, David
Jones, John McGrath, David Mercer, Tom Stoppard,
Kenneth Tynan, and Arnold Wesker.

Phototypeset in 10 on 11 point Plantin
by Carlinpoint Limited, 31 Shelton Street, London WC2H 9HT,
and printed and bound in Great Britain
at the Pitman Press, Bath

Contents

This book
is dedicated to the memory of
David Mercer
and
Ken Tynan

Foreword

by Martin Esslin

If the 'sixties — which started in 1956 — brought us the dawn and the flowering of the new wave of British theatre, the 'seventies, so neatly covered by the first ten years of *Theatre Quarterly,* were a period of consolidation, heart-searchings, and crisis.

There is an old Persian legend about the great poet Firdausi, author of that vast epic poem, the *Shah-Nameh,* being promised by the Shah that he would be paid a *toman* for each line. He completed the poem, many hundreds of thousands of verses, and he was paid. But when he discovered that the sacks of coins that a platoon of porters had delivered at his house contained *tomans* of *silver,* not gold, he felt so hurt that he gave the whole vast sum away as a tip to the porters. In the same way we must be clear in our minds in what currency of theatre we are dealing when discussing the fortunes of 'the British theatre'. The new wave has been and gone, but *The Mousetrap* is in its twenty-ninth year, *No Sex Please, We're British* in its eleventh and, if anything, there are more, not fewer shoddy entertainments for tired business men — and footsore tourists — than twenty-five (or, for that matter, ten) years ago.

But even if we restrict our perspective to the golden rather than the debased currency of the concept of 'British theatre', the situation is by no means encouraging: great progress has been made, but some of it has turned sour, and much of it is endangered from the outside.

What has become of the most promising standard-bearers of the new wave? Osborne has turned from an angry young man into a cantankerous old blimp; John Arden, one of the most gifted of them all, lingers in a self-imposed exile from what he regards as the 'establishment theatre'; Arnold Wesker writes as well as ever, but seems to be excluded from performance in this country; Pinter has lost none of his quality but has become less and less productive; Stoppard and Bond remain active and at the height of their powers. There is something to be thankful for here, but it is not too much.

The main developments of the 'seventies, however, lay in the field of alternative theatre: propped up and nurtured by the various experimental and new writing committees of the Arts Council, this field sprouted innumerable healthy plants during the decade. New styles of presentation — the need to be able to perform in working men's clubs, church halls, and canteens — created new styles of writing and improvisation, and a whole generation of new writers and directors has been engendered by this movement. Many of the personalities represented in this volume sprang from it — Howard Brenton, John McGrath, David Hare, and Snoo Wilson foremost among them.

This is a new generation, very different from the preceding one — more directly politically engaged, more hardhitting. Yet, as the decade reached its end, these writers had increasingly been swallowed up by the establishment theatre, and not always with the most positive results. Howard Brenton in the *Theatre Quarterly* interview here reprinted proclaimed himself 'an anti-Brechtian, a left anti-Brechtian', and went on, 'I think his plays are museum pieces now and are messing up a lot of young theatre workers. Brecht's plays don't work, are about the 'thirties and not about the 'seventies, and are now cocooned and unperformable.' Yet that same Howard Brenton now produces his own 'translation' of Brecht's *Galileo* — somewhat distorted by his desire to make it more left than it actually is — to be put on in a sumptuous, established, quasi-operatic production to the delight of visiting American stockbrokers. And if the same author's *The Romans in Britain* was wrongly — and idiotically — attacked by the prurient *No Sex Please We're British* brigade, it was a sprawling, ill-conceived play nevertheless, overwritten, overgrown, and underthought. Are these the seductions of the lavish establishment theatre?

The 'sixties had seen the founding of a British National Theatre. The 'seventies brought its first profound crisis. The move from the Old Vic into the new building on the South Bank was delayed, over and over again, and the resulting loss of morale, reinforced by the almost total failure of the stage machinery, resulted in an artistic decline of no small proportions. At the same time Britain's parallel National Theatre, the Royal Shakespeare Company, went from strength to strength, consolidating its own style and regularly producing its own star actors out of erstwhile spear-carriers and second gentlewomen. How will the RSC survive its own translation into new lavish buildings in the Barbican?

And is it not ironic that the most highly subsidized, establishment, 'national' theatres should now come under attack from the more radical left elected in 1981 to the Greater London Council, just at the moment when they have become the havens of the playwrights who championed that very left, and so — if theatre is at all effective politically, as they surely believe — assisted its emergence?

Indeed, as the interviews with the writers concerned assembled in this volume clearly show, there *is* an inherent dilemma in such political theatre: there are, on the one hand, the built-in requirements of 'good drama' — that is to say, the need for all the characters to be believable human beings with motivations at least subjectively justifiable, as against the demand of political propaganda for painting them in stark blacks and whites. Too propagandistic a commitment produces, inevitably, cardboard figures and bad drama — and bad drama will inevitably be unconvincing propaganda, while good drama will always also give the other side a fair hearing, and as such displease the pushers of the party line. Brenton, Griffiths, Barker, Hare, Mercer, Bond, and even John McGrath are clearly highly conscious of this dilemma.

In fact, as any thorough study of political theatre in the past clearly shows, plays are not very useful as short-term tactical weapons in the political struggle; but they are immensely powerful in establishing long-term, decisive changes in consciousness — lasting political results.

Even more obvious is another aspect of the matter: the theatre as such — and the established, subsidized sector of it even more so — remains a very elitist institution. The ambulatory, truck-based pioneers of a truly working-class theatre did *not* reach the bulk of the working-class audience; and once the writers of that movement had been swallowed by the establishment sector they lost their foothold in that hypothetical — and idealized — audience for good and all.

Yet what of the genuine medium of our national drama — television? Here there is a truly national, mainly working-class audience, which is being reached by these very writers: McGrath, Mercer, Hare, Griffiths, Barker are or have been television dramatists as much as stage playwrights. The electronic mass media — for radio is also still to be reckoned with — are open and available to these and many other politically-committed playwrights. In spite of their often fully-justified complaints about minor, or major, attempts at manipulating their message, the essence of that message does get through. Indeed, the astonishing expansion of serious playwriting in Britain in the 'seventies owes an immense debt to the mass media: in contrast to America, where serious drama simply does not exist on television, in Britain the electronic mass media provide a sure training ground (and the source of a fairly secure livelihood) for dozens and dozens of highly professional playwrights. In that respect television and radio are highly positive elements in the cultural scene, one of the main safeguards of real quality in the whole field of drama.

And yet, does the fact that so many, and so highly skilful, politically-committed playwrights and directors dominate television drama have any political impact? Again, in the short term, the answer seems decisively: no. Is it that television is watched with such a low degree of concentration? Is it that the serious dramatic material is drowned in the flood of shallow situation comedy and boneheaded police thrillers? Is it that the political message is too subtle, too deeply hidden in the wealth of skilfully observed detail? There certainly seems not much to show for all the devoted work of so many brilliant playwrights. The election that brought in Mrs. Thatcher certainly seemed to point that way.

Here again, we merely encounter the futility of expecting short-term results from political theatre. Over a longer period what matters is the change of consciousness, the gradual *humanization* of increasingly large numbers of people. And in this respect the results already achieved are more than impressive: one only has to see recordings of dramatic offerings of the 'fifties to realize to what an extent the subject matter, the language, and the social range of drama have been widened in the last two decades. It is not only the *Anyone for Tennis* kind of play that has been beaten back into its last bridgeheads in the West End, it is the whole arid, narrow, bigoted, intellectually and morally despicable ethos of an entire way of life that was still dominant in the 'fifties. This is where real revolutions happen — and they *have* decisively happened in this country.

Ultimately this amounts to a merging of form and content: all really good — that is, fully imagined, fully felt, skilfully presented theatre — is deeply political in that it widens perception and consciousness, enables the audiences that are open to it to participate more fully in the lives of their fellow human beings, to develop empathy and sympathy with them, understand their motivations, and comprehend the realities of social and personal existence.

Good, fully realized presentations of the classics can thus be as politically (which is also to say artistically) positive and productive as the work of contemporary playwrights, however committed. It is here that the work of the many brilliant directors this country has produced in the last two decades is of special importance — Bill Gaskill, Peter Brook, Peter Hall, David Jones, to name but those represented in this volume. There are, of course, many, many more.

The live theatre itself may be a minority art — but its impact makes itself felt on a much larger scale: through the mass media, through discussion of the more sensational, outrageous, or titillating events in the press, through the wide radiation of its influence by teachers and other opinion-forming elites. Much, in this context, depends on the level of critical discourse about drama. And it is here that a publication like *Theatre Quarterly* had — and still has — an essential part to play. The daily reviewers in the intellectually more respectable papers maintain, on the whole, very decent standards. But their response is, by its very nature, immediate and impressionistic. To all this a solid source of background information and long-term assessment of trends and personalities is of the utmost importance.

Of all the (all too few) serious theatre journals in the English-speaking world, *Theatre Quarterly* has been the one that fulfilled this task most efficiently, the only one that was free of modish pseudo-intellectualism on the one hand, dry-as-dust academic remoteness on the other; and the only one that strove constantly to back its critical and social insights with thoroughly documented factual material. The selection of interviews with leading theatre personalities of the 'seventies in this volume provides a good sample of the depth and dedication of this endeavour.

The times have gone when the theatre was merely a playground for the shallow and frivolous: the 'sixties and 'seventies have established its claim to the attention of people of high intelligence and serious purpose. Periodicals like *Encore* in the 'fifties and 'sixties, and *Theatre Quarterly* in the 'seventies, did much to change the climate of opinion and to raise standards.

The 'eighties, so much is already clear, will be a period of crisis and violent readjustment. That is the challenge of the new decade: it can only be met through constant and ever-increasing awareness of the problems and achievements of the past, constant and increasing critical insight into the tasks of the present and future. That is what makes publications like *Theatre Quarterly* so essential.

Introduction

by *Simon Trussler*

If, as Martin Esslin rightly suggests, the theatrical 'sixties began as early as 1956, then just as surely had the British theatre moved into a new decade by the end of 1968. When, five years later, we tried to chart in *Theatre Quarterly* the turbulent progress of what was then still called 'fringe' theatre, it soon became clear that the theatrical changes of 1968 were not only a response to but an organic part of a movement for social and political change which had swept the western world.

Pip Simmons, Portable Theatre, the Brighton Combination, Albert Hunt's Bradford group, the original Wherehouse company, and the Welfare State were among the groups formed during those twelve months. The Arts Lab in Drury Lane, Ed Berman's Ambiance, the Roundhouse, the Royal Court's Theatre Upstairs, and the ICA were just some of the new venues which became available in the same period. The Arts Council set up its 'New Activities Committee' in an attempt to comprehend what was happening — and Tony Elliott started *Time Out*, a magazine whose importance in disseminating information about new theatre in London was only fully recognized when, strikebound, its absence from newsstands began severely to affect attendances.

Theatre Quarterly was itself conceived in May 1968 — in part, one of the more sedate sorts of British response to *les événements* in Paris that month, but also an attempt to raise my own spirits, in the wake of a short-lived arts weekly on which I'd found myself involved as theatre editor, and which chose that moment to expire. Persuading a theatre book publisher (appropriately enough, Eyre Methuen) to take the idea seriously took a little longer, and the first issue of *Theatre Quarterly* eventually appeared at the end of January 1971, coinciding with the first-ever extended postal strike in British history — an early response to the 'politics of confrontation' which fired the indignation of many of the writers in this volume.

It didn't seem a propitious omen, and we weren't much cheered by one of the first reviews to appear, following a hasty hand-delivery of press copies from the ramshackle rooms over a paint shop in Goodge Street which served as our first office. Should the magazine survive for a decade or so, predicted an anonymous reviewer in a special issue of the *Times Literary Supplement* devoted to reprint publishing, we'd be just the sort of journal the facsimile industry would be wanting to resurrect — assuming, of course, that by then we'd safely expired. I recalled wryly that my own college library came into possession of its run of *Scrutiny* only when posthumous fame had preserved that once-living organ in printer's aspic.

The later reviews were encouraging in less necrophilic fashion, and I rather liked the *Daily Telegraph*'s description of the editors as 'sober radicals' — a friendly critic's honest attempt to woo readers for us from an unaccustomed political quarter. We weren't too sure about the sobriety, since TQ had been planned mainly in the pubs of the Tottenham Court Road, but we cheerfully acknowledged the radicalism: and, one way or another, the ups and downs of the magazine's existence over the next ten years duly reflected the political mood of the theatre we tried to serve.

For a time — when our first publisher's accountants gave their thumbs down to the venture, after a brave three-year experiment — we even joined the fashionable movement for self-sufficiency. I particularly cherish one issue from that mid-'seventies period, to which I not only contributed my usual share of the editing, but typeset in its entirety on a hired IBM composer, and put into camera-ready artwork at my own desk, with the assistance of a ruler, a set-square, and a tube of Cow gum. Later our methods and equipment became more sophisticated, but I think we all benefited from this experience of 'doing-it-ourselves'.

Although we were grateful for the long association which then began with the University of East Anglia — enabling us to move our subscriptions office to Norwich — there was always a wide gap between the 'academic' image which that name on the masthead perhaps suggested, and the day-to-day struggle for survival in our succession of short-stay premises around London's Seven Dials. But *Theatre Quarterly* continued to straddle the tee-junction of fences where practical theatre, political activism, and academic drama had their awkward conjunction, and I think our 'sober radicalism' helped to steer us clear of any of the narrower ideologies — theatrical, political, or academic.

Is it some measure of our success that the divide between these approaches to theatre today seems less great? Or is it simply that we are all, willy-nilly, now on the same side of the barricades in a struggle that has become ever more politically fraught? This year, savage cuts in university spending have come barely six months after the Arts Council deprived forty of its clients — *Theatre Quarterly* among them — of their grants, with more victims under threat. (And it is another symptom, of far greater severity, but of the same disease, that, as I write, there is rioting on the streets of London, Manchester, and Liverpool, with the list of stricken cities growing nightly.) *Theatre Quarterly* was never under any delusion that the universities, any more than the theatre, could remain calmly detached from the struggle for social change, but we never expected even the most reactionary of governments to tip them so wholeheartedly into the fray.

Just as we tried to reflect the new mood of political concern in the theatre, so we wanted to act as honest brokers between live theatre and the academic kind. It seems scarcely credible that less than a decade ago it was thought unusual for an English-language journal to describe and analyze plays through performance rather than through texts — as TQ regularly began to do in our 'production casebooks', and through reconstructions of notable performances from the past. Now that that approach to performance study has become commonplace, we have started to look at the new vocabulary that it possibly requires — though, as yet, we remain open-minded about the value of theatre semiology. How far the theatre people represented in this volume could helpfully have employed its terminology in describing their work — and how far this would have opened out, how far obscured their intentions — must be for the reader to decide.

Ten years ago, it was, again, a matter of surprise both to the directors and the dramatists we interviewed that we wanted to talk about the 'how' of their craft as well as the 'why' — and not at all about whoever they happened to be sleeping with. We took great pains in our preliminary research — sometimes getting involved in quests for manuscripts which even the dramatist himself had forgotten. (It was, indeed, from such research that our little series of *Theatre Checklists* sprang, offering critical synopses, and other biographical and bibliographial information, about many of the dramatists represented in this volume.)

The interviews themselves seldom took less than three hours, often considerably longer. Usually they were conducted in the subject's own home, but, even then, we often found that the first twenty minutes or so of the taped discussion tended to be the least articulate. So our habit of talking first about a writer's early life not only made chronological sense, but, after a while, also helped to loosen tongues.

Our practice of using at least two (and more usually three) interviewers developed from the initial accident of having three editors — all wanting to chip in — into an invariable policy. Having roughed out beforehand the ground we planned to cover, no single person ever needed to be so mindful of what ought to be asked next that he couldn't follow through an interesting tangent thrown off by some previous answer. Contrariwise, there was always somebody tactfully to steer the discussion back into the mainstream, if some conversational backwater became stagnant. So, in editing, we made no attempt to pluralize the first person singulars in the questions, where these expressed one of the interviewers' own opinions: but we did try to make all the questions as concise as possible — or only as provocative as had proved necessary to elicit a forthright response.

In cold print, this may sound a slightly stilted process: but after a while it became largely instinctive. In any case, theatre people tend to be talkative — and, recording-tape being cheap and recyclable, we always knew we could omit the longer digressions, if these were necessary to clear their own cathartic way forward. However nervous we or any of the interviewers might initially have been, I can remember only one of these conversations which did not conclude with a genuine degree of rapport, or at least of mutual respect. Of the one that *did* end with feathers slightly ruffled on both sides . . . well, whether that can be sensed in print, after our own and the interviewee's corrections, I must again leave the reader to decide — or, in this case, to guess.

It is, perhaps, important to stress that in no sense are these *entrevues véritées*. Such may have a psychological interest of their own, but we were more concerned that our subjects should say what they wanted to say, in the way they preferred to say it, than that all the stutters, false starts, and rhetorical evasions of the spoken word should be faithfully recorded.

In the event, some sort of balance was almost invariably struck in the editing process. A preliminary version was prepared initially from the literal transcripts — cutting irrelevancies and slanders, rearranging material to make consecutive sense, and generally giving the discussion a sequential shape and flow. Sometimes, this version would come back almost uncorrected from the interviewee, but more usually genuine misunderstandings were corrected, elliptic points amplified, and questions we'd forgotten to ask supplied, complete with answers. And the constraints on most theatre people's time served as a built-in corrective against excessive tidying-up, which might have transformed a dialogue into a manifesto. The results, we hoped, were interviews which retained a sense of immediacy, but had the kind of coherence we'd all prefer for our conversations if we thought they were to be set down in some eternal *Hansard* in the sky. The original interviews, as printed in *Theatre Quarterly*, were also, generally, about twice as long as the necessarily condensed versions included here . . .

Although much that has been omitted was of a more topical nature, no attempt has been made here to pretend that these interviews are other than of their historic moment. Sometimes, a director or writer has clearly sustained the direction the interview seemed to suggest: sometimes, there have been shifts of emphasis or direction — and even the occasional U-turn, which, as those urging one on the present government must acknowledge, is not necessarily a bad thing. I have tried in the preliminary note to each interview to sketch in the theatrical and social context of its time, and — especially for the earlier ones — to indicate some of the later developments in its subject's work.

As I write, the future of *Theatre Quarterly* itself remains uncertain. We are producing, somewhat belatedly, the two issues which complete our tenth volume, but as yet are without a publisher for our eleventh. The immediacies of Arts Council cuts aside, it was always the problem of distribution which left us dependent on outside subsidy: and this, too, has its clear political lessons. If some of the erstwhile revolutionary writers in this volume now enjoy the ultimate safety-valve of prestigious production for elite audiences, the establishment has less insidious ways of dulling theatre's political edge. It could not, could it, have been an entirely arbitrary decision that university drama departments bore so disproportionate a share of *their* round of spending cuts?

Theatre Quarterly was given its identity by the three people — all alumni of University College London — who were its founders and first co-editors: Roger Hudson, who left in 1974 to work with the British Theatre Institute, an organization TQ had been instrumental in creating; Catherine Itzin, who left in 1977 to continue her own career in playwriting and directory-publishing; and myself — a lapsed critic with a neo-Arnoldian belief that if the theatre resolutely refused to be organized, it should at least allow itelf to be recorded. Three other people had an important influence in later years — Michel Julian, who became managing editor in 1977, and was chiefly responsible for the success of our campaign to create a new British Centre of the International Theatre Institute; Clive Barker, one of Joan Littlewood's 'scholar clowns', who as associate editor valuably helped to sustain our imaginative drive when I first found myself solo editor; and Malcolm Hay, who contributed much creative thought and practical help as assistant editor from 1979.

In recording my gratitude to all of these, I'd like to add my thanks to Liz Edwards, who ran our Norwich office for five years so apparently effortlessly that we could concentrate on our own London crises; to Sue Papa for her help in the initial work on this book; to Marea Murray, for her assistance with proof-reading and for compiling the index; to Nick Hern, who, as drama editor for Eyre Methuen encouraged *New Theatre Voices* into being — but who also, as one of TQ's earliest contributors, helped to shape the early policy and format of the journal; and, of course, to all the theatre people who gave the interviews which make up this collection.

London, July 1981

NEW THEATRE VOICES OF THE SEVENTIES

1

Bill Gaskill

on directing Farquhar

The career of Bill Gaskill has been almost paradigmatic of the progress of the British theatre since 1956. He first worked in London with George Devine, during the pioneering years at the Royal Court, went on to introduce Brecht to the Royal Shakespeare Company with his Aldwych production of The Caucasian Chalk Circle *in 1962, and in the following year became one of the group of directors under Laurence Olivier who moulded, much in their own image, the National Theatre in its first apotheosis at the Old Vic. Here he continued as associate director until 1965, when he returned to the Court to take over the direction of the theatre following Devine's death.*

During his ten-year tenure as artistic director, Gaskill championed Edward Bond's work in its long struggle against censorship and critical hostility, while also responding to the emerging spirit of the 'alternative' theatre movement — notably, by giving over the whole of the theatre (and often the streets outside) to the memorable 'Come Together' festival of 1970. This, true to its title, did for the first time give the movement a sense that it was more than a fragmented 'fringe', and in 1975 Gaskill himself helped to launch the Joint Stock company, with a policy of actively involving the whole theatrical team in the running of the group, and in the production process.

For many, Gaskill's production of George Farquhar's The Recruiting Officer *for the National's opening season had been revelatory — though, as he himself stresses, it had its roots in Brecht's adaptation of the play, seen during the Berliner Ensemble's influential London season in 1956. I recall, too, a production at the little left-wing Unity Theatre in 1961, which had first fired my own enthusiasm for Farquhar, in whom Gaskill now allowed one to discover a social drive and healthy sensuality refreshingly different from the anaemic posturings of the earlier restoration dramatists.*

By the time Gaskill returned to the National in 1970, to take Farquhar's better-known The Beaux Stratagem *out of the stuffy closet of 'mannered' revivals, the theatre, less certain of its direction, was bringing in star players and prestige directors in a myopic attempt to restore its earlier clearness of focus. When* The Beaux Stratagem *opened, it seemed to have all the hard-edged qualities which had distinguished* The Recruiting Officer *— yet, lacking the constant supervision Gaskill had been in a position to exert over the earlier production, by the time I saw it again, during a special National*

Theatre season in the West End, it had slipped badly, into the well-worn ruts of its leading players' amusing but automatic mannerisms.

This was in the autumn of 1970, by which time Theatre Quarterly *was at an advanced stage of planning, and we asked Bill Gaskill if he would discuss with us for our first issue his approach to directing Farquhar. With my co-editors Roger Hudson and Catherine Itzin, we talked in Gaskill's crowded office at the Court one afternoon in October 1970. Why, we asked him, had he chosen a play by Farquhar, rather than one of his earlier contemporaries, to introduce restoration comedy to National Theatre audiences?*

I think he seems a very grown-up person. I don't feel that he's a bit sniggery, which I do about Congreve sometimes — that for all the brilliance, there's something a bit mean-spirited about him. And there's a kind of pornographic element in Dryden, I think — not real bawdy, but to do with that peculiar semi-poetic sort of metaphor, like using 'dying' for 'coming'.

Yet isn't there something more physical about the sensuality of Farquhar, just because it is less persistently on this level of verbal titillation?

Yes: one's total impression of Farquhar is of someone who is mature. I do think every director has a relationship with the personality of the playwright, even when he's been dead hundreds of years, and I certainly do have this strong affinity for Farquhar.

Why did you decide to do The Recruiting Officer *rather than* The Beaux Stratagem *in the first instance?*

Well, I'd seen *The Beaux Stratagem* in the production in 1949 at the Phoenix, with Kay Hammond as Mrs. Sullen and John Clements as Archer. And this is also a favourite choice of amateur groups — it's a very easy play to perform *reasonably* successfully, and *The Recruiting Officer* was the less familiar play — it hadn't been done in London since Trevor Howard played Plume at the Arts in 1943. And I suppose it was also prompted by seeing Brecht's adaptation, *Trumpets and Drums,* in the Berliner Ensemble season at the Palace in 1956.

Yet there obviously was a new orientation to your production, in the sense that you did strip away the stylistic accretions that had grown up around the play — style for its own sake, as it were.

I think I wanted to do a restoration comedy that was *about* something, and certainly in the recruiting episodes themselves the play offers a kind of socially-critical documentation which goes far beyond that of any other restoration comedy. And, of course, Farquhar does deal with the problems of the working-class people in a way that no other restoration writer attempted. I think this is close to the core of the play.

Did you want to give it contemporary relevance?

I think it *is* relevant, but I didn't want to *make* it relevant. At one time

I considered setting it in the First World War, but before that came to anything Joan Littlewood had done *Oh What a Lovely War*. You have to remember the kind of feeling (which has now disappeared almost completely in the theatre), that almost romantic social awareness of the early 'sixties. For me, it had some relationship to Unity Theatre, which was where I first saw *The Recruiting Officer*, as well as to Joan Littlewood's work. We felt that we had to do plays which had some kind of message, even it we were doing restoration comedy at the National Theatre. You also have to remember that the early work at the National was very much influenced by the Royal Court: both John Dexter and I had worked at the Court with George Devine, and we took three assistant directors with us — and also, very significantly, a certain number of actors. Most noticeable of these would be Colin Blakely and Frank Finlay, both of whom could have played Sergeant Kite and one of whom did. They represented a kind of actor new to the classical theatre, but which we quite consciously wanted to use in a classical company.

And the approach of most of the actors you were working with had been moulded by the then new working-class drama?

That's not entirely true. Bob Stephens was a product of the Court, and so was Colin Blakely: but Maggie Smith had worked almost entirely in the West End and in revue. It is true, though, that when a company's been together for six or seven years — as this had by the time I directed *The Beaux Strategem* — an attitude to plays has been settled which a director finds it very difficult to get inside. Whereas when we did *The Recruiting Officer* we were creating our own company, which knew that it had been chosen by Olivier and Dexter and me. That produced a particular sense of relaxation. *The Beaux Stratagem* was much more difficult to do, and I would say a less enjoyable assignment. Besides, the cast I had for *The Recruiting Officer* was much stronger, both as a group and in individual performances. They were less stamped with any kind of blanket approach to acting than they are now.

You do feel there is a tangible National Theatre style?

I suppose so. But there are also just faults that actors get into. Doing things that draw attention to themselves and not to the characters or the play. Easy misinterpretations. Always attempting to see the thing in terms of the business *they* will do or what *they* can make a part into rather than what the part is. When I did *The Beaux Stratagem* the first thing I did was write to the cast and tell them not to think of it in terms of accents, because I knew that was the first thing they would do playing peasants — put on funny voices.

And yet The Recruiting Officer, *in particular, did achieve a quite distinctive style of its own. There was a certain roughening of the edges, a coarsening of the grain, as opposed to the usual 'mannered' approach: but at the same time there was a greater verbal clarity about the production than is customary in restoration comedy. Wasn't this the intention from the outset?*

Yes, but you see the process from the outside. You think that a director comes along and wishes to change something, that he has a kind of purpose and says, that's wrong, and what I will do instead is this. It's not usually like that. What I myself try to do is to get to the centre of a play — that always means working directly at the text and getting the maximum from it. I don't just mean in the speaking of it well, but in establishing character and situation and the clarity of what the line *means* before anything else. Now the intention of many directors isn't that, whatever they may say: they go after *style*. I think they have an idea of what style is, that you *do* certain things, behave in certain ways. But what you should actually work at in restoration comedy is to make people say it as if it was them speaking, which is not easy. You've got to tell them, this is *you* saying it: it isn't Millamant, it's you. Now say the line as if you said it. It's not an easy thing to do, and it requires a lot of concentration on the part of the actors.

How do you work on this in the early stages?

I do a lot of work on phrasing because actors are not taught about it. You have to tell them all the time that they must observe the full stops and ignore the commas. You have to teach them how a line is made up, and that they must say the line right through without stopping. You have to drill them into doing that so that it becomes natural, and the line becomes the natural channel of expression. Because nowadays we do speak in shorter sentences and phrases, and so you have to teach actors to get used to a long phrase. You have to do this again and again, quite technically, at the same time trying to feed the actors motivations so that they don't become stale or mechanical in what they're doing. But you do have to keep them tied to the text.

The actor who's getting it wrong is doing what?

He's breaking the sentence up into too many sections. Actors tend to make the short phrase the unit in which they work, using far too much stress and trying to milk too much out of a *phrase* instead of seeing the flow of the *sentence* as the unit in which they must express themselves.

Are there any exercises to help actors with phrasing?

No, you have to teach phrasing, like you have to teach rhetoric. It partly comes from a certain literary knowledge: it's like reading music. You've got to be able to show how the line is made up on the page, and how that affects the way the actors should speak it. I learnt a lot about phrasing from Edith Evans when I worked with her on *Richard III*. She always told me that you must ignore the commas, which is an absolutely crucial instruction.

What is the next step in rehearsals — when you start going beyond the full stops, the sentences-as-units, and knitting them together?

I use a version of Stanislavsky, in which I try to find the intention of a line or a speech. The sentence then becomes the channel through which, emotionally, the intention and the situation of the character will flow. The speaking becomes a principal expression of the objective of a particular section of the scene, and so, very early on, a simplified form of objectives has to be allied to the technical work. I tend to do the two simultaneously and jump from one to the other, so that I work internally and externally in the same rehearsal. I think actors rather like this, instead of being made entirely to improvise for a section, and then to work technically.

How important is the plotting at this stage of rehearsals?

I plot loosely, and rather quickly. In *The Beaux Stratagem*, I had blocked it by the end of the first week, and then I changed it all again when I saw the set. The early plotting is really to give the actors something to do with their bodies while I'm working on their voices. It's like sketching: I just say, you come on here and end up somewhere around there. Now let's start. And they come on, moving around a bit themselves if they feel like it. It's better than doing nothing, because actors get very hung up if you don't give them any instructions at all. If the action's in a room, with doors and windows, it's much easier, because then there are specific places one *would* go to. But if it's a rather open stage with little scenery, actors haven't got much they can do anyway, so you encourage them to be as free as possible, without decorating. And then gradually it gets refined down, you try different things and as you work on the inner meaning of a scene so the moves change and alter. I never create a precise blocking in advance. Very few directors do — though Laurence Olivier is a very precise director. He draws plans with red and green and blue passages along which the actors are to go.

At the same time as you're plotting loosely, are you beginning to give the actors some sense of the period — of its social relationships particularly?

I don't think anyone cares a fuck about whether they bow in the right manner or any of those 'quaint' period things. But there are two problems to solve. One is class attitudes, which have changed, and which actors often find difficult to identify: they use over-simplifications of working-class attitudes — and of attitudes towards the working class. For example, take the way the servants are treated: they are always 'fellow', whereas one's equal would be a 'gentleman'. Actors *always* get that wrong, saying 'fellow' in the modern colloquial sense, to describe an equal rather than an inferior. The other problem is that there are certain things which women do now which they couldn't do then — though curiously enough this wasn't such a difficulty in *The Recruiting Officer* because Silvia is such an outspoken and free person. But even in that play there are certain things which are just horrific to us now, like when Balance hears that his son has died and says, 'I was pleased with the death of my father, because he left me an estate, and now I'm punished with the loss of an heir to inherit mine.' In all the writings of that period, until the family became a cult, there were no sentimental relationships between sons and fathers. All that a father meant to a son was that he inherited his property, and the sooner he died the better. This is a very difficult attitude for actors to understand. I think it's something Brecht said, that when money is the object it cannot be the subject. When the object of people is to make money, they're not going to write about making money: they'll write romantic fantasies, which is how they make their money. So the idea of the happy family around the Christmas fire is really post-Dickens, and then you get a kind of dishonesty in art. I don't think there is that kind of dishonesty in the restoration.

One always feels that there is a directness and honesty about the treatment of sexual relationships in Farquhar, though this is not something you find in his earlier contemporaries.

Yes: so that the writing is not, in fact, particularly sensual, but the characters *are* meant to be. It's a very difficult balance to get nowadays because actors imagine that the sensuality should somehow be expressed by what you say, whereas obviously people in those days were extremely physically aware of each other, so that in the plays the writing is often a kind of defence between the individual and the open expression of this awareness.

How much do you work on characterization in rehearsal?

I try not to talk about the characters very much, and to prevent actors from talking about them. It tends to lead to a concept of character as something static, and so to faults in playing. I want the actors to feel all the time as though they are really performing actions. So, to keep the thing in movement, I am constantly setting actors new problems, or keeping them at work on old problems, and continuously assessing the results in the run-throughs. I had a run-through of *The Beaux Stratagem* very early on, just to see that the fluidity was still there. It's terribly important in this kind of play not to get bogged down by over-elaborating any one point in it — you must search, of course, but you must keep it in movement, and if necessary go back later to the search.

Are there strongly-distinguished stages in rehearsal, or is this 'movement' a gradual and continuous one?

I find it very difficult to remember dividing the rehearsals into sections. Some of the things I've talked about keep you in work till the show opens. Often a lot of time is spent stripping-down an actor — saying, do less, do less. Or, say it as yourself. Or, don't wave your arms about, do look out front. This is one thing actors cannot understand — how to use the direction of the theatre, how to take a reaction from someone and, while experiencing it, be aware of showing it to an audience.

There must be moments during the rehearsals when certain discoveries about character or situation change the direction of what's happening? Take the character of Sullen in The Beaux Stratagem, *who was presented, surely, as an unusually intelligent person, not the conventional clown.*

Sullen is a difficult character: he does keep coming on and having a scene and going off again. He's very un-integrated into the action of the play, and his best scene is almost at the end, his long dialogue with Sir Charles. This has a lot of substance to it, but it's as if it's a set piece, there only to set up the divorce properly for the final scene.

Gibbet, on the other hand, seemed slightly fantasticated, almost out of a different play. . . ?

I think you have to be careful about assuming that what is stylistic is not there in the part already. Gibbet *is* a very extravagant character. It's a marvellously written part: but the actor has to make clear that this is the character as written, not self-indulgence. This to some extent is true of Foigard as well: it's like an actor playing an actor on stage, the same problem.

Whilst you try to avoid the dangers of actors indulging in amateur psycho-analysis of their characters, in some way relationships between people — between one man and another, as well as between the sexes — do work themselves out. How?

A lot follows naturally from properly establishing the social relationships. It's sentimentalizing on our part, for instance, to suppose that the treatment of the working class was wicked. It was unthinking, but not wicked: and that's much more difficult to catch, actually. It's much easier to give an actor a strong moral intention for good or bad. It's the thing one used to say about Brecht, you know, that one of the most difficult things to present in a theatre is what is habitual, what people do every day without thinking — the habits and social attitudes they've acquired by *custom*. There's no specific moment at which they have to be suddenly shown: they're just *there*, all the time. The upper-class characters mustn't just be rude to the servants in whispers, for example: they have to be told, you can say what you like about the servants aloud, in their presence, you're not worried if it hurts them. This crops up very often in the play: and you have to get it right, because you can't play a psychological relationship until the social relationship is right. Anyway, to me that's what a lot of plays are really about — just about how people live in a society together. Now the individual emotional relationships usually are so indicated by the flow of the action — simply by *what happens* — that you don't have to particularize very strongly. It's much less difficult to make it clear that two people have fallen in love than that they despise their servants without being wicked.

I can see that this could be clear enough in relationships that form during the course of the action. Yet between Archer and Aimwell, and even between Dorinda and Mrs. Sullen, there is an established modus vivendi *before the action has begun. How do you create the sense of their being confidants — as a 'given' of the situation?*

That's one of the things you have to work towards, producing enough real sympathy between these actors. The danger is that they will play objectives which produce antagonisms: they feel, ah, we must play something strong. In fact there's nothing particularly strong to play. It's very common in rehearsal to find two actors who should be just talking easily, playing against one another. You say, no, really you rather like each other, which is a much more difficult emotion to realize.

Part of the social complexity, I suppose, is that there are also middle and merchant-class characters — tradesmen, like Boniface, the Landlord in The Beaux Stratagem. . .

And his daughter Cherry, who is socially hard to place. I mean, they all remark on how extraordinary she is. . .

Do you regard this as a separable part of the play in rehearsal, a sub-plot perhaps?

No, I don't think of it like that. Cherry in the first part seems all set to be a very important character, doesn't she? It's disappointing that Farquhar didn't find a way of writing a good scene for her in the last part of the play, though: she almost disappears, as does her father. I think they're both marvellous creations.

It's perhaps better sustained, this sense of rich social complexity, in The Recruiting Officer.

That's right. There are very few writers who have been so well able to keep a whole cross-section of society moving all the way through a play.

Probably this is one reason why The Beaux Stratagem *is the easier play to do in a conventional restoration manner.*

Yes, I think so. We had endless trouble, for example, in that courtroom scene in *The Recruiting Officer* where all the villagers are present: it's late in the play, a central scene, and you need really good actors, realistic actors, in the smallest parts.

The Royal Shakespeare Company's recent production of The Relapse *perhaps illustrated the kind of 'deeply romantic' approach to restoration comedy one could describe as the opposite of your own. . .*

They all wore black and silver, and huge wigs up to here, didn't they? I thought it was appalling: like a nightmare. It was a new kind of fantastication of design and presentation — to do everything in that colour scheme of black and silver and pink and silver. I don't think they had any feeling that social context was important, and I don't think that they would ever say it was. I think they are interested in theoretical, abstract concepts of what a play is.

This could never be of any value in approaching Farquhar?

Nor any restoration comedy. All of them are plays about people at a certain time in society, about people's social behaviour. You can say Shakespeare's mythical if you like, but you can't say Farquhar has any mythical or allegorical elements. Not for one second.

Is this a positive defect in the RSC, or just a limitation on the range of work they should attempt?

Well, I think it is a defect. I think when you stop remembering how people live and how they behave it's always a danger sign. You need to be pulled back.

You don't attempt to create any sort of abstract quality in your own productions? Not even, say, in occasionally placing actors to make pretty stage pictures?

Sometimes. It's really more like a painter trying to isolate a single moment through the relationship of one person with another.

Do you place actors so as to emphasize power relationships, the dominance of one person over another?

Yes, but in a realistic not a symbolic way, inasmuch as these things are expressed in life. Then the symbolism is inherent, it doesn't need to be stressed. I had great pleasure directing the recruiting scene in *The Recruiting Officer.* It was very difficult, but finally I thought it was one of the best scenes I've ever directed. I felt absolutely satisfied with the relationships of those four people — Plume, Kite, Pearmain, Appletree — on stage.

And you obviously relished directing that slightly set-piece scene at the beginning of The Beaux Stratagem — *the arrival of the stage-coach.*

Yes. We spent really too much time on that. To get it even half-way right was a nightmare. And to *keep* it right. . . ! The group scenes are of course always the most difficult to keep up to scratch.

Did you find you could keep a closer eye on the progress of The Recruiting Officer *in the repertory, as an associate director, then, of the National Theatre?*

Well, yes, but also we had better assistant directors: we had people who were *only* assistants, not in the production as well. When you have assistants whose job is to monitor the production, it is easier to maintain standards. I think they've rather slipped on this at the National.

Do you think that the National Theatre has lost its sense of direction since the earlier days?

I think the invitation to Jacques Charon was the beginning of the end. The moment you pay homage to that kind of theatre, you are wide open to influences that are wrong to a British National Theatre. I think it is without an absolutely clear sense of purpose at the moment — not that a National Theatre should ever be too exclusive, but neither need it be too catholic. I've never felt that a National Theatre needed or ought to be an International Theatre.

2
Kenneth Tynan
the critic comes full circle

Like Bill Gaskill, Kenneth Tynan had been recruited to Olivier's team for the opening of the National Theatre in 1963 — as literary manager, the nearest the British theatre thought it seemly to approach the role of 'dramaturg' on the German model. When Roger Hudson, Catherine Itzin, and I talked to Tynan in his South Kensington flat in September 1970, he had just been eased into the lowlier role of 'consultant', and his residual loyalty to Olivier and the National sat uneasily with the concern he evidently shared with Gaskill at the direction the company was taking.

We'd wanted to include an early interview with Tynan in TQ because, in his own career, he seemed to have epitomized the sort of critical-cum-practical approach to theatre we hoped the magazine would itself encourage. By this time, however, he was more readily tempted into discussing the merits of sexually-titillating theatre — as, presumably, displayed in his erotic revue Oh! Calcutta! *just then launched into its long West End run — or defending the artistry of bullfighting.*

Born in 1927, Tynan had, true to his middle name, peacocked his way through drab, post-war Oxford, and his early critical writing in the old Daily Sketch *and* Evening Standard *was full of articulate enthusiasm for the virtues of heroic acting — as celebrated in his first book,* He That Plays the King, *in 1950. But as weekly reviewer for* The Observer — *more or less continuously from 1954 to 1963 — Tynan's discovery of his own social conscience coincided happily with the emergence of the earliest 'new voices' in British theatre: and, more than any other writer, Tynan at that period gave coherence and a sense of shared purpose to all those concerned with making theatre a force for social change.*

Without undue modesty, Tynan admitted the centrality of his critical role as we weaned the conversation away from the virtues of masturbation and matadors. Though his health slowly declined, he continued to keep a steady eye on theatrical developments — as the interview later in this volume on the work of Peter Brook amply demonstrates. But this, for health reasons, was increasingly at a distance, and it was in California that he eventually died, in the summer of 1980. In his now legendary notice of Osborne's Look Back in Anger, *Tynan had written that he could not love anybody who did not want to see the play: when I learned of his death, I wondered if I could love anyone of my own generation who did not shed a tear at his loss.*

My own concern for the theatre didn't really begin as anything more than an intense fascination with birds of bright plumage — exceptional and irreplaceable individual performers who can produce an indelible emotional or intellectual effect upon an audience. It fascinated me to try to reproduce the fingerprints left by these giant personalities on my consciousness, and that's what I took to be the role of criticism. Then, primarily as a result of seeing the Berliner Ensemble in its early days, I came to a different concept of theatre, the theatre militant, which told me not only about the crisis of the individual, but the crisis of a society. And I was and am convinced that that sort of theatre is the most important.

But now, with the infiltration of the ground formerly belonging to theatre by the other media and arts, I've had to define a little more closely what I believe to be the areas still available to theatre in the future. I think in the last ten years in England the Arts Council and the British theatre in general have tried to hold a long, thin line. Now I believe the time has come to let theatre withdraw geographically and artistically to the ground that it alone can hold — to what one might call citadels of theatre. Geographically, to large population centres, instead of trying to hold every outpost and every village; and psychologically and artistically, to the ground where theatre can most assuredly provide effective opposition to the other arts. One of the ways in which theatre still has a unique role to fulfil is in providing an arena for the exceptional performer — the person whose god-given or life-developed gift is to be able to mould the consciousness of a thousand people in a room at the same time. The other media do not allow this person any leeway. We have seen the exceptional comic doctored, spayed, tamed, domesticated, into situation comedy on TV, and the experience just isn't the same as seeing Lenny Bruce live, or Frankie Howerd live, or Sid Field live.

Another area the theatre ought to hold is the one we began in a very tentative way to explore in *Oh! Calcutta!* — the area of human sexual response, on a social rather than an individual scale. Whether one can discover anything worthwhile about human reactions by removing sexual embarrassment and shame in this way, I don't know. But I think there are many more experiments to be made in this field: the presence of the live performer generates a sort of electricity that very few erotic films can, and the intimacy, the *pressure* of the live event can have exciting, startling, revealing, and of course often titillating results. I don't reject the word titillating, which means to tickle pleasantly.

Politics is a third area, and for factitious reasons I think the live theatre can do much more in this field than the other media. Films for commercial reasons fight shy of politics: they say people don't want to see political films, and so except for fairly low-budget or enormous propaganda movies, you very rarely get a genuinely political film. Secondly, television is either state-controlled and therefore totally propagandist, or, like our own, meant to be impartial and so emasculated eventually — because the other side has to be given equal time to reply. One of the few areas in which the independent political viewpoint can be expressed with no censorship and a quite untrammelled directness is the theatre, and I don't see why it shouldn't become a sort of political cockpit.

How many plays in your own experience reached an audience as directly in this political manner as you would now wish them to do also in an erotic manner?

All I can talk about are the ones that have reached *me* directly. The early repertoire of the Berliner Ensemble — *Caucasian Chalk Circle, Courage, Die Mutter, Arturo Ui.* I was reached by the *Marat-Sade*, but I felt that its politics had been rather betrayed and distorted by the brilliance of Peter Brook's direction. It's quite true, it's very hard to think of an example of political or sexual theatre that has as yet totally worked in changing one's consciousness. Now the best sexual experiences that I've had in theatre were all a long time ago in the very best of the burlesque houses in the United States. The old Howard Theatre in Boston had an extraordinary tradition of stripping, which was on a much higher level than the average burlesque house. But even in the burlesque theatres which were supposed to arouse you to a great pitch of sexual delight, the ushers would be walking up and down the aisles with torches to see if people were masturbating — you see, the dual standard. Similarly, in the political theatre there would always be police waiting outside in case one should march out and take over the Houses of Parliament. Society has its means of preventing with one hand while it encourages with the other.

Theatre is also — and this is the last of the four areas I feel it remains best at filling — wonderfully equipped to refute the McLuhanite heresy. In many of its forms theatre is still a stronghold of the word, and I think will remain one, perhaps even more so than in the past. So those are four jobs I think the theatre can do that the other arts cannot or will not do so well.

I remember that when the Grand Théâtre de Panique did their own version of Arrabal's The Labyrinth *you yourself reacted against their rather intrusive physicality. . .?*

Yes, I was rather irritated by that production. One naked actor was clambering across the knees of other people in my row towards me, and I did have a momentary impulse to get out my cigarette lighter and give him a hot foot. . .

So that you were, in fact, objecting to being brought into close physical contact with an actor, which I should have thought was also an essential ingredient of a truly erotic theatre.

Yes, let us be quite clear about this. I don't want to legislate for any audiences younger than myself, perhaps mine is the last generation of voyeurs. But I do have a tremendous respect for the spheres of activity of the artist and the interpreter, and I want to be the watcher. I want to be involved in the activity *only* psychically. I am a very bad participant — I was the child at pantomimes who refused to join in the community singing. I can't sing, why should I sing? And in that same Arrabal production one of the actors approached me and asked me to tango. Now I don't tango, and I explained this, whereupon he made a farting noise at me and said I was a spoilsport. That I think was an invasion of my own rights. Audiences do have civil rights, and this was an infringement of them.

This presumably means that you are out of sympathy with the activities of the Living Theatre?

Yes, completely. I admired a lot of their earlier work and I admired *Frankenstein*. I didn't like *Paradise Now*, though not only because of the hectoring of the audience. It's particularly infuriating if you've spent the morning drafting an ad. to abolish laws against pot, if you've taken part in a noontime discussion directed towards the abolition of censorship, if you've spent part of the afternoon talking to American army deserters about how to obtain legal recognition in this country, and then you've had a quick discussion with a Trotskyite group about an underground magazine — then to go to the Living Theatre and to be seized by the lapels and held personally responsible for the laws against pot, for the laws restricting the issue of passports, for the persecution of socialist minorities, just makes me want to say, oh, fuck off, I've had enough of this without you accusing me of it. That's my personal gripe against the Living Theatre — and also the curious, whining, masochistic tone of their voice, which I find highly unsympathetic.

Recent developments in theatre do seem to have been shifting it more in a McLuhanite direction. I'd like to agree with you that the theatre will remain a stronghold of the word, yet isn't the recent tendency towards non-verbal performance?

Yes. And I know that to people like Jeff Nuttall this is the theatre of the future, but it's had its heralds for a long time now. Happenings and the theatre of cruelty one first began to hear about in the mid-'fifties and every couple of years a book on the underground and the explosion in the arts comes out and says this is the theatre of the future, and yet you never seem to see anything happening very much. You get Nuttall writing 'Pete Harringay, one of the greatest junk-sculptors in Deptford, put on this marvellous happening in a garage and it blew our minds.' Now I went to the happening fifteen years ago in Hounslow, and it was the same garage, it was the same happening, but it still shows no signs of taking over the theatre, though no one's tried to stop it.

I remember when I first argued this with people like Ken Dewey and

Allan Kaprow I was finally forced down to saying, look, if I get run over, is that theatre? And they would say, yes. And that was to me a breaking down of a valuable frontier I would have preferred to have kept up, the frontier between what is intentional and that which is fortuitous. Now where that which is fortuitous takes over you have what is called human life, which I find riveting. But where the intentional intervenes in the fortuitous you have what we may possibly call art, though I don't like the word. I do think it's a valuable distinction, since a form of theatre that breaks it down is going to be so indistinguishable from life as to be non-theatre, but there did come a point when 'art' meant too many things to too many people. When I for instance first went to a concert of John Cage, when I met and knew action painters for the first time, when I saw happenings for the first time, and I found their supporters and detractors both throwing the word 'art' at each other — 'this isn't art' and 'this is art' — the whole thing seemed to revolve around the definition of a word rather than the analysis of an experience. I felt at that point, any word that has to take under its wing such disparate things as a butterfly being let out of a box by John Cage, and the Beethoven Ninth, is not a useful word.

Have you on the whole felt happy about the later eddyings of the new wave, or do you feel that it's not really kept up its initial momentum?

It's a purely journalistic concept that artistic waves break and then retreat. And only playwrights who read too many papers stop writing their own kind of play because they're told the ebb tide has begun.

But it was surely in part because playwrights did read the papers that there was a certain new activity in the theatre after Look Back in Anger . . .

There was activity on the part of people who saw what I and many other people wrote about it. People began to think, 'Ah, that play I wrote last year the one I'd locked up in the cupboard — now there's a chance for it.' But the plays were there, even if only in embryo: John's was just the first to be done. And *then* the real newspaper readers came in, the hoard of imitators, like the little Pinteretti that are turning up everywhere now. But I don't think that there was a new wave, so I can't think that it's lost its impetus. I think the picture's much more interesting and blurred than that. When there *are* a great many writers writing in the same way, I think it's probably bad for the theatre. A lot of the best writers in English are spending their time in the cinema, which is all right. When they have something that only the theatre can say then they will come back to the theatre. But there is no question in my mind that if I was twenty now and I was a writer, I would not go into the theatre. Except for my masterpiece. I would give my talent to the other media and my genius to the theatre.

Yet ten years ago there was still a certain feeling of coherence about working in the theatre, a feeling of moving in the same direction, though by many different means and with many different playwrights doing the leading. This coherence now seems to be lacking. Do you think what has taken its place is equally worthwhile?

Playwrights never give coherence to a movement in the theatre — only critics and directors do that. Except when you get a playwright who becomes his own critic and spokesman like Arnold Wesker. But on the whole a playwright like Osborne or Pinter will make his own direction and it's really of no great concern to him whether others follow.

But this is still begging the question, because you after all helped to give a certain coherence to the late 'fifties.

That's what I was about to say, being reasonably immodest. I tried to articulate a welcome for a sort of play that had not been common in the English theatre in the years before I was a critic. And I don't find a great many critics writing nowadays who are pointing as many signposts as I tried to do: instead of saying, this room is quite well-furnished but this other room is empty, they are merely saying, this room is quite well-furnished, and not pointing to the empty rooms in the house. That I feel sure is one of the critic's jobs, and I don't think there are many doing that at the moment. But then I didn't have to come to terms very much, as a critic, with the theatre of total gesture, the theatre of total improvisation. The Living Theatre was coming in as I was going out as a critic, so I never had to find an aesthetic to embrace it.

I think this is part of the problem nowadays, to identify the empty rooms.

Sure. Because some of them perhaps ought to be left empty. And that's a critic's job too, to say, get out of that room, it's contaminated.

Do you have regrets that you aren't any longer yourself writing criticism?

None at all. I did it for twelve years, and so did Max Beerbohm. I think that's long enough. After that you are recording not what is actually happening to your sensibility but what you think ought to be happening to it, or what once happened to it. After twelve years of seeing four or five plays a week your reactions have been so trampled on that it takes years of convalescence. You are left with a clear knowledge of what you liked, but the vocabulary of disapproval has begun to pall. Suddenly you become — at least I became — much more interested in concocting the recipe than in being a rented palate.

What were your reactions on being asked to be Literary Manager of the National Theatre?

Well, obviously I knew what Sir Laurence was up to. He's an expert politician. Like Abraham Lincoln. In his first cabinet Lincoln included one of his most virulent opponents, and the man said, 'Why are you doing this Mr. Lincoln?' and Lincoln said, 'Because I'd rather have you inside pissing out than outside pissing in.' But I'd known Larry for a long time, we'd had many conversations about what form a National Theatre should take. And another thing I think he knew was that there would be no direct competition between him and me — he would know from the first that I was not a contender for the job of being Director of the National Theatre. I am not an actor and I am not at the moment a director, so we would not find ourselves at loggerheads. He would also know that any advice I gave him would be disinterested, in that if a production is a success I don't get the praise and if it's a flop I don't get the blame. We complemented each other because he has all the practical skills that an actor and a director could have, and I presumably have the theoretical knowledge: where he was strong I was weak, and vice versa. He almost to a fault protests that he isn't an intellectual, and I almost to a fault protest that I'm not a participant. It's true that I've sometimes been nettled by his reluctance to delegate authority and he's been annoyed at my obtuseness and stubborness and obduracy in pressing causes that he has no sympathy with: but we have never had any bad blood, so the combination has worked out rather well.

How did you begin to tackle — even at the mechanical level — the problem of being confronted with the whole body of world drama, and from this choosing what was to be performed in the first season, the second season, and so on?

Sometimes we sit and argue all night, and we draw up charts and make plans and issue little memos to each other. A little booklet was rather prettily printed, called *Some Plays*, which was simply my own list of all the plays in world drama that could possibly, conceivably be worth reviving in Britain in the second half of the twentieth century. Interestingly, it wasn't a very long list, although I did all I could to make it exhaustive and included everything that might have the least claim to revival. We use this as a reference book when we are planning the repertoire — it's an easy and portable way of finding out what plays John Lyly wrote, or Anzengruber, or Aphra Behn.

Sir Laurence takes the actors' point of view, and his tendency will always be to keep the ensemble together by looking for the right parts for them. My tendency has always been to look for the right plays and the right playwrights, and such differences as we've had have usually occurred when these two aims haven't overlapped, so that we sometimes find ourselves doing plays to make actors happy that were perhaps not plays we ought to have done, and sometimes we've done plays to make playwrights happy or to make *me* happy that we oughtn't to have done. But on the whole the overlapping has been considerable, and greater I think than either of us expected when we first went into this.

You also have advisers who read scripts and give opinions on them?

We have readers, and all of the twenty odd plays that we get each week *are* read, but it's very rarely that we get more than one that's worth even a second reading, and we've never I think put one on. We've either commissioned, or we've known the authors and said, can we have your next play? This is what happened in the case of Peter Nichols. It's simply a case of long, long all-night debates. And the difficulties involved in running a continuing, accumulating repertory are geometrically greater than those of running a seasonal repertory. You have to think of parts for an actor not only for one season but for the next season. You have to know that certain actors will be leaving you, so that if a production is to remain in the repertory other actors will have to take over their parts — and a continuing rep where a play may be in the repertory for five or six years means that the parts have to be re-rehearsed by lots of other actors.

When a new actor joins the company, it's part of his job to take over parts already played by other people. And the time needed to rehearse the replacements for these plays is enormous. We've found that we have to have somebody who does almost nothing else but work out the availability of our actors. I mean, how many hours per day can somebody re-rehearse this play, understudy that part, play a new part in this play, go to the Young Vic to do something on Saturday, then go on tour the following Monday to Newcastle? It's really a computer job, running a large company which has a continuing repertoire.

What ways are there of preventing a play that may be in the repertoire for five or six seasons from going stale? How can actors be stopped from slipping into instant mannerisms, easy ways of getting laughs?

We haven't found the answer to that. We do call re-rehearsals constantly. When a play has been out of the repertoire for even as little as three weeks we have a special dress rehearsal of it before we bring it back in, and new actors are constantly being rehearsed into important parts. But when a director comes back to a production after a year, say, in the States, almost inevitably he will call a rehearsal 'to take out the improvements.' It's a built-in hazard of theatre. All one can say is that whenever the actors know Sir Laurence is out front they tend to revert to the original performance, and we let it be known that he's out front quite often when he's in Brighton.

My impression is that more actors have remained for longer periods in the National Theatre's company than in, say, the Royal Shakespeare's, and that there is a strong rapport amongst these actors — yet nothing like the same sense of directorial continuity.

Well, the Royal Shakespeare is much more a director's theatre, and this, parenthetically, may be the reason why I prefer the National as a place to work: there is not so much scope for a literary manager at the RSC as there is in an actors' theatre like ours. I've always been a great supporter of the bringing in of outside and indeed foreign directors as often as possible. But I was very sad when John Dexter left, because I think he's one of the top six English-speaking directors. He was a tremendous fire in the company's belly, and without him I think a certain impetus was lost. Bill Gaskill always wanted to have his own company, and we all understood when he went to the Royal Court. But you're right, we do need new directors.

Do you follow any particular guidelines in commissioning new plays? Is there any reluctance to accept commissions?

We've tried asking authors of the stature of John Osborne to do adaptations of lesser-known classics, with varying success. But if I was a young author I would undoubtedly prefer to write for TV, because the seed I'd planted would tend to come up much more quickly. I'd finish my script in May, and it could well be seen nationwide in July. In a theatre that has to plan as far ahead as we do, it might not be seen for twelve or eighteen months, and I'd by then be that much older and have gone on to other things. This is a tremendous problem. One TV playwright whom I won't name said to me when I tried to commission a play from him, 'Why should I expose my work to the fangs of twelve critics in the national press after only nine hundred people have seen it? In television sixteen million people have seen it before the critics get their hands on it.' There, on television, he gets an untainted response.

Would you describe any writers as distinctively National Theatre playwrights, in the way that there are Royal Court playwrights or Aldwych playwrights?

No. I would hate a playwright to come to us and say, 'I think I'm writing your sort of play.' That would really mean that we had failed to fulfil our brief. The Royal Court is entitled to have a special sort of play, the Royal Shakespeare is, Joan Littlewood is — but the moment *we* have a special sort of play then we're limiting ourselves too much. I think we have to leave all the doors open, whereas they're entitled to slam some.

So this means that you have to suppress personal preferences to some extent in settling your repertoire — perhaps even bend over backwards to be catholic . . .

No, it means simply that the National Theatre has no preconceived identity, which is marvellous . . .

But you have an identity. Do you have to conceal it?

Ah. *Officially* I have no identity. Of course, I would be very sad if a play that supported apartheid was done at the National Theatre, and I would do what I could to prevent it. Similarly, a play that supported the American action in Vietnam would be unlikely to find me rooting for it. And if a play that involved mass audience participation was proposed for the Old Vic I would probably vote against it. Of course, I might lose the vote in any of these instances. But I can't think of a play that's been critically applauded in the English theatre in the last ten years that we wouldn't have given very sympathetic consideration to.

Failures in production, rather than failures relating to the quality of the writing, often seem to come back to the problem of finding the style to fit a particular play. Fielding's little burlesque, The Covent-Garden Tragedy, *in* Triple Bill, *for instance, seemed to me to fail because nobody really knew how to play a mock-heroic, burlesque style.*

Now this is a rather invidious thing to say. There is a theory that actors know more about how to make actors act than non-actors do. Sir Laurence being an actor and a director has a splendid and often rewarded faith in the ability of actors to direct. On that particular occasion, maybe because of the choice of subject or a failure to match subject and director, it didn't work. But I agree with you that in other circumstances it could have worked.

Before the National Theatre opened, you remarked in an interview upon the absence of a tradition for acting the comic classics in this country. Since then, I'd feel that the National has had some success at least in solving the restoration problem. . .

Yes. I think in *The Recruiting Officer* and again in *The Beaux Stratagem* Bill Gaskill — and to a lesser extent Peter Wood in his *Way of the World* — did find a way of taking the dust and varnish off those particular plays. I don't think we've solved the Molière problem, though. . .

Or the Jonson problem? At least, to judge by what I considered the Royal Shakespeare's quite disastrous Bartholomew Fair?

I didn't see that particular production, but the fatal thing has generally been that the comedy of humours in this country has developed along the lines of the *Goon Show*, so that a Jonson play comes to be considered a field day for clowns — what Ivor Brown might have called a gallimaufry of eccentrics. I'm not asking for strict social realism, but I should like to see a Jonson production which didn't have so many grotesques in it. Another difficulty is that many of Jonson's very serious preoccupations — with certain aspects of religion, for example — don't mean a great deal to us now. His Jacobean world is one to which I don't think there's a precise modern equivalent. I laughed very much at Guthrie's modern dress *Alchemist* at the Old Vic a few years ago, but that was an eccentrics' field-day really, and I didn't like his *Volpone* at the National. It may be that eccentric comedy in this country has now veered away from social satire into surrealism, into *Monty Python's Flying Circus.*

Of the range of plays that you've done, in which forms and which areas do you think you've had most success?

I think we've been best at certain sorts of humane, ironic comedy. That may be because it accords with the spirit of the age: the Zeitgeist is not, I should have thought, sympathetic towards the totally tragic. The commonest intelligent response to the age in which we live seems to be an ironic one, since it's consonant with some sort of civilized poise. And the sort of talents we've nourished have tended to make a joke of it. I think that's absolutely natural. That kind of play, whether it's the intellectual irony of *Rosencrantz and Guildenstern Are Dead* or the rather more emotional ironies of *The National Health*, or comedy like *The Recruiting Officer* and *The Beaux Stratagem*, those are things we've been really best in — plus sudden eruptions from Sir Laurence, as in *Othello*. I think Maggie Smith's performance in *The Beaux Stratagem* is perhaps the most consummate bit of female high comedy I've ever seen, and one knows that she wouldn't have been able to do that if she hadn't played Desdemona, *The Master Builder*, and so on. The Maggie Smith who came to the National Theatre was a gauche girl. The Maggie Smith who's at the National Theatre now is a fully mature and ripened actress.

My own hope when you gave up full-time criticism and went to the National Theatre was that you would eventually write some latter-day equivalent to what Lessing attempted in the Hamburg Dramaturgy: *recording the impressions of the critic in the theatre but not quite of the theatre.*

Well, I'm writing a book on precisely those lines, about what I've learnt in these last seven years of working on the other side of theatre, both at the National Theatre and in the commercial theatre with *Soldiers* and *Oh! Calcutta!* But I may not want to publish it until, or unless, I leave the National, because there's a certain element of inside information in it which one probably wouldn't want to publish if one was still there. Yes, one is making notes, a full record is being kept, but this isn't perhaps the time to publish it. To write about an organization that is still paying one's salary imposes certain restraints of vocabulary, however small the salary and however large the vocabulary.

What kind of development do you personally anticipate taking place at the National Theatre over the next few years?

The National Theatre has been in existence now for seven and a half years and a certain replenishment is I think necessary. It may be that there are people connected with the organization, myself included, who have been there too long. Peter Hall once said the maximum time that any ensemble should stay together without renewal was five years. I think that's an arbitrary figure, but it is true that one needs new directions, new infusions, every so often.

3

Edward Bond

the long road to Lear

It was appropriate that Edward Bond should have been the first dramatist we interviewed for Theatre Quarterly. *Having suffered in the mid-'sixties from the merely scandalous interest in the censorship battles over* Saved *and* Early Morning, *Bond was by this time being subjected to the quieter indignities of critical hostility and audience apathy. Just as* Encore *magazine had banged the drum for John Arden a decade or so earlier,* Theatre Quarterly *now began to sustain, through production casebooks and occasional critical bromides, its own campaign for the recognition of Bond's preeminence among the newer theatre voices. Insignificant though our efforts were in comparison with Bill Gaskill's sturdy championship of the work on stage, they perhaps made some small contribution to the present climate — even though it now permits critics to praise the later work with faint damns, in the firm but entirely mistaken belief that back in the 'sixties they, too, had been welcoming an emergent genius.*

Genius or not, Bond's originality and sheer formal range are beyond question. Finding an early and natural home with Gaskill at the Royal Court, his work ranged from the spare social realism of Saved *through the almost imagistic precision of* Narrow Road to the Deep North, *to the broad epic sweep of* Lear, *the closely-textured domestic comedy of* The Sea, *and the picaresque tragedy of* The Fool. *More recently, such plays as* The Bundle, The Woman, *and* The Worlds *have found a variety of homes, and seen a shift to a less idiosyncratic socialism in the underlying — and now sometimes overlaid — political philosophy of the work.*

But at the time of this interview, in June 1971, Lear *had yet to go into rehearsal at the Court — though Roger Hudson, Catherine Itzin, and I had had an opportunity to read the script before we talked to Bond in the garden of his home in rural Cambridgeshire. Though his earliest produced play,* The Pope's Wedding, *had had an East Anglian setting, it was, however, in the seedy London suburb of Holloway that Bond was born in 1935. He was evacuated to Cornwall on the outbreak of war — and later to his grandparents in the Fens — but it was only with reluctance that he talked of these early years, and we asked if this was because they had left little influence on him.*

They obviously had an enormous influence on me, which is why I am not prepared to talk about them. Disruption of that sort makes one aware of all sorts of things that one normally wouldn't be — just the change from London to the country was so striking that it brought one up abruptly.

You'd never really got out of London before?

No. And actually to see a field for the first time when you had no expectation of ever seeing anything like that — well, it's a very startling experience. And it made me very aware of people. They were all talking this strange Cornish dialect — it might have been Japanese or something. So one was very much aware that certain facets of experience lacked the values that I think one would normally attach to them. That is, if I'd lived all my life in London, I would have sensed what to feel about certain things when they happened: one would have been taught the responses. Being put into a strange environment created a division between feeling and the experience of things. If there is any one reason, I dare say it's because of that that I'm a writer.

You were more conscious of this kind of change than of the dangers of the war as such?

I certainly had no conception of being removed from danger into safety — I would have seen it the other way round, of course — and at first the war itself came through as something heroic. This is the way it was taught to a child, anyway — there were these very brave people involved in a titanic struggle somewhere or other. The whole thing came over as an adventure story, and I was rather disappointed not to be more deeply involved. But there were one or two things that contradicted that impression — from the descriptions of Hitler, for instance, he just behaved in a way that I could not imagine. He was a human being, yet he was behaving in a way which was inhuman, grotesque. It created in one's world an image of total evil, you see, which was very curious because it wasn't explained by anything which one had experienced before. If this man was Hitler, who was the nearest Hitler to me? That was the sort of problem it posed, so that one expected everybody to be potentially explosive in the way that Hitler was.

The other thing that affected me very much was wanting some tangible evidence of the war. One occasionally saw dogfights and so on up in the sky, and I remember walking along a road and seeing two aeroplanes hit each other, and I was terribly excited about this: it was marvellous, these great toys going smash in the air, two little silver aeroplanes miles off. And I remember running down this hot road towards them, and suddenly out of the aeroplanes two men appeared — sort of thrown out, these two little black figures in the sky. Two parachutes opened, and these men sort of stood for a moment in the sky, before they started to fall, jerked up by the parachutes. It stopped me dead in the road, and made me realize that in fact what one had been talking about was human beings, and what was important was the fact that there were men operating those toys, and perhaps there were bodies up there at that moment.

Were you with your family at this time?

No. The whole of my relationship with my family was one of suspicion — after that sort of background it had to be.

That background was what — working class?

Lower working class. But not London working class — my parents had come up to London during the depression because they couldn't get work on the land. My father had been a farm labourer in the country, and he did various kinds of labouring jobs when he was in London.

What sort of education did you have?

Very little — it was interrupted by the war, in any case. When we went down to the country the problem was just to organize the children into some sort of passive obedience. I would say I had no formal education at all, even when I got back to London — what was obsessively in the minds of everybody in the school was obedience, and some sort of conformity.

This was what kind of school?

A secondary modern school in Holloway.

London just after the war is a place and period that rather fascinates me — perhaps because I just start being able to remember things, the bomb sites, the queues. Did these have a particular impression upon you?

Yes, although what I felt much more about the end of the war was just enormous relief that in fact one wasn't going to be killed. It had been like a sort of lottery — would your number come up? And one had survived. When a doodlebug came over and we had to hide in doorways, we would have these discussions about whether we should run towards it or away from it. These were real problems, we certainly felt in danger. In the mornings we used to go out and collect shrapnel in the streets, and find that houses where one had been had been bombed.

I remember once that I was walking along a road and there was suddenly this enormous sort of bang which one can't describe, you know, because it's so . . . a noise almost inside you. I went along to the park and saw all the trees stripped bare, and picked up this little bird with its head blown off. I would think, very much, that was one of the reasons why I wrote that scene in *Saved*. There was always the possibility that violence could really explode. Nowadays I listen to undergraduates talking about using violence for this or that end, and it's all terribly unreal. The first time they actually hear a pistol go off in anger, it'll be a great political education for them.

How politically aware were you yourself at that time?

Well, I don't quite know why, or where it came from, but from quite a young age — about twelve or something — I know I was anti-Conservative, although my family were politically in a sort of limbo.

And you left school as soon as you could?

At fifteen, yes.

Had you begun to write while you were still at school?

My education really consisted of one evening, which was organized by the school. They took us along to a play at the old Bedford Theatre in Camden Town. We saw Donald Wolfit in *Macbeth*, and for the very first time in my life — I remember this quite distinctly — I met somebody who was actually talking about my problems, about the life I'd been living, the political society around me. Nobody else had said anything about my life to me at all, ever. To begin with there was just this feeling of total recognition. I *knew* all these people, they were there in the street or in the newspapers — this in fact was my world. And also out of the play I got a feeling of resolution — that there were certain standards. My reactions were absolutely naive, but I knew that if one could maintain these standards they could work in social situations and produce certain results. So that after seeing that play I could say, well, yes, now I know what I have to do, what it means to be alive.

What did you do when you left school?

Oh, I went and worked in various sorts of factories, things like that. They're all jumbled up in my mind now — making bits of aircraft, cars, and things. Apart from two years in the army, that went on until . . . until I started writing plays, I suppose when I was about twenty-two. But I went on working until *Saved* was produced.

Did you write many plays that never got as far as production?

Yes, I did. About fifteen — I've never counted them.

Do you think of them now as apprentice work, or as something more?

They were well-meaning and incompetent — totally incompetent. And rather embarrassing to read, I should think.

Were you trying to get them staged, though, at the time?

No, I wasn't. I think one realized, in a way — anyway, it wasn't that I wanted to get the plays produced: it was a personal thing. Now of course I want to get them produced, for a variety of reasons, but that is something extra. It's very helpful to me, actually to see a play that I have written — just to see it once. It gels the experience, and I can go on to the next thing.

You've said that the theatrical climate of the late 'fifties did stimulate you in a way — any particular writers?

Really, I saw absolutely everything that was on for a couple of years, but obviously what mattered and what intrigued one was what was happening at the Court. There was some relevance there that was lacking in other theatres.

The Pope's Wedding *was the first of your plays to be staged. Did you feel that here, at last, was something fully achieved? How, in fact, did it get to be staged?*

Before *The Pope's Wedding* I had sent one play to the Royal Court, but I think that was just in a desire for contact with other writers, to see what on earth they felt about it. Then I sent *The Pope's Wedding* — it somehow worked. I didn't mind it being produced.

Why did you decide on deeply rural Essex as the setting for The Pope's Wedding?

Well, I didn't have a car, and it was the nearest really rural area I could get to. I went there one weekend and made notes — it's near London but it's really very rural.

Was the language part of the puzzle you were solving in that play?

No, I think the language was more of a distancing device. It enabled me to see the characters with an objectivity I might have lacked if they were talking like the people next door to me.

The stoning of the hut and the unseen murder do seem to work towards a peak of violence, rather like the stoning of the baby in Saved, *or the putting out of the eyes in* Lear . . .

What you see in *The Pope's Wedding* is a sort of identity of opposites, I think. You see two completely separate worlds, and then, when they are brought together, they are the same world. At that time there were a lot of rather metaphysical plays with tramps in them who just sort of came on and said strange things . . . and I think it was an attempt to humanize for myself that image, which I felt was very powerful. I remember going to the Tower Theatre at Canonbury, seeing this strange figure in Ionesco's *The Killer*, stamping round the stage . . . that sort of image was very much in my mind.

The important thing is not to be intrigued or puzzled by images, but always to understand them. So that what I wanted to do was to try and get inside the image, and see what it was all about. That is what Scopey does in the play, and in the end he kills a man and wears his clothes in order to find out. And of course there's nothing there. The truth about this man's charisma, you see, is that it's based on nothing.

In Saved *one felt that the act of violence, instead of being an act of individual frustration as it was in Scopey's case — an inability to find out, even by committing murder — was much more a representative occurrence. Given those circumstances, this could have happened to almost anybody, which is what made it so terrifying.*

A play doesn't exist on its own. It has to be taken in relation to our factual knowledge about human nature, or to the past political nature of a society. So that one is always part of a movement, and what I hope happens in *Saved* is that an audience better realizes the nature of its society, what the nature of its problems are, and therefore what sort of solutions are needed. If you believe that people are innately wicked, then one solution is to say, well gas them. Somebody as recently as Bernard Shaw could openly say that. And if you *do* believe that people are innately wicked, it's a logical and defensible position. I can't believe that people are innately wicked at all.

Why is Saved *set in south London? The whole feel of it is exactly right, it really is south London rather than north, yet that was not where your own background lay . . .*

South London is slightly newer and I always get the impression, whether it's true or not, that it's more industrialized. I've got a feeling too that it's physically flatter — there are those miles and miles of long straight streets that always look the same. I used to call it the brick desert, and this feeling of being in a desert of bricks seemed to be absolutely right for the play. As to why it wasn't north London — and you're quite right, it couldn't be — I think that quite often one feels the need to see something at a bit of a distance, just to see its relationship to oneself better.

Do you think that there has been a feeling of continuity in your own work, from the early plays to Lear?

Oh, absolutely. As a writer one should sense that one is not writing separate plays but a series of plays, and it's very important that one should have a feeling that they belong together. You can trace a line from Scopey to Lear direct — I mean, Scopey is obviously Len in *Saved*, and then when he becomes Arthur in *Early Morning* he gets split up into two because the image just can't be contained in one person, and in *Narrow Road* the images grow even further apart, so that instead of seeing the closeness one must look at the distance. But the curious thing is, in *Lear* I think Len has finally been . . .

Exorcised?

Well, Lear is not Len. I don't think Lear is Len.

Just lately, there's been a rather insistent skeleton, too — a character who dies but goes on clinging, and somehow has to do it all over again. The Gravedigger's Boy in Lear, *of course . . .*

I suppose there is. Occasionally I've pulled funny faces in front of a mirror, to see all the other people there are in me, and it's very strange . . . I'm putting on my Len-like face now . . . There is a certain sort of struggle in people about various parts of themselves, some of which as one gets older one has to get rid of. And if one can't get unity between these various personalities, then one can't achieve coherent action. And so in *Early Morning* it's very important that Arthur should be able to get rid of George, because he's a sort of acceptable, socialized version of himself. It's apparently very difficult for him, but when he does finally get rid of him, then he can act. And of course it's very important for Lear too that he should get rid of this other figure: he has to disown something of himself, this instinctive thing he calls the Gravedigger's Boy. That, incidentally, was the image from which the play grew — this image of the Gravedigger's Boy. In some senses he is much older than Lear, and Lear recognizes this — he has been in his grave, and Lear, who is a very old man, has still to go towards it.

Why can't the Gravedigger's Boy die — the second time?

Well, it's quite complex for Lear, because he recognizes that this person did live in a workable society, did have everything he needed — a field where nobody troubled him, food, water. Admittedly his wife has been trained by a priest somewhere and she's worried, but Lear can't any longer live and operate in that way at all, though he can only rid himself of it with a great deal of nostalgia because it must have been a way of life with a great deal of beauty and happiness about it. So all societies must resign themselves to the loss of their golden ages, I suppose. Anyway, Lear has this clear vision of a golden age, which his own political activities have helped to destroy — his insistence on building his wall to defend his kingdom — but he has also to recognize that its loss is irrevocable. It doesn't mean accepting compromises or not fighting for what is important, but that there are great dangers in romanticizing and clinging to the impossible. Some things are dead — but they die with difficulty.

You've rechristened Goneril and Regan in your version, yet Bodice and Fontanelle do remain Lear's daughters, whilst Cordelia, who keeps her name, is no relation to him at all, and she emerges at quite a different point in the action. Is this just the way things happened, or was there a more conscious intention?

One of the very important things in the play was to re-define the relationship between Cordelia and Lear. I don't want to make this seem easy or slick, but Cordelia in Shakespeare's play is an absolute menace. I mean, she's a very dangerous type of person, and I thought that the other daughters, though I'm not excusing them, were very unfairly treated and misunderstood. What I wanted Lear to do was to recognize that they *were* his daughters — they had been formed by his activity, they were children of his state, and he was totally responsible for them.

I don't really remember why I changed the names except that I wanted to make it very clear that I wasn't just lifting the characters whole out of Shakespeare's play. In fact my version turns out to go back more faithfully to the original source, though I wasn't consciously aware of this when I was writing. I wanted to explain that Lear was responsible, but that it was very important that he could not get out of his problems simply by suffering the consequences, or by endurance and resignation. He had to live through the consequences and struggle with them.

Those consequences involve a great deal of physical suffering, and violence executed on stage — more, certainly, than in Saved, *and more realistically put over than in* Early Morning. *Obviously you regard this violence as an essential element in your plays?*

Well, as a society we are destroying ourselves through violence. All people say is, we must do something about these violent people, let's hit them harder. Or, look at those wicked Russians, we must make bigger bombs. Russell before the last war said that society could never survive another war, but in fact society did, so people keep thinking it wouldn't actually destroy us next time. But it could and will. Violence just *is* the big problem of our society — in the way that sex was the problem that haunted the Victorians. And what we must not do is make violence pornographic. Now the Victorians made sex pornographic, which meant that they could then use it for political ends. Sex became not a natural function, but something to *use*. Now, the whole of our society is bent on glamorizing — and *using* — violence. If you turn on your television set, you see a programme about somebody killing somebody else, and Mrs. Whitehouse says, how dreadful, it shouldn't have been made. But then the ads. come on, and there is a government commercial for killers, saying what a marvellous life it is in the army. Come and be one of the boys, go sailing in the Mediterranean, be taught how to use a sten gun — be a man.

So there is no doubt about it that we live in a very violent society. My plays are all concerned with the problem of violence because it is *the* consuming problem — the one that will decide what happens to us all. And what I have always tried to make clear in my plays is that violence in itself is not a danger to any species. The way it operates for instance in that garden out there, or in the jungle, may be deplorable but is not catastrophic. With human beings, all our mechanisms are biological, and if I get upset something happens inside me and I have to act. If I am threatened, I will hit back. All violence is basically defensive — the lion isn't angry when it goes hunting any more than you are angry when you go into a restaurant. So what we have to worry about is the violence that goes with anger — the violence that is triggered off when one is threatened.

Now if you threaten an animal it will become aggressive. If you cage an animal so that it can't behave in a normal way, so that it always feels threatened by the things around it, it becomes violent. And if you threaten human beings all the while, they become violent. No animal can be subjected to too much noise, for instance, because noise means danger. We have the same function in us — we don't like noise. We are living on top of motorways. Biologically we cannot function. There are H-bombs in the air all the time. The human being today is always in a state of tension and of being scared and frightened, and is therefore aggressive. And the sort of political community we have is based on utilizing this aggression. It's got nothing to do with the world of nature at all, where aggression functions in a protective way. A competitive society must destroy itself. There is no alternative, because this is the whole dialectic of violence — I threaten you, you threaten me, and finally you have to carry out your threats, otherwise there is no credence behind them. And also because aggression creates fear and this leads to more violence and this has an escalation of its own. So that if society goes on as it's going on now, it will destroy itself. Not will it, could it, might it — it *will*.

In other words, the capacities that we've developed over the last few million years are no longer the right tools for our environment. Forgetting whether or not it's a good thing that we live in a technological society — and I don't think it is — we have to ask whether a government will have enough knowledge to be able to manufacture the human beings it wants. It might be that it will *have* to start developing, genetically, people who are stupid — or stupified. Even now, most of capitalist society is a process for manufacturing consumer drugs — because nobody would want these extraordinary things they consume like mad if they were living a natural life. Right: so you spend all your life as a slave, producing tranquillizers to make slavery bearable — yes? It is possible. It might happen in a few years' time that governments will be trying to make people take drugs. And the awful thing is that it is speeding up so quickly. If I'd been a labourer in this village three hundred years ago, and returned fifty years ago, I could have lived very nearly the same life. I could have worked on this farm, I would have known what to do. If I came back now I'd be totally lost, and either have to starve or go around pinching things.

How do you set out to make an audience respond to this violence as you intend, so that it doesn't merely add to the pornography of violence with which they're saturated from their television screens?

Well, I don't think that my plays really are violent, though *Early Morning* might be an exception. They have moments of violence, which are usually set in an atmosphere that is quite different — the dismembered body of Shogo appearing at the end of *Narrow Road*, for instance, which isn't a violent play. It is not even *about* violence — it is about the kind of situation in which violence occurs. Even in *Saved*, where they talk very aggressively, it's really a joke. They never take violence seriously, nobody in the play takes violence seriously. Violence happens there in the way that it happens to an audience — there aren't those sort of scenes where somebody goes and buys a sword, or slips in the poison. So that I think the violence comes as a surprise because the play is about other things. But it isn't introduced in order to make those other things interesting, but as a consequence of them.

I can see that that's true of all the plays except Early Morning — *but there the violence surely* isn't *counterpointed by any sense of normality, of continuity, but almost* becomes *the continuum in which the action works . . .*

Yes. I think that's true. I hadn't thought about it in that way before, but it's almost as if Arthur has made a list of all the things that aren't normally on one's list, as it were. It's very important that he goes through all these circumstances and sees them in great detail, you see.

Did you find that the censorship trouble which especially affected Early Morning, *and all the off-the-point publicity surrounding that and* Saved, *had an adverse effect on the work you were able to do?*

Curiously enough I don't think it did. Of course on a personal level it was unpleasant, and I think it was about the most humiliating thing that could happen to a writer to get a script back from the Lord Chamberlain with all those blue marks on it. But Bill Gaskill was absolutely determined to put *Saved* on.

How does an idea come to you for a play?

The plays come up like milestones on a road, with a sense of inevitability. You write one and think you're solving all the problems, but then, as soon as it's finished, more crop up . . . Before starting *Lear*, I read a certain amount of biology, quite a bit of history and politics, and all the rest of it. I don't know whether it did any good, but somehow one wanted the confidence of its support before one made any statement. Then I wrote that story called *The King With Golden Eyes* — that was one of my notes, as it were, for *Lear*. And I write a lot of poetry — which was very strange, it really came like a flash.

I used to be able to see the shape of the poem on the page. I would start writing the first line, and only when I'd finished that would I know the second line. And by looking down at the paper I could see the shape — it was very curious. But don't misunderstand this — not psychic, or anything. It's just that if you think about a character or subject for months, there's a kind of backlog of impressions stored up, and at moments they crystallize into something. I used to get into what I called my *Lear* mood . . . a character was coming thumping down the garden path, and I had to go out and meet him. But there's nothing strange about it.

Did you make more specific notes about the characters or the action before starting work on Lear?

No. And nobody else but me would see the relevance of the notes I did write. They are part of getting into the mood, and just occasionally something will come. The business of the autopsy, for example — originally that was going to be carried out on one of the daughters by her husband, but this was too complicated and unnecessary, and would have meant that the husband would have had to change sides and so on. But the scene happened because I had these people chatting away inside, and one of them said, there is the man who could do the autopsy on his wife. So that's how that originated. But a lot has to be discarded because it seems terribly important or funny at the time, but becomes unsuitable in the play.

Do you write whole scenes that have to be discarded?

No — but I often find that I have to write one *more* scene to make the action clear, because one feels that the audience needs some help. In *Saved* the scene where the baby is on the bed was added after the play was written, and is really unnecessary — nothing happens that isn't made plain somewhere else. But somehow I felt that before the killing it was necessary to sum things up for the audience. And in *Lear* there was the scene in which the daughters are polished off, in the camp — this could have been done in a few lines, but I sort of felt that a scene between them was needed.

All your plays — at least all you've allowed to be staged — share this distinctive episodic quality, or at least a great fluidity of scenic structure. Did you begin to write more conventional three-act plays with nice beginnings, middles, and ends, and then slowly evolve a less traditional shape? Or how did it happen?

I think I started by writing a three-acter — one would have done — but I soon discovered that I couldn't tell the truth in that long-winded sort of way any more. It didn't relate to my experience at all, which was much more a series of sudden reverses and changes. And I felt it was important not only to know what was happening in the room I might happen to be in, but also what was happening in that room over there, that house down the road. So that in order to say something useful about experience now, one has to keep track of all these things. The plays keep an eye on what's going on, you know — I think that's what my structure does.

Do you do much re-writing after you've produced a first draft?

I find the actual business of writing almost physically painful, like touching something hot. I can perhaps type half a page, and then I just have to get away from the bloody typewriter. So in the first draft I really only take glimpses at the subject — write it all down very quickly, and it's a lot of old rubbish. But at least I can say, look, there's a draft, you can work on that. Then I go through several drafts, perhaps up to ten, something like that.

To what extent are you aware of the audience when you're writing a play?

Oddly enough, not at all. If you're in a bicycle race you have to *assume* that you can ride a bike — if you're always thinking about how you're doing it you won't win. So one must be aware of how certain things work with an audience, but not let this awareness get too much in the way. My justification for saying that my plays ought to have an interest for society is that I am a typical member of my society, and so my problems are the problems that everybody else has to solve if they're not going to die, or be killed, or be very unhappy. Now I have written very committed plays, but I couldn't work by asking, what's the audience going to think about this, or, what must I tell the audience this week? Of course, if one's going to write a play for the Campaign for Nuclear Disarmament, as I have done, one assumes that it's going to relate somehow to politicians and bombs — but that's just part of what one is setting out to do. Provided one is interested enough in a subject, it is possible to write for a particular occasion in that way.

I was rather struck by one stage direction in the CND play — that the director must get his pig from a slaughterhouse, and not have it killed specially for the performance. Did this indicate your awareness that there are people working in the theatre today who'd rather fancy the chance of slaughtering a live pig on stage . . .?

There are tendencies of that sort. I can have sympathy for thugs, but I certainly don't intend to excuse them, and anybody who would want to kill an animal as part of a ritual on the contemporary bourgeois stage strikes me as a bit cretinous.

Even the burning of the butterfly at the end of US?

Did they burn a butterfly? They ought to have been kicked up the backside.

Can I ask about titles? Saved *is fairly explicit — or ironical, according to taste — but why* The Pope's Wedding? *And why* Early Morning?

The pope's wedding is an impossible ceremony — Scopey's asking for an invitation for something that isn't going to happen, that *can't* happen. In *Early Morning* — well, in part there's the pun on *mourning*. And, because I thought the play might be taken to suggest something catastrophic and final, I also wanted to make clear that it was meant to be just the opposite . . .

Your own brand of pessimistic optimism . . . Because happiness in your plays comes through in rather strange and oblique ways, doesn't it? Particularly in the early plays, it only seems to be possible when people aren't doing anything very much . . .

Well, there really is so little happiness about. It's extraordinary how unhappy so many people are — they don't know what happiness is or how to look for it. They seek it in all the substitute happinesses that capitalism produces, and all they find is some sort of tranquillizer. We've got rid of our television set, and it's such a relief, it really is — we'd turn it on, and there'd be this man saying, we're going to Venus, we're going to Mars, and he was mad, absolutely mad. I think if one is at the scene of an accident then that dictates one's behaviour in that situation, and so when one is living in a society which is really a sort of awful accident, then it is very difficult to find the time and the impulse to write about people who are just happy . . .

Yet there is a certain quality of happiness about some of those quiet scenes in Saved. *How do you think an ideal audience, coming out of the theatre, would have responded to that play?*

Well, if they come out saying, oh, what dreadful people, they all ought to be locked up, that's not what I'm after. Perhaps they should be asking, are these facts really so? And if they are, we must find out more about them, and do something about them. I would like people to have seen something that they might have read about in a newspaper, or even have been involved in, but not really understood — because they see it from a partial point of view, or whatever — suddenly to be able to see it whole, and to be able to say, well, now I can understand all the pressures that went into the making of that tragedy: when I come to judge that situation, my judgement will be more accurate, and therefore the action I take more appropriate. And I would like them to be so strongly moved as to *want* to take action.

As Brecht was trying to do?

Yes, and he did die so opportunely, didn't he? Just before the Hungarian Revolution. He missed the main scene. But I think he would have left, or been kicked out. He certainly couldn't have gone on in that set-up very much longer.

You've called Brecht's plays naive melodramas. Is that a blanket condemnation?

They really are so naive, it's not true. I rather admire Brecht, actually. I think his naivety covers painful knowledge. The nearest thing to a Brecht play in English *is* the Victorian melodrama, with its wicked landlord and pure labourer's daughter and all the rest of it. Do you remember the girl who gets raped by the stormtroopers who comes on and says, I am a proletarian girl and therefore I am not surprised. And he will condemn the nazis for doing things he is quite capable of praising the communists for doing. The end can never justify the means in important matters, and certainly shouldn't for a writer.

At the other extreme, how do you feel about a playwright like Beckett?

He's a writer I admire very much, but I think it's wrong to make a cultural hero out of the man. One can say, all right, you've lived through a time of enormous and extreme suffering which your plays capture very well: yet a writer has to do more than this. In Beckett's plays there's no earthly reason why Beckett should ever have written them, and every reason why he should go and kill himself tomorrow. And yet he doesn't, he goes on writing plays — so they can't be true to all his experience. And a writer has to be true to his experience and not tell himself lies, even comforting ones.

Do you think of yourself strongly as 'a writer?'

I have a sense of literary responsibility, if that doesn't sound too pompous . . . no, it doesn't, a writer does have responsibilities, and I accept them.

4

David Jones

on directing Gorky

The Royal Shakespeare Company did not much figure in the annals of the new theatre in the years immediately following 1956, and even after Peter Hall joined the company as artistic director in 1960, and found it a London home at the Aldwych for non-Shakespearian work, its interest in new British writing was at worst eccentric, at best intermittent. A season of new British plays and of major foreign work at the Arts Theatre Club in 1962 was the earliest of the sporadic outbursts which, over a decade later, led to the regular studio seasons of new plays and revivals at The Other Place and The Warehouse.

To the Arts Theatre season a young television director named David Jones had contributed a production of Boris Vian's The Empire Builders: and of the relatively small team of regular directors for the RSC, which he quickly joined, David Jones went on to become identified with its most productive author-director relationships — with David Mercer, the subject of a later interview in this volume, and with a dead Russian dramatist, Maxim Gorky, previously known in this country, if at all, as the author of just one play, the doss-house masterpiece The Lower Depths.

Ironically, The Lower Depths — first produced by Stanislavsky at the Moscow Art Theatre in 1902 — had been one of the plays in the RSC's Arts Theatre season. But it was with Enemies, written in 1906, that David Jones himself first came to Gorky in 1971 — bringing to it, as he revealed when he talked to us, a number of the lessons he had learned during rehearsals for his British premiere of Günter Grass's The Plebeians Rehearse the Uprising in the previous year. Then, in 1972, came David Jones's own version of The Lower Depths, again in fruitful collaboration with the translating team of Jeremy Brooks and Kitty Hunter-Blair, and he went on to direct productions of Gorky's Summerfolk in 1974 and The Zykovs in 1976.

Terry Hands confirmed the company's adoption of Gorky as a sort of posthumous house dramatist with The Children of the Sun in 1979. What gave the work of this Russian writer — whose lifespan from 1868 to 1936 made him the only dramatist of significance to straddle the Czarist and Soviet periods — its immediacy for British audiences in the 'seventies? And how had David Jones tackled the problems of acquainting British actors with what it felt like to be living in the rigidly stratified Russian society of the turn of the century? Roger Hudson, Catherine Itzin, and I talked with David Jones in the small Bloomsbury garret which served as Theatre Quarterly's first office, soon *after the Aldwych opening of* The Lower Depths *in June 1972. Why Gorky, we asked? And what had led David Jones to direct two plays by him within a twelve-month period?*

Enemies, the first one we tackled, was thrown up by a process rather than by accident. Jeremy Brooks, as RSC Literary Manager, was combing the whole field of the classics, and in particular looking — because that is our policy — for the neglected or unknown plays that haven't been done for a long time. Since the inception of the National Theatre, we've seen their job as doing the magnum opus of any particular world dramatist, and ours as either to rediscover a lesser-known work, or to find a dramatist who hasn't been done for some time. Gorky, obviously, had been put completely to one side compared to Chekhov in English theatre. In fact, I can't claim any previous knowledge or enthusiasm for Gorky — *Enemies* was simply the play, out of five put forward by Jeremy, that he recommended most strongly.

Though you didn't know Gorky's plays before, were you particularly interested in that period in history — the culture, the country?

I knew a little about Bloody Sunday, but in terms of detailed background knowledge of the Russian social situation — and the whole build-up from 1904 to 1906 to that main outburst — I was pretty well illiterate.

But you were personally in sympathy with the political and social attitudes of Gorky?

Over the last three or four years, I've found plays that do not have a social or political context curiously rootless. I'm not really interested in working on plays that exist in a total fantasy situation. This feeling came out of working with David Mercer on *After Haggerty*, and out of the work I did on Günter Grass's *The Plebeians Rehearse the Uprising* — exploring the attempts in the post-war Iron Curtain countries to set up a new society. It was necessary for the actors playing in *Plebeians* not to take a stock western view of repression and terrible living conditions, because it was quite clear from the content of the play that these people *believed* in a way of shaping a new society. To get a group of English actors, and, indeed, to get myself to understand that situation, pitched one not only into what happened in East Germany from 1945 to 1952, but made one go much further back to the roots, to find out why Marx thought that Germany was the country that was going to become communist first of all. *Plebeians* made me respond to this feeling I was finding in myself then, that theatre should be connected to and should explain certain things about the way we are living. Gorky came to me at just the right moment, when my political awareness was growing, when my interest in doing larger-cast work was growing, when I was wanting to do something on a fairly big and complex level.

I suppose, too, there's always been a slight tug in me towards the naturalistic mode. So when *Enemies* arrived, it had, of all the plays I've read, an immediate impact, even in a slightly inferior translation. It seemed that the characters, even the smallest ones, were absolutely crystal clear and three-dimensional, beautifully understood and realized — I was very excited by the vitality and energy of the piece. Compared to Chekhov — towards whom I am respectful but not wildly enthusiastic — this had an energy and a vitality and a sort of roughness which was much more my cup of tea. The other thing which appealed to me immensely was the thematic point that the play was about a society on the brink of a revolution it was not ready for, didn't anticipate, and didn't understand. It seems to me that the revolutionaries in the play, with a few exceptions, are untrained and unready for the situation — and certainly the well-meaning liberals in the big house just don't understand what's hit them. Immense social chasms were opening up between the two groups, which had always been there, but which had been glossed over by a social routine. This was something that I could see beginning to happen in England, something that had been happening in America. For that reason the play was a very ironic and timely one to be doing.

How did you begin to communicate these attitudes to a group of actors?

We did do a lot of background reading about the historical pattern leading up to Bloody Sunday, about the rights and wrongs of that situation, and then, because the play breaks up into three worlds — those of the owners and the privileged, the workers, and the police — I split the actors into three groups. Actors playing policemen did all the background research on the police — how they worked and what their power structure was. The rest of the company didn't know about any of this research. Each individual worker took away a Stalin biography or a Trotsky biography, and then came back and had to say what were the salient factors. In fact, the workers were the most difficult to hit the right tone with. I realized about two days before the opening that they were continuing to play them in a rather idealistic, romantic way — they were playing them as if they knew 1917 was going to happen. So I had a session with them one day which I thought was going to be twenty minutes. I'd called all the workers together in private, and I had the factory-owners waiting to rehearse their scenes. In fact the session went on for an hour and a half. When we came out, the other actors were furious because they'd been kept waiting and they said, what the fuck have you been talking about? We said, we're not going to tell you — and we got this natural, extremely valuable aggression. They knew the bloody workers had got a secret. This actually set up vibrations over the next two nights of performance, which were very valuable.

Did you use the police investigations in the same way?

Not in such crystal-clear terms. Because the last act of *Enemies* is a strange one. In a way Gorky's written a comedy act, in that Captain Boboyedov is a clown buffoon figure in one sense: but I believe that if you're writing in Russia in 1906, where the Secret Police are a fact of life, you can afford to turn a character who's got that influence on the action into a clown — because everyone knows that he's formidable, even though he is a clown. I found the most difficult thing to get English audiences to understand was the degree to which, however great your integrity or position, you have to keep your nose clean in a police state. I remember the last act of *Plebeians*, when the official party poet comes back, taunts them, and makes them listen to his speech in the square: Peggy Ashcroft in particular had immense difficulty. She said, well, I just would not stand here and listen to this man. One had to go through time and time again what the repercussions would be, exactly what it meant in terms of imprisonment and deprivation. And I foresaw the same problem with *Enemies* so we did a lot of film research for it — I used Jancso's film *The Round-up*, although it had nothing to do with that period of Russian history, because I felt that it conveyed the atmosphere of a totally impersonal police state where you cannot question anything.

We also saw the whole of the Gorky trilogy — the three films by Mark Donskoi, *My Childhood, My Apprenticeship,* and *My Universities,* based on Gorky's autobiography. That seems to me the best introduction to Gorky, not so much in terms of historical specifics, but in terms of spirit. The actors in both *Enemies* and *Lower Depths* were slightly lukewarm after the first part of the trilogy — they said, this Russian acting is very extravagant, isn't it? And, they let their hair down too much. By the second and third parts, they were understanding that there was a temperamental difference, and that's what they'd got to try and achieve as English actors — an ability to move quickly and in extremes from a tragic mood into a comic mood, or to be absolutely vicious to somebody one moment and terribly sweet the next. It's a sort of volatility of temperament which is not English — English actors as a rule want to smooth out their emotional shape. I tried to encourage them to have the nerve to be extreme, exploring emotional limits to the characters, behaving in a peculiar and inexplicable way socially on occasions. The other films we showed were Pudovkin's *Mother* and Eisenstein's *Strike*, which were about the pressures in Russia at that time.

On *Lower Depths*, we saw quite a bit of modern documentary material about Rowton Houses and meths drinkers. The phenomenon has hardly changed from Russia in 1906 to England in 1970. Those particular alcoholic down-and-outs use the same strange poetic turns of phrase, have the same veering between intense aggression and intense, maudlin self-pity. The similarities were much more remarkable than the differences.

What was your reaction to Stanislavsky's making his actors get first-hand experience of a doss-house?

They all had to make contact with a tramp in some sort of way, and talk to him for about half an hour. A great deal didn't emerge from that, to be honest. Maybe we should have done more . . . I don't know. The only way it would be at all valid is if they had spent a week doing a Jeremy Sandford tramp-round, staying in various spikes, up and down the country. We *did* do a lot of swopping of personal experience, and people were very frank if they had had any contact with the wrong side of the law or bumming off people. One actor, who's very straight and honest normally, suddenly told, with some difficulty, a story which didn't reflect much credit on him. At the end of it, Heather Canning said, I don't believe you, you've just made that up. This response set up a valuable cross-current, because in *The Lower Depths* there is always the question, do I trust you or not? The play is about truth and lies.

How do you work with the actors once you get to the script?

The first week or ten days we soak in the background, no script at all. Then there is a reading period — we read the first act, we talk about it, we go back and read it, we read each act twice. That is useful for bringing out a few points about character and text early on. But I don't like imposing too much at that stage — one wants the actors to make the discovery. Then you start doing it. Both with *Enemies* and *Lower Depths*, I did no blocking as such. Although once you've made decisions on the bed-spaces in *Lower Depths*, or once you've made certain decisions about how the court-martial is conducted in *Enemies* — where the people sit — a lot of the physical action becomes inevitable from then on. In *Lower Depths* particularly, it was important the actors had an environment, and had to find out about living in that room — just as one has to find out about living in a barrack-room.

So you don't block a play in any sense?

I always used to. If I go back to the time of *Saint's Day* or even *Belcher's Luck* and look at a copy of the text, I've got a little diagram of the set on the left-hand page all the way through, and little crosses and arrows with 'A moves here', and so on. There was a time, a long time ago, when I got rattled if we departed from that. Then I just had the blocking there as something to fall back on. Only on these last two have I completely abandoned blocking. I don't believe you can do that with every play — *Plebeians* had to be much more highly organized in terms of numbers on stage. But with *Enemies*, in particular, where often there were not more than four-handed scenes, you could give the actors a situation and say, right, let's see how it develops. *Lower Depths* eventually settled into a mode which the actors discovered. If I realize they're not finding a physical solution, I will suggest one, or if they find one early on which they are pleased with and I think they're getting set in, I will change it so they've got to start reacting in a different way.

The actors could deal with this flexibility?

The *Enemies* group, two thirds of them fresh from doing Brook's *Dream*, had no trouble at all. The *Lower Depths* group, in a sense slightly more conservative in their approach at the beginning, tended to say, 'Is that all right?' and I'd say, 'It's all right . . . if it helps you relate to that person.' The eradication of the wrong sort of theatrical consciousness took much longer with the *Lower Depths* group. John Wood adapted very fast — when he did *Enemies*, it was his first show with the company. He's an incredible actor in rehearsal for taking risks and trying strange things, but when we came about the third time to his first entrance in the breakfast scene, he said, 'That chair has moved.' I said, 'What do you mean?' He said, 'That chair is not normally there.' And I said, 'Well, no, but something different has happened before.' He said, 'Well . . . it does affect what I'm doing,' and I said, 'I know it does, it may be different every night.' And Brenda Bruce said, 'This is the Royal Shakespeare Company — some nights I'm not even on, John.' John was marvellous, within fifteen seconds you saw him dealing with this mentally, and he made a complete wipe in his work method, and changed. But he did it, *voomph*, like that, you could see it happening.

What happened on *Enemies* was that — once we were secure about the psychological shape — even after we opened, certain pieces would change completely: scenes like the one between Sintsov and Tatiana — Ben Kingsley and Helen Mirren — when he's asking her to 'hide something' for him. Helen sometimes would be by the chair, and sometimes she'd decide she didn't want to stay near him. So she'd go right over by the tree, and Ben would adapt accordingly. Eighty per cent of the time the change worked as well as anything one had officially set, and had the advantage of being absolutely fresh and of the moment. I think you can only do that with certain plays.

There's one rider I would add. Blocking has become a dirty word . . . People say, oh, nobody blocks nowadays. That seems to me irresponsible. I do believe that one of the key ways in which a director affects the communication of a play is in actual physical placing. I think it's sometimes crucial where an actor is — the distance from the audience, whether he's up, down, how he's relating to other characters. Just as, if you're directing a film, camera angles are not just visual effects, but means of communication. But I also tend to believe that, in this sort of play, if you get the foundation of the physical life of the scene right — *where people are* — the pattern that evolves thereafter can come out of the actors.

Getting an actor into character . . . did you have sessions where you explained *a character?*

I don't sit down a great deal and analyze background. I think actors resent the director moving too far into the Stanislavsky background of a character. Obviously if an actor's hitting the wrong note in a scene, one's got to start examining what he's bringing onto the stage at that point. The key thing I'm interested in with actors is them expanding their intellectual and emotional horizon — basically, getting them to trust vulnerability, which is to do with playing together as well as on their own, which is to do with the part being fresh each night. The actor's instinct is to get a security, to get something set, to repeat something because he knows it works. A lot of the rehearsal process with me is not letting them rest on that, saying, maybe that could be more interesting, maybe that could be taken further, you're near that, but actually I don't quite believe you're interested in that situation. There is a lot of talk about motivation, but one tries to dramatize the motivation rather than sit down and coolly analyze it.

Do you improvise?

Very little. If I'm absolutely honest, it's because I don't know enough about it to use it very fruitfully. I'm much more interested in trying to release the actors on the text, by actually sticking with those words, because I believe that the words themselves often open doors.

You don't get them to do a scene using their own words?

No, I haven't done that at all, because I think both the Gorkys are very formal written texts. Particularly with the upper-class characters in *Enemies*, there is a kind of Edwardian style about their way of talking, where, if it is translated into modern terms, you're actually losing nuances. . .

When you work, how far do you break down the script . . .?

The normal practice with all RSC directors, and probably with all directors, is to break it down into blocks which tend to be about four pages in length, and tend to be timed to the arrival or departure of a new actor. This is really just to make for smoothness of rehearsal calling. The danger of it is, unless you get to your run-through at an early enough stage, the play is a series of little one-acters. I've got a rough rule of thumb: I know it takes me about a quarter of an hour to do a page, so I will allow an hour's rehearsal for four pages of the script. I go through quite methodically from the top of the play working through to the end, and then go back to the beginning again over a week or a week and a half, whatever it takes.

What happens during one of these sessions?

The card game in *Lower Depths* gave us endless and I think unnecessary trouble, because we kept changing our mind about how we wanted to tackle it. The actual playing of the card game used to take up forty-five minutes, and then we had quarter of an hour left to discuss the scene. You learn that there are certain actors who absolutely loathe it. Therefore, you begin to know that certain sections are going to take longer because, although the problems are not actually any greater in that section, there's a particular psychological problem with an actor. I said very little for the first fortnight of *Lower Depths*, except to make general suggestions. If they asked me things, fine, but I'd very rarely jump in and say, don't you think if . . .

Or the point about this is . . . Then in the third week, once they'd begun to get something firm, I either began to reinforce and build that, or to question it strongly.

It's dangerous to comment too early, because an actor's got to have a period where he can thrash about and try different voices and try different physical lives. Sometimes there are things one will leave entirely to the actors. With *Lower Depths* I said from the beginning that I was going to start the play at 7.20 rather than 7.30 — they would have to be in bed on the stage by 7.15, and the getting up would gradually start. Now, on that, I didn't say anything, except to Peter Geddis as Bubnov, who I wanted to wake up first, and to Morgan Shepherd — that when Bubnov had reached a certain point, Kleshch starts. At the first full run-through in Manchester at the beginning of our provincial tour, I said, right, we start. And Geddis played for ten minutes getting up — it was a complete Beckett mime on its own.

Why did you decide to do that? That was very effective for me . . .

The company are curiously divided on it. Half of them think it makes their work terribly hard when they start that act. All of a sudden Gorky whips the curtain up and you're in midstream. But I felt that to get an audience to appreciate the drabness and the depression of that way of life, you needed them just to sit and smell the atmosphere for ten minutes — to have two people completely locked in their isolated selves, getting up and trying to cope with a new day, was a sort of valuable addition, a gloss on Gorky. I did the same thing to a lesser extent with *Enemies*, which starts in the script immediately with the dialogue of the clerk about the cucumbers. It's a morning, a new day, there's an elaborate ritual of laying a table for rich people. The plays are aspiring towards the condition of a novel in the sense that in both of them you should feel that there is an existence before and after the play.

It struck me in Lower Depths *that the first and the final act had close affinities, not only in terms of setting but of story and action. The second act is very different. What sort of thinking went into the handling of that?*

When you read the play, it's the middle act that makes you most nervous, because it's the act where they are just sitting around and talking. Except at the end, where there's the outburst — which is a Gorky device, very similar to what he does in the first act of *Enemies*, where you have discussion, discussion, discussion, then, pow, there's an explosion. It's a similar pattern, but all the talk at the beginning of *Enemies* is concentrated on a particular issue. The talk in the second act of *Lower Depths* is much more Chekhovian, and Gorky's description of it is very emotive — he says there's the first sniff of spring, the snow has just melted, there's the black elder which hasn't yet budded in the background. He describes the fact that there is this vast red fire wall at the back — in fact, one translation of the word used for the back yard is 'the waste land.' And what one wanted — even when they move outside — was the feeling of total sterility about the world: they are still enclosed and trapped. They are in the open, and yet they have no escape, although it is the act in which people talk most strongly about getting away, about going on the road, where Luka says, right, I'm going to move on now, and where for a moment it looks as if Pepel and the girl may get together and move on.

But you're right back in the rat-cage again by the last act. When you've got a scene that appears very static and short on narrative, you either say I'll do everything to disguise that, and then do all sorts of interesting things, or you say, no, this is a curiously still scene, which is a series of stories, starting with Nastya's story. And it has the vast cornerstones of Luka's two stories. That's what you've got to embrace — it's got to be people sitting down listening to a story. Then one added the tension of saying, but it doesn't work if you're an absolutely captive audience. The people telling those three stories have got to earn their audience. I think it's indicative that Nastya had such a rough ride on her story — it's also obviously deliberate in Gorky that Luka's first story is just to one person on stage, and then with his next story he begins to draw people into it.

Did you work with actors individually on those set pieces?

I worked with Gordon Gostelow, as Luka, and to a certain extent separately on the two, very little with Alison Fiske's Nastya. You've got to be aware of the architecture of the stories, which are the two most polished bits of translation in the whole play. It took me a week to convince Gordon that if he got a word wrong he was in trouble. Because they are cases where Jeremy has managed to achieve an inevitability of text, which you piss about with at your peril. At the same time the stories have got to be related to the people on-stage. In Natasha's confessions Richard Pasco as the Baron, rather than listening in a sort of generalized sympathetic way — 'interesting little girl' — suddenly one day began to behave strangely and cross to her in a predatory way. I said, what were you thinking about? And he said, I don't know, I suppose I was fancying her a bit. We then very subtly built on that, what she says about death and being frightened — and it betrays a sensuality of nature underneath. There's an undertone which she doesn't understand as a character, that he only just flirts with, thinking, let's find out what you are like and maybe you're a potential victim for me later on. That sets the tone.

But it is fatal if they start playing the surface of it, if they say, oh, this is our quiet magic moment, or anything like that. You've got to rediscover it each time. I drove Alison fairly strongly on the rhythm of the last breakdown section, and I certainly had to work very hard with Gordon in terms of getting him to observe the deliberation in the final build-up of his stories. Whereas the Russian story from his own life he tells in a lively way, the story of the 'virtuous land' is a sort of set piece that's really got to have the old Russian folk-teller inevitability about it.

Did the elements of violence affect your casting?

There is a certain amount of viciousness and strength required from Pepel, from Vassilissa, from Kostylyov, but I particularly wanted Kostylyov to be not a heavy landlord but a sort of manic clown figure, rather like the grandfather in the Gorky trilogy. That's what we were aiming towards. I had quite a long battle with Heather Canning because she didn't want to play Vassilissa as the stereotype of the virago lady. But you've *got* to play it at certain points. I had the same kind of problem for a while with Sara Kestelman, as Kleopatra in *Enemies*: she kept saying, you've got to be joking about that act one curtain. I can't actually stand over a dead body and say, 'Well, murderers?' flat out, it's got to be thrown away. And I said, no, she *sees* herself playing that moment.

The most violent moment in *Enemies* is the body of Mikhail falling across the breakfast table. The most difficult thing to do on a stage is to persuade the audience that somebody's dying — to get the emotive effect of someone dying, the ugliness of it. That was something I had a hunch about. We didn't plot it. I said to the actor, will you bring him on and land him near that table. I don't mind if you fall across that table. By then we'd got rehearsal plates. Everybody reacted to the violence of that moment, the plates falling on the floor and getting smashed. And, curiously, that bit — which looks like a very orchestrated moment — literally happened.

I also believe passionately that Gorky's plays are in the end optimistic. With *Lower Depths*, he is taking the blackest, most deprived situation, the most damaged human beings, and yet out of that comes Satin's speech on how man can fly. It's romantic if you like, but it seems to me a positive statement, and the energy that's in the writing has to be embraced. To do a flat, grey 'I will arouse the social indignation of the audience' production would be wrong. Gorky said to the Moscow Art actors, after he had seen a run-through, 'You're all asking to be pitied, you're saying let's have a little kopek out of your charity. In fact what you've got to do is frighten the audience and make them aware that there is an existence other than theirs.' The awful difficulty is to get a well-heeled London theatre audience to make that imaginative jump.

5
David Mercer
before the difference began

Like David Jones, David Mercer first worked in television, but it was in the theatre that the creative partnership between the two men flourished, and Jones eventually directed four of the six plays Mercer wrote for the Royal Shakespeare Company. Following Mercer's tragically early death in 1980, at the age of 52, David Jones wrote that he 'demands in my mind the same love and esteem I feel for Gorky. They share a generosity of spirit, a desire for change, and a savage compassion for those who must be changed.'

Mercer was, then — more than the socially ambivalent Osborne or the aspiring autodidact Wesker — very much the voice of the dispossessed post-war generation: able to take advantage of new opportunities for social mobility, yet always aware of the tug of working-class roots. His early television trilogy The Generations *showed how such a conflict affected one family, in its personal relationships and political feelings: yet, as the setting of the trilogy's final play in Eastern Europe suggested, Mercer fully recognized the global implications, alike of commitment and complicity, under the nuclear cloud.*

His first full-length play to reach London, in 1965, was Ride a Cock Horse: *it became a prestigious West End success, and a star-vehicle for Peter O'Toole, reflecting in this reception, as in its theme, Mercer's own predicament as a northern working-class writer, well aware that he had helped to create the very Hampstead cultural milieu he also despised. His work continued to combine a deep and wide-ranging social concern with a sense of his own displacement within the class system — in which, eventually, he felt himself* démodé *as well as* déclassé. *'As a writer in England', he told David Jones a month before his death, 'I've become invisible'.*

But the loyalty of Jones and of the Royal Shakespeare Company ensured that his later work had its opportunity to batter away at jaded critical sensibilities. His last play to be seen at the Aldwych, Cousin Vladimir, *set down a Soviet dissident refugee amidst a clutch of middle-ageing British alcoholics, and his last play of all,* No Limits to Love, *seen posthumously at The Warehouse, shunted a gay teutonic psychoanalyst into a North London* ménage à trois. *Such combinations of booze, bed, and political battlefields were entirely characteristic of his work.*

When, in the summer of 1972, Roger Hudson, Catherine Itzin, and I talked with David Mercer (in Hampstead, of course), his reputation still rested as much on his work for television as on that for the stage, and it is a mark of the ephemerality of the medium that, only a few years later, the titles of the television plays should now sound so much less familiar. As Mercer himself affirms in the interview, this was a period of transition for him. Thus, his most recent work at that time, After Haggerty, *had been, he thought, a sort of gathering together of 'strands going back into the past', and he sensed that, for the future, 'the preoccupations of my middle age will begin to express themselves' — a coming-to-terms with death among them.*

But because the concerns of his work up to that time had been, as he agreed, more closely autobiographical, we inevitably talked at some length about his own early life. Born in Wakefield, in the West Riding of Yorkshire, David Mercer was the son of an engine-driver, and he told us that this put his family, in their own estimation, a cut above the coal-miners of the area.

They thought they were upper-working-class, highly repectable — and very ambitious for their children. I had one brother, five years older than me, and he went on to grammar school, and then became a scientist. But I twice failed the exam, so I just went straight from elementary school to work at the age of fourteen. Mind you, there was a sort of inverted social cachet about it, because if you went to grammar school it meant you were probably a cissy. Then I started work as a path-lab technician, the great dictum in our family being, do owt as long as tha doesn't get th'ands mucky.

Were you ambitious for yourself?

I think I was totally retarded — emotionally, intellectually, in every conceivable way. I'd had a rather severe illness when I was about seven or eight, which had confined me in a plaster cast from collar-bone to ankles — it was completely painless but completely incapacitating. And the result of this was an extraordinary kind of timidity and passivity towards the world. The only compensating factor was that I became a fluent reader — the content was shit, but the fluency was terrific. I think I plodded along at school, and then for quite a long time at work, just as a kind of dourly functioning animal.

You weren't writing at all?

I wasn't doing *anything* at all, not even playing games. The only physical thing I was allowed to do after the illness was swimming — it's still the only kind of exercise I take, no longer because of the illness, but because I'm bloody lazy.

Were your parents at all politically involved?

My father was political in the sense that he was completely pro-union, and thought the Labour Party was right for the working man — but in a completely unintellectualized or rationalized way. My mother was a sort of Lawrentian type, the dominator of the household who took most of the decisions. But certainly not political.

Were they religious?

Partly ritualistically, partly traditionally, my family were originally Methodist, but for reasons which remain quite mystifying to me they switched to low Anglican when I was quite young: so I was brought up to go to church and believe in God and say my prayers. Then there came a time in my father's life, in his middle years, when in his dark and inarticulate fashion he must have undergone some sort of crisis, because he went through a period of saying, when tha's dead, tha's dead, and that's all there is to it. But it merely took the death of my mother to sling him back into the arms of Christ. I don't think I ever believed it, though I dutifully went to church twice on Sunday. I was even a choir boy, bizarrely enough, until I got thrown out for some act of skulduggery or other. I was thrown out of Sunday School too, I was even thrown out of the Church Lads' Brigade. It's been a ludicrous contradiction, that whereas all my life my instinct has been to defer to other people, to conform, to be what they want, anything for love, peace and quiet — especially peace and quiet, and love if possible — at the same time I've had the most remarkable tendency for outbursts of insolence and violence, and impropriety, as it would have been construed in those days. I think I was thrown out of Sunday School for trying to get my hand up a little girl's knickers, which given my personality as well as the historical and social circumstances was outrageous . . .

Did you have any feelings about the outbreak of war?

I certainly didn't understand it. I think I became most aware of the war when I went to work, because the hospital in Wakefield had been commandeered by the government for military patients, and so we had people brought in from war theatres all over the world, smashed and broken, diseased and gangrened. And that really hit me quite hard when I look back on it, the sheer human destruction of actual flesh and bone, the loss of blood and eating away of tissues. Of course, there's a morbid element introduced very early in your training as a lab technician in a hospital, because this includes doing post-mortems. So I was at my first post-mortem at the age of about fourteen and a half, and by the time I had qualified I was doing two post-mortems a week, for over a year. Even at the age of seventeen or so I can remember going to bed on a post-mortem day shaking with tears, sobbing, devastated by it.

Did a medical job save you from being called up for the army?

In fact I went in just before the end of the war, as a volunteer — partly out of a sort of utterly mistaken patriotism, partly — with hindsight — out of a blind urge to get out of the Wakefield environment, and partly, I suspect, as a kind of self-proof thing, just to show that I *could* go in there and fight. Only, of course, they were short of path-lab technicians in the navy, so I went on being a path-lab technician. I was shore-based for eighteen months, then, after the war, I went to sea in the *Vanguard*, the only ship in the Royal Navy that had a path-lab — it had been used to take the royal family to South Africa, and had everything. But we used the path-lab most on the way back, when we had a great many cases of VD out of a crew of a thousand.

Was the self-proof working?

I had a lot of trouble with the timidity bit. But in the navy at the time there were a lot of people who had been drafted maybe after failing their first or second year university exams, and among them were one or two equally sensitive, equally fearful individuals. So I made a few contacts which began to lead me in the direction of realizing the huge cultural world and the huge stratified social world which existed, and to give me some kind of perspective on it and an ambition in it — of wanting, after all, to get to university, which I was able to do because of the ex-serviceman's grant. So when I came out of the navy I went back to school in Wakefield and took what was then called matriculation in a year, in order to get to Durham University.

What did you study at Durham?

Well, I went up there originally to do chemistry, still limping along in my brother's tracks, but I had this swellingly urgent wish to become a painter, and spent the whole term at University College, Durham, painting on the banks of the river instead of going to the labs. Finally I went to the master of my college and said that I was terribly sorry, but I didn't think I wanted to be a scientist after all. He was a real liberal, classical high tory of the best sort, so he got on the blower to Newcastle, to the art school, and they asked me to go round there with some paintings and drawings, and took me in. I did the B.A. in Fine Art at King's College, Newcastle, and that's really when I began to read enormously as well, in politics and psychiatry and history and philosophy, in a completely random way of course.

I think that's when I began to make the connection between political philosophy in terms of Marxism and the circumstances under which I'd been born and brought up. What started out as the 'us and them' thing that working-class kids had, and working-class parents too for that matter, was filled out by political self-education, and it rapidly developed into a sort of crude Marxism. But this is during the period from 1949 to 1953, the height of the Cold War, and there was also this necessity to develop a knowledge of Stalinism as well. So I grew up simultaneously with a feeling that Marxism-Leninism was the basis for a coherent political philosophy, and at the same time with a horrified awareness of what had happened to the Bolshevik revolution, and what Stalinism meant. Like most people of my age I was deeply influenced by people like Orwell and Koestler. I never had any illusions about Stalinism, which meant that I never considered joining the Communist Party.

But the Campaign for Nuclear Disarmament later became a focus for your political activity?

I think it became a focus and to some extent a mystification. Because to concentrate on the issue of nuclear weapons was an un-dialectical thing to do. I perhaps still hadn't properly understood the dialectical approach to history, and so I was a bit impressionistic in my politics, the communist-without-a-party idea. I couldn't see any development of communism to which I could give my allegiance. I was driven and drove myself into an abstract position. So I went to Paris for two years and started by burying myself in painting. Then I realized I wasn't ever going to be an important painter — and if I wasn't going to be a good painter, I didn't want to be a painter at all.

So you started writing instead?

Yes. When I'd been at King's College, Stanley Eveling was a postgraduate student there, and editor of the college magazine. He printed a few stories of mine, and it was partly through his influence, and partly from this accumulating alienation from any idea of myself as a painter, that I started writing. And one day in Paris I just said to myself, you are not going to be a good painter, stop. So I burnt all the canvasses, and started writing interminably bad novels — about wandering, homeless, stateless heroes.

Were you trying to get the novels published?

My first novel was sent by a friend to Sonia Orwell, who was with Weidenfeld and Nicolson at the time, and she asked me over to meet her, and I thought I'd really hit the big time. She gave me a delightful lunch, and was extremely charming and bright, and then informed me as I tottered away a bit drunk that she thought the novel was dazzling but unpublishable. So I didn't really make much effort after that to get anything published, and the shift from novel-writing into plays actually came about through a nervous breakdown — back in London in 1957, living in friends' flats, split marriage, face turned to the wall. Finally, one day I realized that it was going to be suicide if I didn't do something about it. I had sufficient functioning left in me to be aware of that, and I staggered into the Tavistock Clinic one day — I must have been looking like all hell — saying, 'Can somebody help me? Will somebody help me?' And they immediately took me in and gave me all kinds of interviews and tests and God knows what, and finally I ended up being interviewed by the head of the British Institute for Psychoanalysis, who, putting his fingers together the way they do, these people, said, 'Well, Mr. Mercer, we've finally decided after our investigations and tests that you are (pause) a suitable case for treatment.'

They got me into analysis at the British Institute of Psychoanalysis amazingly cheaply, five days a week for two pounds. So I started teaching in order just to live and eat — and pay for analysis. You begin to create a very primitive form of stability out of the sheer need to pay for your analysis. It was during the first year of psychoanalysis that I started writing plays.

What were you teaching?

I started off by teaching English to foreign students in a private school. By this time I'd met Jon Silkin, the poet, and we were sharing a flat with about a hundred other people, it seemed, in Hampstead. Jon was working in this school, and he got me a job there, teaching English solidly six hours a day, for twelve pounds a week. And through the process of analysis, and delving back into the past and re-experiencing primal relationships and all the rest of it, it suddenly dawned on me that the wandering, homeless, stateless person in the novels was in fact myself. Then in the middle of analysis, when words came to me, when ideas came to me, they ceased to come in a narrative form and began to occur as images and as speeches. And one day I went to see *A Taste of Honey*, and read in the paper that Shelagh Delaney wrote it because *she'd* been to see a Rattigan play, and thought, if you call that good playwriting, I can do better. And after I'd seen *A Taste of Honey* I thought, well, if that's a good play, I'm bloody sure I can do better. So I wrote a play in 1959-60, which became the first of *The Generations* trilogy, *Where the Difference Begins*. It wasn't simply a question of going back to childhood, to one's mother and father and sibling and all the rest of it, but also the recognition that perhaps the first thing you can properly do as a writer is to deal with what you really know about. So that play was very much to do with my own circumstances. It was also the play that got me taken on by Peggy Ramsay, when she was given a copy of it through a friend.

It was written as a stage play?

Yes, and in fact it was optioned several times by Oscar Lewenstein. But I believe he thought that the whole northern working-class thing was beginning to work itself out, in the way that the West End tends to adopt a fashion and then imagines it's somehow been dealt with.

But apart from A Taste of Honey *you hadn't yourself been influenced by these plays?*

It's all hack now, but I really was tremendously affected and infected by *Look Back in Anger*, because it simply burst the doors of the bourgeois middle-class theatre wide open. But while we were waiting for Lewenstein to make up his mind Peggy Ramsay sent the play to the BBC, where it was read by Don Taylor. He got quite an obsession about it, and more or less pushed it through. And even by the BBC's own standards it was quite successful, because it seemed to get a response from ordinary working-class people, who knew the scene, whilst the middle classes and the students and so on responded to the political and social implications. So the BBC made their by now well-known promise, that what I wrote they would do: and this was reinforcing, tremendously reinforcing, and tended to keep me in television drama for some years. They were paying me enough to live, so I stayed with the BBC, and more or less with Don Taylor, for four or five television plays before I got into live theatre.

Did you conceive The Generations *as a trilogy from the start?*

No, the idea really evolved during the first play. The central figure is obviously the old working-class feller, and how his contact and communication with his children is disrupted through their being educated. Then Don Taylor and I almost simultaneously got the idea that maybe a play about the children would be a good thing. By that time I was pretty deeply involved with CND and the Committee of One Hundred, and so I wrote *A Climate of Fear* — then *The Birth of a Private Man* evolved naturally from that, and was related to my growing disillusionment with the anti-nuclear movement.

How far is there an element of reportage in these plays — how far are they autobiographical, really?

The first play was very much so, although I now think that the father is vastly idealized. My father is really a reactionary working-class racist bigot, although he still thinks he's Labour.

Much more the father in After Haggerty . . .

Yes, he got his come-uppance in *After Haggerty*. I had to 'do' him.

No guilt feelings about that?

Of course there are. I feel guilty about taking to pieces or dissecting a character with whom I have obviously complex and contradictory relations and feelings. At the same time, I don't think anything has ever stopped me from using actual characters, if they fitted into the scheme of the play. You know how characters come out — that curious mixture of what they are in life and what their dramatic necessity is — so I suppose one's plays are always in some sense autobiographical.

You don't use actual situations, or what people have actually said?

I never collect, as it were, people's speech. I'm much more concerned with the invention than the recording of speech. As a matter of fact, I think in quite a few of the plays where speech appears to be naturalistic it's really very formal and stylized. Even in *Where the Difference Begins*, when the old working-class father's talking, he's only talking what *seems* to be day-to-day northern dialect — in fact it's highly structured. But it's a completely unconscious process. I really don't understand what conscious intention in writing is, at any level. I don't know what a character is going to say, I don't know what a scene is going to contain, I have only the vaguest ideas about the events in a play. It really is a question of sitting down and hoping.

I can remember personally feeling rather depressed by your work at that time —

having felt with Where the Difference Begins *and* A Climate of Fear, *here at last is a writer who can deal with politics in plays without either preaching or being nihilistic,* The Birth of a Private Man *seemed suddenly to negate this position, and then it was almost irrelevant to* A Suitable Case for Treatment.

But it was relevant. I think that if you are intellectually and emotionally committed to a particular ideology, as I was and am to theoretical communism, and yet find no way of becoming active in the world which is consistent with your beliefs, this does create just the kind of split that is dramatized in *A Suitable Case for Treatment*. Morgan, remember, was the son of a communist working-class family, and perhaps turning the whole thing into a joke and resorting to fantasy was his only way of coping with the situation . . .

All the same the transition in those early plays from direct political consciousness to a sense of total estrangement does seem abrupt . . .

I think *The Birth of a Private Man* signals the coming preoccupation with madness, with people who can't live in society without either getting locked up or put away or forfeiting the love and affection and care of people around them . . . the mavericks, I suppose.

Although, curiously, the plays about madness have somehow a more objective quality than the first two parts of the trilogy . . .

Yes, I think I was becoming much more aware of the individual as embodying an entire social area with political associations — and it was after *A Suitable Case for Treatment* and *For Tea on Sunday*, which is another television play about a nut, that I began to read Ronnie Laing. And in the way that when I was in college Marxism-Leninism had made sense of what the working class and the 'thirties and all that were about, now Laing seemed to be making sense of a whole lot of questions about sanity and madness that, particularly in my own case, were very closely related to the political questions. At that time, anyway, Ronnie thought of himself as a Marxist too, and I was looking for a synthesis between the problems of the individual in society and the problems of the society that produces the individuals.

Did Laing co-operate in the writing of In Two Minds?

He was official consultant on it. After all, I'm not a trained psychiatrist and I was writing in territory of which he had a great deal of clinical experience. It was a completely invented piece, by the way, it wasn't a Laing case-history — though it had all the characteristics of one. Laing was in any case ethically prevented from giving me access to his files. But once you've grasped the Laingian idea of the schizogenic family, and if you can write, then you can invent a schizogenic family which has its counterpart in the real world but which is inevitably viewed from a Laingian position (which I still hold *vis-à-*

vis the theories of madness). I don't think there was any plagiarizing involved. There was a mutual fertilization: I was very impressed with his ideas, and he said that he was very reinforced to find that somebody had intuitively been writing about characters in a way that he recognized as making sense in terms of his clinical theories. But I invented every single word and I didn't even know, when I was writing, that it was going to be given a documentary treatment by Ken Loach. I thought we'd be in the studio, with actors and constructed sets.

You seemed to be exploring the technical potential of television much more fully by this time — especially in the last play of that early bout of writing for television, And Did Those Feet.

Yes, the things that happen in *And Did Those Feet* — how on earth could one get them across? Lord Fountain leaping about the countryside on his horse and crashing every third hunt and breaking a leg, things like that, and the scene in the zoo where the twins let all the animals out, or on trapezes in the swimming bath full of toy animals.

Yet despite the fluidity in your TV work, your earliest plays for the stage, The Governor's Lady *and* Ride a Cock Horse, *seem well within the normal conventions of live theatre. Did you feel yourself more convention-bound when you began writing for the stage?*

I think it's part of the medium. Working in the theatre was for me, for some reason which I can't quite define, curiously traditional, at least until *After Haggerty.* If the plays are worth anything, they're worth something for what is said and done, not for how — but of course the whole tendency in contemporary non-bourgeois theatre, as I suppose they would call it, is towards the *how*, towards feeling and sensation in the literal sense, light and sound and colour and movement and emotion and participation. I'm personally quite repelled by this particular development in the theatre.

Hence that extrapolated parody of the Living Theatre in After Haggerty . . .?

Well, yes, that was a bit wicked of me, but more or less expressed how I felt about it. I had gone through the experience of being at *Paradise Now* at the Roundhouse, and having Julian Beck screaming and yelling at me to be free. Now the idea of being tyrannized into being free strikes me as being rather contradictory, and I was really rather turned off by the Living Theatre, and by various other things going on in the theatre — *Vagina Rex and the Gas Oven* was another deadly experience for me. A lot of it I kind of admire and appreciate, particularly Berman's street theatre and Agitprop and so on . . . at the same time, I guess, whether it's my age, my generation or whatever, to me it's a development out of which can come only a social meaning rather than an artistic result. The on-the-hoof and participatory kinds of theatre have become therapeutic social rituals in which people may or may not be able to experience new things and releases within themselves, rather than what I would call an artistic experience. I guess this does really set me apart from the younger generation.

I used to do a great deal of travelling round the universities. I virtually packed it in two years ago when I had rather an unpleasant experience at Essex University, at their so-called Revolutionary Be-In. I regard this as being my personal failure, not what they were like, but my sudden slump afterwards. Well, you know, fuck it, if they don't want to talk, if they just want to have 'happenings' and scrawl slogans from Plekhanov to Regis Debray all over the walls and burn a car in the campus . . . One lad came up to me — I was with John Arden — and they threw a smoke-bomb in the auditorium, and this kid said 'That is a more meaningful event than anything either Arden or you could say.' So Arden diffidently said, 'What does it mean then,' and he replied, 'It means what it means, man.' Arden and I rather shiftily ambled out.

Ride a Cock Horse *certainly seems very much a play for the previous generation* . . .

It was the inevitable play for many people who become what's termed successful — out of a life in which they were originally destined to be utterly 'other'. If I'd been born into any other family, or at a slightly different time, I might well be down the pit now, or a clerk in the town hall, or whatever . . . And *Ride a Cock Horse* was the play you write when you finally realize that the links are broken, that you have no positive connection with what you've left behind, and no positive relation to what is now possible. And yet of course one is unconsciously still deeply related to the past, so that the two major characters in that play are really the mother and father to whom Peter is constantly praying, as a sort of convention to enable him to say rotten things about them. That's still the only way he expresses the past. He can't live in the environment which would relate him to the past, nor can he tolerate the environment into which his talent and hitting the jackpot with a novel brought him.

How did the breakthrough into live theatre actually happen?

I suppose I really broke in with *The Governor's Lady*, which was produced in the same year as *Ride a Cock Horse*, although it was originally a radio play. I must really have felt that I had to come to terms with the parallel process in me to the one in *Ride a Cock Horse*. I was also beginning to become obsessed and rather anguished by the question of the relationship between men and women, the male chauvinism thing . . . I think I was already dimly Women's Lib years and years before it became a social carry-on — partly because I was one of the great guilty, and probably still am. The trouble is that however intellectually men recognize the complicatedly awful position of women in society, the more primitive male instincts and assumptions, and the whole weight of history and tradition, still urge men to relate to women in a primitive way. My personal life has been a history of wrecked and failed relationships with women, and perhaps that had to get into a play too.

Belcher's Luck seems to be in those terms a kind of act of revenge on an overwhelming parent — very, very forceful most of the way through the play, yet finally getting his come-uppance . . .

Yes, I think the wrong person got killed in *Belcher's Luck*.

It's a very curious play. It always seems to me the odd one out in your work. What was the impulse behind it?

Obviously it's a metaphor for England and its class structure — there is this *déclassé* in the character of Belcher's son, the unclassed person who is educated and committed to nothing and no one, and so can speak freely and be a bit dotty with it. Yet the one thing that characterized the traditional destiny of the English working class is that they always lose out — in fact this applies to the working class anywhere, even in a revolutionary country, they are always cheated. In the case of the Bolshevik revolution it was obviously due to the complex results of Stalin coming to power. Under capitalism it's the enormous resilience and strength of the owning class and the ruling class. I guess I wanted to present that simply as a metaphor — here is this huge, bull-like, sexually virile, strong man who is in a master-servant relationship, virtually seduced into overthrowing the king figure by the nephew, and then the nephew turns round and overrules him, because he's still an employee. Then there's the rather dubious and corrupt association between the *déclassé* working-class son and the new kind of upper-class modern figure, of the kind which now has a very powerful presence in business and technology. Now what the old man's niece wanted in *Belcher's Luck* was really to possess this crumbling, decaying old England, and do a white-hot technology bit on it: and there is some curious collusion between the swollen middle class created by post-war education, and the traditional middle class and upper-middle class, because the ex-working-class people on the whole have accepted middle-class values and objectives.

Your next stage play, Flint, *has on the face of it another metaphorical sort of hero, a minister of the Church of England who's randy and agnostic . . .*

Yes, that play is really about the obsolescence of institutions, and the contradiction that we create institutions which are intended for our communal benefit, be it material or spiritual, but which become huge kind of road-blocks in the way of the development and evolution of the society. So that I guess I could have written *Flint* in the context of the Communist Party, or in the context of ICI, but I chose the Church because it is such an abiding institution with such a long history, in such a hypocritical position in our society, which has perhaps ossified even further than the various institutions of political democracy, and because it would simply be more available to people than if I'd narrowed it down to the CP or something else.

You've never yourself been tempted by the certainties of institutionalized religion any more than by those of the institutionalized Communist Party?

I've always been rather overawed by the Catholic argument from design — that if there's a watch there must be a watchmaker. I can pound my way through it philosophically, wearing my Wittgenstein clogs or my logical-positivist clogs, but at the same time the argument seems to me to have a kind of inherent grandeur and necessity, before which one day I might crumble, though I think my immunity is pretty high.

One senses that your next stage play, After Haggerty, *and the Kelvin trilogy on television, represented some sort of summing-up of your own work and development so far . . .*

Yes, I think that the Kelvin trilogy and *After Haggerty* in its way were summing-up plays, gathering together strands going back into the past, both personally and artistically, and they may represent the end of one particular direction for me. I'm in the middle of a new stage play at the moment, and I find that I'm searching in a more painful way than ever to create an invented world, in which the preoccupations of my middle age will begin to express themselves. *Haggerty* and the Kelvin plays do represent the end of about ten years' development of certain themes and autobiographical preoccupations, and what's going to come after is I think going to be much, much more subjective in all kinds of ways.

And formally more experimental?

Probably, yes. This last television play, *The Bankrupt*, is a very weird piece, I think. I really don't know what I feel about it. It still contains bits and pieces of the past, but it contains also a movement away. There's nothing more salutary than a developing sense of death, really — of coming to terms with death — and I think when you get into your forties, you begin to have a relationship to death which is qualitatively different from when you're a younger person. Obviously, anybody can die at any moment, but when you're into your early middle age that sense of the possibility of dying at any moment ceases to be a question of all the accidents that could overtake you, or the diseases that you might accidentally have, and is supplanted by an increasing sense of the death contained within you, as an inevitable biological process. I would hope to develop one or two comedies of death, and comedies of relationship to death. I think death is something I've got to deal with now.

6

Tom Stoppard

ambushes for the audience

Even back in 1966, deciding on an evening's entertainment from the plentiful offerings on the Edinburgh Festival fringe presented an invidious choice: but almost as soon as the curtain in the Cranston Street Hall had risen on the Oxford Theatre Group's production of a new play by a previously unknown writer, Tom Stoppard, one sensed that here was something out of the usual run of undergraduate jeux d'esprit. *Not that* Rosencrantz and Guildenstern Are Dead — *which by the following spring had found its way into the repertoire of the National Theatre — was lacking in the better qualities of a* jeu d'esprit, *for Tom Stoppard has never been reluctant to treat the most erudite of ideas as his playthings. Though given to bouts of seriousness — on the relationship between art, politics, and revolution in* Travesties, *or on the rights and wrongs of so-called press freedom in* Night and Day — *Stoppard's unquenchable delight in combining the resources of the English language with the potential for philosophical paradox usually spills well over such possible constraints.*

Stoppard himself makes an interesting distinction in this interview between his 'nuts and bolts' comedies, such as After Magritte — *a joyous attempt to carry off a 'comic coup in pure mechanistic terms' — and his more complex works. But he concedes that, even in these longer plays, no 'single, clear statement' emerges — rather, there's a 'series of conflicting statements made by conflicting characters,' who 'tend to play a sort of infinite leap-frog'. Interviewing Tom Stoppard was rather like that.*

As a dramatist, he has had little experience of failure, and such dramatic sports as The Real Inspector Hound *or* Dirty Linen *have enjoyed even longer runs than the limitations of playing in repertoire allowed* Travesties *or* Jumpers. *Finally, with* Night and Day, *Stoppard played according to the West End rules, and won a long run at the Phoenix Theatre. It remains to be seen whether he will continue to tap the slightly more naturalistic vein of that play, or return to the bedroom philosophizing of* Jumpers — *'love among the logical positivists', as no less an authority than A.J. Ayer approvingly dubbed it.*

Tom Stoppard came to our old Goodge Street office to talk with Roger Hudson, Catherine Itzin, and myself, one cold morning in January 1974, just before Travesties *went into rehearsal for the Royal Shakespeare Company. Born in Zlin, Czechoslovakia, in 1937, he'd left that country with his father, mother, and elder brother just before the outbreak of war.*

That's right. My father was employed by a very large shoe company, Bata, as company doctor — they transferred many of their employees to different parts of the world, and we went to Singapore.

And it was there that your father was killed after the Japanese invasion, when you were — what, four?

Yes — it was women and children first, and he remained behind, while my mother and my brother and I were evacuated to India.

How much do you remember of all this?

I've very little recollection of Singapore, but vivid memories of India, for which I have a huge nostalgia. But I've never been back. I imagine I'd be fairly disillusioned and despairing if I did, with the population increase, for one thing.

Were you 'poor whites', or reasonably well-off?

Neither, really. My mother was manageress of the Bata shoe shop in Darjeeling for some time, and we never seemed to be particularly short of money. I suppose we were just living the ordinary sort of life of a working mother with two sons. But quite soon after the war my mother remarried — an Englishman in the British army in India, name of Stoppard.

A step-up to the sahib class?

Well, the lower-sahib class, I suppose, though I don't remember feeling in the sahib class — except perhaps towards the very end, when I was older. I went to an American school, but Indians went there too — all nationalities did, in fact.

And the family moved to England in 1946 — anticipating independence?

No, my new father came from England, and was simply going back there now the war was over — simply as a soldier going home. The first school I ever went to was an English convent, and English had always been my own language.

Your step-father left the army?

Yes — he was, and is, in the machine-tool business, and this involved moving from place to place at first, as he moved up the machine-tool ladder. We lived in Derbyshire and Yorkshire, and somewhere else too, I think, before moving to Bristol round about 1950.

But you were away at preparatory and a boarding grammar school — a 'privileged' education?

Well, the chief influence of my education on me was negative, and whether that had much to do with it being privileged is open to doubt. I left school thoroughly bored by the idea of anything intellectual, and gladly sold all my Greek and Latin classics to George's Bookshop in Park Street. I'd been totally bored and alienated by everyone from Shakespeare to Dickens.

Had you been expected to try for university?

I suppose in a notional sense everyone at Pocklington was. But don't get the wrong idea — it wasn't a school where everyone wore boaters and communicated in Latin, just a grammar school in a small Yorkshire town.

What age were you when you sold the books to George's?

For eighteen shillings, something like that . . . I was seventeen, and it took about another five years for me to start buying them back — not the same books, but books.

In between, you started in journalism?

Yes, this was while the family was still living in Bristol, so I joined the *Western Daily Press* straight from school, in 1954, living at home on £2-10s-8d a week. I stayed with them till I got sort of poached by the *Bristol Evening World* in 1958 for another couple of years. It was during this time that I started wanting to write for the theatre.

Why for the theatre, rather than novels or poetry, do you think?

Historical accident. After 1956 everybody of my age who wanted to write, wanted to write plays — after Osborne and the rest at the Court, and with Tynan on the *Observer*, and Peter Hall about to take over the RSC. In a sense I was writing plays for Tynan and Peter Hall.

And A Walk on the Water *was the first.*

Yes. I was on holiday in Italy, and it struck me that I was never going to start writing unless I did something active about it, so when I got back I handed my notice in, making sure I had two weekly columns for bread and butter while I was writing the play, which I did in the second half of 1960.

How easy a play was A Walk on the Water *to write?*

I wrote it very easily in about three months, and I was astonished with myself — every day there was more done and less to do, and I hadn't stopped, and instead of getting harder it was getting easier. I was working in a sort of panic because — at my ripe old age it's hard to believe, but at that time it seemed incredibly important that I hadn't done any of the things by the age of 23 that I'd intended doing by the age of 21. So I was doing everything two years late, and really had to get down to it. I was living with a very nice family in Bristol, paying very little for my board and lodgings — in a sense, it was the good old days, from the point of view of life's complexity, though as it turns out the new days are good too.

I gave the play to the Bristol Old Vic, naturally, as I had lots of friends there, though I don't think I did anything with it for a while. But the whole thing was very amorphous, it was just a way of getting it assessed, as though there was never any possibility of it being performed. Ah yes, and then my life was changed. I asked someone at the Bristol Old Vic if they knew of an agent, and they recommended Kenneth Ewing, who handled the literary side of Fraser and Dunlop. So I sent off the play to him, and he didn't have my phone number or something, because I had one of those Hollywood-style telegrams that change struggling young artists' lives. I had never had ten quid in a lump sum before, and within a fortnight I was given a hundred pounds and Tennant's had an option on the play, and they were discussing various actors, all of whom were knighted. The option was for a year: a year later back came the play.

And in the meantime . . .?

I was writing theatre reviews for *Scene* magazine, which lasted eight or nine months, and that of course got me to London. One room, scratching a living, not writing much apart from a few short stories — three of which Faber eventually published. Another one which they didn't particularly go for I turned into the radio play *M Is for Moon Among Other Things* — the one about Marilyn Monroe's death. I was also hired by the *Daily Express* in some sort of showbiz category, but that got overruled by someone higher up. Fortunately, though, it was just about the time that *Scene* folded that I was managing the transition to living off playwriting, because *Walk on the Water* was bought by one of the commercial television companies. One television play then was worth about 150 weeks' rent to me.

All this adds up to . . . what, four years between the writing of that play and Rosencrantz and Guildenstern?

Yes, I began writing *Rosencrantz* in 1964. But that wasn't because I was in any sort of despair or sulks, I was just busy or lazy. I don't think I got too overwrought with disappointments over *Walk on the Water,* though my memory *is* very good at erasing things I'd rather not remember. Also, very conveniently, just after *Scene* folded, and after *Walk on the Water* had been done on TV, Charles Marowitz was asked by some Germans if he knew any promising young playwrights, because the Ford Foundation was financing a kind of annual cultural picnic in Berlin — part of the general effort around that time to keep Berlin alive in every sense, I suppose. So between May and October they had this colloquium, which in 1964 was to be for young playwrights. We were fed and housed in great comfort and just asked to get on with it. Of course, it was quite incapacitating.

This must be the occasion Charles Marowitz describes in Confessions of a Counterfeit Critic — *one of the confessions being that he thought the early version of* Rosencrantz *you sketched out there was quite hopeless . . .?*

Oh yes, what I wrote in Germany, if I remember — and I'm trying to forget — was just a sort of Shakespearian pastiche. It was Kenneth Ewing who gave me the idea, driving back from some abortive attempt to get ABC Television to commission a play from me — all my ideas were 'too downbeat,' they said. But he suggested that it should take place in England, and I remember writing a version — maybe the one Charles read — in which they got to England, and King Lear was on the throne . . . I mean, the whole thing was unspeakable. But it did contain some of the dialogue which still exists in the play.

Can you trace the progress of the play from that embryonic version to the one put on two years later at the National Theatre?

Not very adequately in terms of my intellectual process. What I do remember is that the transition from one play to the other was an attempt to find a solution to a practical problem — that if you write a play about Rosencrantz and Guildenstern in England, you can't count on people knowing who they are and how they got there. So one tended to get back into the end of *Hamlet* a bit. But the explanations were always partial and ambiguous, so one went back a bit further into the plot, and as soon as I started doing this I totally lost interest in England. The interesting thing was them at Elsinore.

Were you still looking on it as a play about a play — Hamlet — or a play about these two characters . . .

By this time I was not in the least interested in doing any sort of pastiche, for a start, or in doing a criticism of *Hamlet* — that was simply one of the by-products. The chief interest and objective was to exploit a situation which seemed to me to have enormous dramatic and comic potential — of these two guys who in Shakespeare's context don't really know what they're doing. The little they are told is mainly lies, and there's no reason to suppose that they ever find out why they are killed. And, probably more in the early 'sixties than at any other time, that would strike a young playwright as being a pretty good thing to explore. I mean, it has the right combination of specificity and vague generality which was interesting at that time to (it seemed) eight out of ten playwrights. That's why, when the play appeared, it got subjected to so many different kinds of interpretation, all of them plausible, but none of them calculated.

What was calculated?

What was actually calculated was to entertain a roomful of people with the situation of Rosencrantz and Guildenstern at Elsinore. The chief thing that added one line to another line was that the combination of the two should retain an audience's interest in some way. I tend to write through a series of small, large, and microscopic ambushes — which might consist of a body falling out of a cupboard, or simply an unexpected word in a sentence. But my preoccupation as a writer, which possibly betokens a degree of insecurity, takes the form of contriving to inject some sort of interest and colour into every line, rather than counting on the general situation having a general interest which will hold an audience.

With hindsight, do you think Rosencrantz was more a play about, well, existential problems posed by bit-part characters in Shakespeare, or was it, maybe subconsciously, asking questions about more general, more 'real' philosophical problems?

First I must say that I didn't know what the word 'existential' meant until it was applied to *Rosencrantz*. And even now existentialism is not a philosophy I find either attractive or plausible. But it's certainly true that the play can be interpreted in existential terms, as well as in other terms. But I must make clear that, insofar as it's possible for me to look at my own work objectively at all, the element which I find most valuable is the one that other people are put off by — that is, that there is very often *no* single, clear statement in my plays. What there is, is a series of conflicting statements made by conflicting characters, and they tend to play a sort of infinite leap-frog. You know, an argument, a refutation, then a rebuttal of the refutation, then a counter-rebuttal, so that there is never any point in this intellectual leap-frog at which I feel *that* is the speech to stop it on, *that* is the last word.

That's curious, because I would have thought it could be said of quite a few of your plays, the more recent ones particularly, that they are solutions to problems, in a quite precise though often a very comic sense — After Magritte, for example, The Real Inspector Hound or Artist Descending a Staircase . . .

If you're thinking of a situation as being a metaphor for a more general confusion then of course that's true of *After Magritte*; but that's not an intellectual play, it's a nuts-and-bolts comedy.

How conscious are you before you start that this play is going to be a nuts-and-bolts comedy, and this other play's going to have philosophical complications?

Wholly. You see, I've only written four full-length plays, one being *Walk on the Water*, which doesn't really count in this respect. Now the other three — that includes the new one, *Travesties* — are in this area of trying to marry the play of ideas to comedy or farce. At the same time, I don't think of myself, I don't think of any writer, as ploughing that narrow a field. *After Magritte* and *The Real Inspector Hound* are short plays and they really are an attempt to bring off a sort of comic coup in pure mechanistic terms. They were *conceived* as short plays. The one thing that *The Real Inspector Hound* isn't about, as far as I'm concerned, is theatre critics. I originally conceived a play, exactly the same play, with simply two members of an audience getting involved in the play-within-the-play. But when it came actually to writing something down which had integral entertainment value, if you like, it very quickly occurred to me that it would be a lot easier to do it with critics, because you've got something known and defined to parody. So it was never a play *about* drama critics. If one wishes to say that it is a play about something more than that, then it's about the dangers of wish-fulfilment. But as soon as the word's out of my mouth I think, shit, it's a play about these two guys, and they're going along to this play, and the whole thing is tragic and hilarious and very, very carefully constructed. I'm very fond of the play because I didn't know how to do it. I just got into it, and I knew that I wanted it somehow to resolve itself in a breathtakingly neat, complex but utterly comprehensible way.

I find it very interesting, this combination of your not knowing what's going to happen and of knowing exactly what's going to happen — or exactly what you want it to come out like, anyway.

Well, for anyone who is actually familiar with *Hound*, I didn't know that the body was Higgs, and I didn't know that Magnus was going to be Puckeridge. I mean, as soon as I realized the body had to be Higgs and, later, Magnus had to be Puckeridge, as solutions to the probems in writing that play, it made sense of all the things I'd been trying to keep going. But it's a sort of risk operation, that particular play. *After Magritte* was worked out very carefully.

There's something equally careful about how many of your plays operate, yet one does wonder very much how the more eccentric situations germinate.

Before *The Real Inspector Hound*, I wrote a sort of goon-show version of it, which had no kind of structure — it was just a situation of two people watching a whodunnit and getting involved in it. I wrote that in Bristol after *The Gamblers*, and then didn't finish it and kept it about, and brought it out again in 1967. But I have enormous difficulty in working out plots, so actually to use *Hamlet*, or a classical whodunnit, or another play (which I'm afraid I've just done again) for a basic structure, takes a lot of the pressure off.

I suppose even plays like Albert's Bridge *or* If You're Glad I'll be Frank *also rely on . . . not so much familiar situations as familiar metaphors — painting the Forth Bridge, and the faintly ridiculous concept of a 'speaking clock', in those cases.*

Yes — in fact *If You're Glad* actually had its origins in a series the BBC were contemplating, which I don't think ever happened, about people in absurd jobs which didn't really exist, and the idea of doing one about the speaking-clock girl occurred to me then. For me, it is such a relief to get an idea! I know there are writers who are not going to live long enough to do justice to all the ideas they have, but to me it's like being struck by lightning, and I feel just as powerless to *make* it happen — even, as it were, by hanging about under trees in thunderstorms.

You clearly don't feel yourself part of a 'movement', and your plays could hardly be called social or political. Does this mean you have no strong political feelings, or simply that they're not what you want to write plays about?

Look, can we clear a few decks to avoid confusion? I'm a professional writer — I'm for hire, if you like — as well as being someone who pursues his own path in his writing. Latterly I have been able to stick to accepting the kind of jobs which happen to lie on my own path, but in the past I've written all kinds of stuff, everything from 70 episodes of a serial translated into Arabic for Bush House, to a one-off spy thing for Granada. Furthermore, the plays which I do from pure choice are not all of a kind either. I find it confusing to talk about 'my plays' as though *Hound* and *Jumpers* were the same sort of thing. Obviously, the two have things in common — for example, *Jumpers* is a serious play dealt with in the farcical terms which in *Hound* actually *constitute* the play. Much the same is true of the play I have just finished, *Travesties*, which (and this is pertinent to your question) asks whether the words 'revolutionary' and 'artist' are capable of being synonymous, or whether they are mutually exclusive, or something in between.

Okay. So forget the Arabs and *Hound* and whatever, and here I am as the author of *Jumpers*, *Travesties*, and of my next unwritten, unthought-of play which we will, optimistically, assume represents perfectly the kind of theatre I am interested in. That's 'my plays'. Next — 'political plays'. Well, here are some plays which I have seen or read in the last year or so and which I assume all go into your political bag: Hampton's *Savages*, Griffiths's *The Party*, Fugard's *Sizwe Bansi is Dead*, and his *Hello and Goodbye*, Hare's *The Great Exhibition* — and *Slag* if you like. I haven't seen Brenton's *Magnificence*, only the earlier ones, but there was another very good Griffiths — *Occupations* — and then the combined work, *Lay-by*.

Well, there are political plays which are about specific situations, and there are political plays which are about a general political situation, and there are plays which are political acts in themselves, insofar as it can be said that attacking or insulting or shocking an audience is a political act (and it *is* said). There are even plays *about* politics which are about as *political* as *Charley's Aunt*. The term 'political play' is a loose one if one is thinking of *Roots* as well as *Lear* — I mean Bond's — as well as *Lay-by*. So much so that I don't think it is meaningful or useful to make that distinction between them and *Jumpers*, which obviously isn't a political act, nor is it a play about politics, nor is it a play about ideology. There is an element in it which satirizes a joke-fascist outfit but you can safely ignore that too. On the other hand the play reflects my belief that all political acts have a moral basis to them and are meaningless without it.

Is that disputable?

Absolutely. For a start it goes against Marxist-Leninism in particular, and against all materialistic philosophy. I believe all political acts must be judged in moral terms, in terms of their consequences. Otherwise they are simply attempts to put the boot on some other foot. There is a sense in which contradictory political arguments are restatements of each other. For example. Leninism and fascism are restatements of totalitarianism. The repression which for better or worse turned out to be Leninism in action after 1917 was very much worse than anything which had gone on in Czsarist Russia. I mean, in purely mundane boring statistical terms, which sometimes can contain the essence of a situation, it is simply true that in the ten years after 1917 fifty times more people were done to death than in the *fifty years* before 1917.

The boot, in other words, was on the other foot, and how, but the point is not to compare one ruthless regime with another — it is to set each one up against a moral standard, a consistent idea of what constitutes good and bad in the way human beings treat each other regardless of class, colour, or ideology, and at least my poor professor in *Jumpers* got *that* right. Even before I read Lenin it always seemed to me — well, curious, that while he was in a Czsarist prison, and in Czsarist exile, he managed to research and write his book on the development of capitalism in Russia, and receive books and magazines, and write to friends, all that, whereas — well, compare Solzhenitsyn.

People tend to think of Stalinism as being something else, a perversion of Leninism. That is an absurd and foolish untruth, and it is one on which much of the Left bases itself. Lenin perverted Marxism, and Stalin carried on from there. When one reads pre-revolutionary Lenin, notably *What Is to Be Done?* but also all the letters and articles in which he railed against the early Marxists who had the temerity to disagree with him, one can see with awful clarity that ideological differences are often temperamental differences in ideological disguise — and also that the terror to come was implicit in the Lenin of 1900.

The great irony about Marx was that his impulses were deeply moral while his intellect insisted on a materialistic view of the world. His theory of capital, his theory of value, and his theory of revolution, have all been refuted by modern economics and by history. In short he got it wrong. But he was a giant whose shadow still reaches us precisely for the reason that, wrong as he was in detail, the force he represented sprung from a sense of universal moral justice. He realized which way things would *have* to go, and then he put together a materialistic theory which was quite irrelevant, like sticking scaffolding on a moving train.

It was only a matter of time before somebody — it turned out to be Bernstein in 1900 — somebody with the benefit of an extra fifty years' hindsight, would actually point out that Marx had got it wrong, but that it didn't matter because social justice was going to come through other means. Bernstein reckoned that the class war wasn't the way, that human solidarity was a better bet than class solidarity. And this argument between 'hards' and 'softs' constitutes a great deal of radical argument today. It is not an argument about tactics — that's just surface dressing — it's an argument about philosophy. I mean Bernstein stuck his banner on the grave of Kant. So I'd like to write a play which would pertain to anything from a Latin American coup to the British Left, and probably when I've done it I'll still be asked why I don't write political plays.

If you are, perhaps it would be because your plays — to date, that is — are so philosophically opaque that they don't really make clear statements. I'm thinking particularly of the philosophical element in Jumpers.

Opacity would be a distinct failure in that play. I don't think of it as being opaque anyway, and I consider clarity is essential. On the other hand, if you mean that the mixing up of ideas in farce is a source of confusion, well, yes, god knows why I try to do it like that — presumably because I *am* like that. Plays are the people who write them. Seriousness compromised by frivolity. It gets up a few people's noses, but that's not important. At the same time I'm making all this sound much more self-confident than I feel. The thing is, if my plays were the end products of my ideas, they'd have it all more pat, but a lot of the time I've ended up trying to work out the ultimate implications of what I have written. My plays are a lot to do with the fact that *I just don't know.* This is something I tried to bring to the surface in a TV *One Pair of Eyes* programme, but to me it is even more evident in the thickets of dialogue. Few statements remain unrebutted. But I'm not going to rebut the things I have been saying just now. One thing I feel sure about is that a materialistic view of history is an insult to the human race.

Isn't there a danger that one just ends up with the conclusion that all political art is perhaps well-intentioned but impotent, so why bother?

The possibility of political art having a political effect in close-up, in specific terms, certainly exists, though I can't offhand think of an example of it happening, but it is in any case marginal compared to the possible and actual effects of, say, journalism. On that level, one *World in Action* is worth a thousand plays. Come to think of it, *Cathy Come Home* could be cited, though I don't know if it *changed* anything. But when Adam Raphael broke the story in the *Guardian* on wages in South Africa, within 48 hours the wages went up. Now Athol Fugard can't do that. God knows he can do things which Adam Raphael will never ever be able to do, but it is self-evident that the situation provokes a very important question, whether it is better to be Adam Raphael or Athol Fugard.

The plain truth is that if you are angered or disgusted by a particular injustice or immorality, and you want to do something about it, *now, at once,* then you can hardly do worse than write a play about it. That's what art is bad at. But the less plain truth is that *without* that play and plays like it, without artists, the injustice will *never* be eradicated. In other words, because of Athol Fugard, to stretch a point, the *Guardian* understood that the Raphael piece was worth leading the paper with, worth printing. That's why it's good and right that *Savages* has a long run in the West End. All kinds of people have said to me, how ridiculous to sit in the theatre and watch this, how pointless, how useless — what they were saying in effect was that Hampton's play wasn't going to save a single Indian, but that is to misunderstand what art means in the world. It's a terrible reason for *not* writing *Savages*.

At the same time, Hampton's plays, and Fugard's plays, are absolutely different from yours.

Of course. Fugard writes out of his experience as a white South African living against the current in a white supremacist regime. I write out of my experience as a middle-class bourgeois who prefers to read a book almost to doing anything else. If you say, then Fugard is much more important, I'd say, yes, of course he is! He's very much more important than me, just as he's much more important than the gang of playwrights who think that waving your cock at the audience is a revolutionary act and makes a play 'political'.

You said that in Travesties *you asked the question whether the terms artist and revolutionary could be synonymous — did you come to any sort of conclusion?*

The play puts the question in a more extreme form. It asks whether an artist has to justify himself in political terms *at all*. For example, if Joyce were alive today, he would say, juntas may come and juntas may go but Homer goes on for ever. And when he was alive he *did* say that the history of Ireland, troubles and all, was justified because it produced *him* and he produced *Ulysses*. Okay. So clearly one now has to posit a political prisoner taking comfort from the thought that at least he is in the country of Joyce, or of Homer, and to ask oneself whether Joyce, in moral terms, was myopic or had better vision than lesser men. And my answer to that question is liable to depend on the moment at which you run out of tape. Of course one feels uneasy in trying to work out questions that involve *oneself*, in terms of authentic geniuses, but it helps to clarify the issue. How do you measure the legacy of a genius who believed in art for art's sake?

Your plays are evidently at least moving *in the direction of 'issues'.*

Jumpers still breaks its neck to be entertaining as well, which was the intention, and it's still the way I tend to write things, though I think it's gradually becoming less so. With *Rosencrantz*, whatever lessons could be drawn from it, they were all just implied, and not necessarily by me at that. *Jumpers* was the first play in which I specifically set out to ask a question and try to answer it, or at any rate put the counter-question.

The way you've been talking am I right in thinking that you feel that it's your full-length plays which constitute your more important work, and the shorter the play the more occasional it is?

Yes, in practice. But I've been asked to do a short play now, and though I've no idea what I'll do, if anything, there's absolutely no reason why it shouldn't be a serious play. I think actually that it probably isn't a matter of length, it just happens that at the time when I wrote the short plays my inclinations were slightly different.

How far do you involve yourself in the first production of your plays?

Wholly.

And does the play itself undergo any change in the process?

Some, yes. One day, when I was out for ten minutes, Peter Wood cut a scene in two and played it backwards, and it was better. So we kept it. That was in *Jumpers*.

Normally you're there all the time to make sure things like that don't happen?

No, I sit there to *do* things like that if they're necessary. I'm free about that sort of thing as long as I'm there, and pretty rigid about it if I'm not. I think of rehearsal as being a very important part of getting the play right. Of the directors I've worked with, I had very good rapport with Robert Chetwyn, and with Peter Wood, and that is the main thing — it's not that somebody is born to direct your plays, or that they particularly understand them. I always feel it's like what Evelyn Waugh said about the Second World War, that the great thing was to do it among friends. Getting a play on is so awful, the important thing is to spend it among friends.

7

Peter Hall

on directing Pinter

*When Laurence Olivier stepped down from the artistic direction of the
National Theatre in 1973, the succession to that office of Peter Hall appeared
pre-ordained. This was the theatrical* enfant terrible *who had succeeded in
bringing Beckett's* Waiting for Godot *into the West End in 1955, and went on
in 1960 to shape the Royal Shakespeare Company into a true ensemble. At
Stratford and the Aldwych in the 'sixties, he politicized Shakespeare for his
generation, notably in a pacifistic* Troilus and Cressida *(momentously
coinciding with the Cuban missile crisis), the reworking with John Barton of
the history plays as* The Wars of the Roses, *and David Warner's* Hamlet.
*His other work with the RSC ranged from the drawing-room metaphysics of
Albee's* A Delicate Balance, *to the breathtaking, stage-brimming romp of his
brilliantly orchestrated* Government Inspector.*

*It was also at the Aldwych that Hall had directed for the first time plays by
Harold Pinter — the one-acter* The Collection, *and* The Homecoming. *The
association continued there with the double-bill* Landscape *and* Silence, *and
with* Old Times — *but by then Hall had handed over the direction of the RSC
to Trevor Nunn, true to the feeling he'd expressed some time earlier that the
natural life of such a permanent company was seldom more than ten years. In
1975 he led the National Theatre company from the Old Vic to its purpose-
built, triple-auditoria home on the South Bank, and here the relationship with
Pinter — and, indeed, with John Bury as designer — continued, with
productions of* No Man's Land *and* Betrayal.*

*Whatever one's feelings about the rights and wrongs of the existence of the
concrete colossus that is now the National Theatre — conceived as it was in an
age of affluence, but nurtured on scarce funding in a period of austerity — it's
arguable that the sheer bureaucratic burden that its running imposed on Hall
had some detrimental effects on his work as a director. But when Catherine
Itzin and I talked with him for TQ in July 1974, it was in the sprawling clutch
of Waterloo prefabs which served before the move as the administrative outpost
of the Old Vic, and here he entered into the discussion with articulate
enthusiasm.*

*It was, we felt, an important interview, since Pinter himself talks very
rarely about his own work, and then elliptically. But Hall had by this time
become securely established as Pinter's rightful interpreter on stage: and while
it would be wrong to try to pin down meanings too precisely, it was, surely, still*

valuable to talk about methods. We wondered, though, how the association had begun — relatively well into Pinter's own career, wasn't it?

In practice, yes. But Pinter had seen my production of *Godot* back in 1956 or 1957, and Michael Codron sent me *The Birthday Party* when it was first going to be done. I didn't know who Harold Pinter was, but I liked the play enormously. I couldn't do it though, because I had commitments in New York that year: and then when *The Caretaker* was sent to me, I couldn't do that, either, because I was just setting up the new companies at Stratford and the Aldwych. But I did put £250 into the production of *The Caretaker* at the Arts, which I think was capitalized at £1000 or something very low, and it earned me a surprising amount of money — it's one of the few times I've made money out of investing in plays, a hobby I've long since given up! I then put most of the money back into the film of *The Caretaker*. So there were these very early possibilities for association with Pinter, which didn't come to anything.

Can you remember now how you reacted when you first read The Birthday Party *by this unknown dramatist?*

Well, I heard the voice of Beckett, without any question, and the voice of Kafka — the horror, the terror of the unknown. But I did think the play was rather too bound by its own naturalism: you know, the three-act structure, the French's acting edition set. That was why I was so thrilled when I read *The Caretaker*, which seemed to have reached a point where the form was uniquely the dramatist's own. I don't think *The Birthday Party* is quite free from being a 'rep' play.

You didn't see the short-lived first production, presumably?

No — I remember actually coming back from New York on the Sunday morning after the opening, and reading Hobson's review. He was the only one more or less to get *The Birthday Party* right, and there in the same paper was the news that it had closed the previous night.

How well did you like Donald McWhinnie's production of The Caretaker?

I certainly liked it well enough to ask him to do I think three productions with the RSC. I didn't think it was quite hard enough, actually. It was a little explanatory — perhaps Pinter needed to be at that stage.

By the time you eventually co-directed The Collection *with Pinter for the RSC, he had written quite a few other radio and television plays — why did you choose to stage* The Collection *in particular?*

He hadn't got a new play ready at that time, and we were trying to find something from among the other pieces which would be viable on stage. We decided to do it together for a number of reasons. I think it's true that Harold actually wanted to learn to be a director, and thought that collaboration would be a sensible way to begin. And I was very involved at

Stratford that year, so I couldn't have considered doing a full-length play, even if there'd been one. I think, too, he also wanted to see how I responded to his stuff directly.

And how did you respond to The Collection?

Well, working on Pinter's plays over the years, I'm conscious, retrospectively, of having developed a technique, an approach, a way of going about things. I certainly didn't have that when we began *The Collection*. I don't think I was fully at home with it as a technique until about half-way through the rehearsals of *The Homecoming*. But it was very much part of the same world as working on Beckett — making the actor trust what is given, making him accept the premise of the words. That goes as much for the architectural shape of the words as it does for any resonance they may have for the actor emotionally. And since you cannot actually ignore or change the words, you may as well start from there. The parallel to me is with music — don't get me wrong, I don't think if you merely sing the right notes, you make any sense in human terms. You don't in opera, you don't in Pinter. But if you sing the *wrong* notes, you are going to make nonsense. And certainly, even in *The Collection*, there was a great discipline required of the actor, to trust the text.

It's always seemed to me one of Pinter's more paradoxical plays, in that it's all about the search for verification, trying to pin things down, yet there can't really by a 'right' answer as far as the audience is concerned. . .

Well, I think you have to take an attitude yourself about what happens. You may decide the audience should not be let in on the total secret. *Old Times* belongs to the same world. What is truth? What is memory? What actually happened?

But you think it is possible, at least for the purposes of the actors, to say what actually happened?

Oh, yes. You must. Or what happened for one particular actor. It may be different from one actor to another. Certainly, for the audience, part of the problem was to keep the enigma intact — I mean, of what actually happened in Leeds in *The Collection*. All you can do for the actors is to discover what needs to have happened in Leeds for each of them, so that their behaviour will make human and emotional sense. And if you ask Pinter what happened in Leeds, he does say, 'What needs to have happened in Leeds? What does it say?' Well, that's fair enough, I think. Pinter productions which remove the ambiguous, the contradictory, the enigmatic, actually become very simplistic and boring. The image lacks complexity, and is then *unlike* memory because it is uncontradictory.

On the other hand, don't you think that if you have a play like The Collection, *in which there is an objective truth out there somewhere to be found, and the characters are searching for it, isn't there an inevitable danger of removing the enigma for the audience? That they will get so concerned about what 'really' happened that they lose track of what seems to me the most interesting aspect of* The Collection, *which is the shifting relationships between the characters?*

Yes, I agree. I'm not really very qualified to talk about *The Collection* at this distance of time. I no longer know it very well. But the same gradual unfolding of problems goes on in all the other plays. Teddy's marriage in *The Homecoming*. . . where does that girl come from? Does she really come from quite near the house? What actually happened in *Old Times* — I mean, who was in love with whom? I think it's no accident that Pinter is fascinated by Proust, and the shift of memory — the fact that your reporting of this conversation will be totally different from mine, and yet we're both accurate within our own obsessions.

He traded, I think, on ominous vagueness at times, in the early work. His advance as a dramatist is that he's become more and more concrete, making plays depend on the strong dramatic conflicts which underlie *The Homecoming*, or *Old Times*, or even *Landscape*. At first sight it is an enigma, but the situation, if you attend to the play, is blindingly clear.

Can you describe the process of work on the play?

I can speak about how I work on a Pinter play. It doesn't mean to say this is *the* way. And I must make absolutely clear that although Harold and I have had a long association and I've directed a number of his stage plays, and we've worked together on films and so on, it is a totally pragmatic situation. I would hate anybody reading this to think *this is the way to direct Pinter*. This absolutely is not true: it's the way *I* direct Pinter. Having said that, my working arrangement with him has been, over twelve years, that in front of the actors — and I stress that — he can say anything he likes about what I'm doing, and the production, and the rights and wrongs of it. And in front of the actors I can say anything I like about the text, and the rights and wrongs of that. But I am the final arbiter of the production, and he, obviously, is the final arbiter of the text. I think this has, on occasion, been very tough on the actors, because we do develop a kind of Tweedledum and Tweedledee act, and we are, I think, very good for each other. But that doesn't necessarily mean we're very good for some of the actors surrounding us. It's all a bit high-powered, it's very wordy, and we split hairs with great glee. The scrutiny can get a bit much. But Harold will never say, 'You should do *that*.' He will say, 'That isn't right,' which is something quite different.

Is there an example of that you could give?

Well, let's take *The Homecoming*. The problem there is that the biggest bastard in a house full of bastards is actually the man who at first sight appears to be the victim — that is, Teddy, the brother who brings his wife home. He is actually locked in a battle of wills with his father and with his brothers, and of course, with his wife, during which, in some sense, he destroys his wife, and his family, and his father, and himself, rather than give in. He is actually the protagonist. Now, it's very easy for an actor to fall into the 'martyred' role in that part, because Teddy says so little — just sits there while all the other characters are speculating about his wife's qualities in bed. But this is the point — it's a tremendous act of will on his part to take it, and if he was actually feeling anything uncontrolled, he wouldn't be able to do it. It wasn't until Michael Jayston did it in the film that I realized how hard Teddy actually had to be, and how much in control he was. I'd felt it, but I hadn't pushed it far enough. And Harold was always saying to me, during the two stage productions, 'That's not quite right.'

So my approach to a Pinter play is first of all to try and expose the underlying melodrama of the text. I try and find out who does hate who, and who loves who, and who's doing what to whom, and in the first stage of rehearsals play it very crudely.

Does this mean that you try to find what is actually happening, in fact, in so far as there might be a fact?

Yes. There is a fact. Certainly there is a fact. Why, in *The Homecoming*, is Lenny so obsessed from the word go with destroying his father? Talking about his cooking and his rotten meals and so on. Now that must not, in my view, be played with any kind of heaviness: but the underlying feeling is one of absolute naked hatred. Because I think at the base of a good deal of Harold's work is the cockney game of taking the piss: and part of that game is that you should not be quite sure whether the piss is being taken or not. In fact, if you know I'm taking the piss, I'm not really doing it very well: and a good deal of Harold's tone has to do with that very veiled kind of mockery.

Now, actors can't play veiling until they know what they're veiling, so we play mockery, we play hatred, we play animosity, we play the extreme black-and-white terms of a character. That stage of rehearsal is very crude, but it's a very important stage, because unless the actor understands what game he is playing, what his actual underlying motivations are, the ambiguity of the text will mean nothing. People who think that all you've got to do in Pinter is to say it, hold the pause and then say the next line, are wrong. The mystery to me is that there is a communication in the theatre which is beyond words, and which is actually concerned with direct feeling. An actor who says to you, 'All right, I may be feeling that, but unless I show the audience that I'm feeling it, they won't understand,' is actually wrong. If he feels it and masks it, the audience still gets it.

Would it be possible to illustrate that in terms, say, of how Harry and Bill related to each other in the early rehearsals of The Collection?

Well, that marvellous slum-slug speech, *that's* taking the cockney piss, absolutely. He is masking his hatred and self-disgust by the level of the mockery he is expressing, but he has to have it inside. So I think the crude melodrama is very important to find and to discover. Harold usually stays away from those rehearsals. The melodrama begins to alter as soon as the actors start speaking the words and start relating to each other.

Do you find the actors have very definite feelings initially, even if they're wrong ones, rather than just feeling confused?

It very much depends on the actor. You see, because he has such a distinctive voice, very quickly there came to be a 'Pinter style,' which is external. Actors know you speak Pinter in a dry, clipped way, and you hold the pause, and you don't inflect very much, and you don't show very much emotion. It's wrong, of course — a convention, nothing more. Like saying play Chekhov sad, or Shakespeare with a lot of lung power. But, very early on, one felt actors making Pinter patterns, and that's really dreadful — though I suppose it's better than actors trying to 'normalize' Pinter's speech rhythms, because the first thing I say to actors when we're beginning a Pinter play is 'Look, don't mislead yourselves into thinking that if there's a pause there, there shouldn't be a pause there, or, if there's a silence, there shouldn't be a silence, because there should. Our job is to find out why. And don't, in order to make it comfortable, turn a full-stop into a comma, or break it up in a colloquial way different to the way he's written it.'

I actually believe that Beckett and Pinter are poetic dramatists, in the proper sense of the word: they have a linear structure and a formal structure which you'd better just observe — don't learn it wrong, don't speak it wrong, you can't, you mustn't. But there are various things that you can exercise. One of the greatest influences on Pinter, obviously, is the early Eliot — particularly in the repeated phrase, the catching up of a phrase and repeating it over three sentences, keeping it up in the air, like a ball. Now, that is often written in three separate sentences: but it has to make a unit, and you don't find that unit till about the third week. So at the beginning it is better just to observe absolutely accurately what he's written.

I also know that the intensity of the feeling underlying Pinter's text is so very extreme, so very brutal, that you have to explore this melodramatic area that I was speaking about. And this of course raises the question of where the actors live in relation to each other, physically, because until you start letting loose the naked feeling, you don't know the answers to very basic questions, such as, are eyes necessary, or are they not? Are they part of the weaponry?

My vocabulary is all the time about hostility and battles and weaponry, but that is the way Pinter's characters operate, as if they were all stalking round a jungle, trying to kill each other, but trying to disguise from one another the fact that they are bent on murder. And whether you can see a character's face or whether you can't, whether you hold his eyes or not, is absolutely critical — and that to a very large extent comes out of the actor's psyche, once the feelings are being generated. So I wouldn't have anything to say about the physical life of a Pinter play until the emotions had been released, because I wouldn't know what they should be. Equally, Pinter deals in stillness, in confrontations which are unbroken, and I believe it mandatory to do as few moves in a Pinter play as possible. You don't want moves up to the drinks cabinet, or across to the table, in order to 'break it up,' or to make it seem naturalistic. It isn't naturalistic.

You mention cockney piss-taking as a recurrent element in Pinter's plays. Are there other important features they share?

If anybody breaks down in a Pinter play, it is catatonic. . . total. A breakdown is a sign of great, great weakness — the end of the world. So most of the characters preserve their cool, however hot their cool is inside. Equally, physical violence can suddenly be unleashed, which is an expression of the tensions that have been developing beneath this often very urbane surface, and people crack each other over the head or beat each other up or kill each other. It's there in that sudden unleashing, that total breakdown of Deeley at the end of *Old Times*.

The other recurring characteristic concerns his treatment of women. It is very sensitive and well-observed — he creates wonderful women; but always one feels it's a *man* looking at women, the feminine enigma remains.

But isn't there a difference here between the younger and the older women? The older women seem to be observed more from the inside — the older women in Landscape *and* Silence, *for example.*

Yes, I think you're right. He has a more romantic approach to them, a greater compassion and understanding. I think Beth is an astonishing creation of regrets — very feminine, very romantic. But the women in his plays who remain sex objects — sexually active, attractive to men — are all enigmatic, and dangerous, in some sense.

What is the next stage in rehearsal?

The next stage actually is to try to analyze exactly what games of hostility each character is playing with the others. Because they all play games, all the time. They all tease each other, they all try and get rises out of each other, they all try and disturb each other by saying the opposite of what the other one was hoping or expecting. This reaches its obvious climax in *Landscape*, where one character is apparently totally oblivious of the other, although she obviously hears every word he says.

One of the worrying things for actors in Pinter is that you can never trust what is said to be literally true. It is much safer, in fact, to assume that it is a ploy, rather than the truth, unless you can actually discover that it is the truth. So when the actors have found how to wear their hearts on their sleeves and actually show their emotions, you then have to start a process where they hide their emotions, because to show emotion in Pinter's world is, as I've said, a weakness, which is mercilessly punished by the other characters. You have to construct the mask of the character — because all Pinter's characters have masks — though it's no good having a mask unless you know what's underneath it. But the mask almost never slips. It's exactly like that Marceau mime, where he's laughing, and the mask gets stuck in the grin, and you know his heart is breaking underneath. Now, his breaking heart is what you feel, but he doesn't actually indicate that his heart is breaking at all. That's very like acting in Pinter.

So, the second stage is to find how to disguise the emotions which are quite evidently being felt. When Ruth returns with Teddy and comes downstairs in the morning and the father is so dreadful to her and to his son, 'having tarts in the house at night,' the obvious realistic reponse would be to break down left and bury your head in the sofa, or whatever. But he beckons her over to him, the father does, and she crosses and looks him in the eye, and he says to her, 'How many kids have you got?' 'Three.' 'All yours, Ted?' Now, by any normal standards of improvisation, Ruth should be playing that scene hysterically, but she isn't. The alarm is underneath, but totally masked.

And the actress knows why she isn't hysterical?

Oh, of course. Because she's taking the old man on. If the old man is making that kind of challenge, she is accepting it. It doesn't mean to say she's not upset, underneath her mask, just as in the last section of the play, when Teddy is deliberately pushing the family, they retaliate with the proposition that his wife should be put on the game, as a dreadful joke at first, to see if he'll crack. And he is saying throughout the last twenty minutes of the play, 'You live your joke. Go on. You want to put her on the game? You needn't think I'll object. *Put* her on the game.' He's dying inside, because he doesn't, of course, want to lose his wife. But again, the mask is not allowed to slip.

There's one little crack at the end of the play, the most difficult moment of the play, when he's leaving the room, and Ruth says, 'Don't become a stranger.' It is very difficult to play. That's the first and only time she calls him Eddie, which is obviously the intimate and familiar name. It is all there, and it's all very. . . calculated is the wrong word, because I know Harold to be a deeply instinctive writer, who writes very quickly once it's there to be written, and it would not be true to say that he works it all out like an intellectual game.

Are you partly saying that there are really no weak characters in Pinter's plays — weak in the human sense? Ready to give in and to react naturally?

No, I don't think so. Uncle Sam is very weak, but he's also very sly and very cunning, because he knows the dangers of the game. That's why, when he makes the final revelation in *The Homecoming*, that 'McGregor had Jessie in the back of my cab as I drove them along,' there's nothing for him to do but keel over, pass out, the pressure is so much.

I do think that Harold has recognized from the beginning of his writing that if, say, I'm sitting in this room on my own, I'm in a totally relaxed state — I don't know how my face is behaving, I'm not concerned about it, I'm not presenting myself to anybody. A knock on the door, by you, is sufficient to make my face form a pattern, even before you've actually entered, and from that moment on, neither of us, either by word or by deed or in physical relation to each other, are expressing what we are actually feeling. We are modifying ourselves in relation to each other, and all the modifications, the signals of modern behaviour, are aimed at preserving the mask. We are playing a game — that is, social intercourse.

Pinter has worked from that premise, and taken very dreadful situations, usually, dreadful confrontations between people, which are about territorial battles, or battles over people. And where Pinter on the stage goes wrong, is if the actors stop playing the game, if they actually show what they're feeling, because it becomes ludicrous — you know, those unfortunate laughs you can get in Pinter when it's played without underlying truth. Suddenly, something quite apparently serious is said, which pulls the rug away from everything. Now, Pinter *is* very funny, mainly because you can't believe people can maintain these signals, these masks, and it's so shocking, it makes you laugh. But if an actor indulges himself and actually drops the mask, and says, 'I want to show the audience that I'm breaking my heart,' the whole scene collapses.

I think it's at this point, as you manufacture the masks, that you have to verify, in a very particular way, that you are saying what Pinter says, and hitting the rhythms that he wrote. It's no good doing it earlier, because then you apply it like a funny hat to the actor. But once the play is beginning to live, you cannot be too meticulous. What Pinter wrote is always better than what a lazy actor will come up with. Now, this may seem a very small and pedantic point, but most of our actors have a fairly easy-going, not to say contemptuous, attitude to what a dramatist has written, and for the average playwright, writing the average colloquial flim-flam, it doesn't much matter whether you say 'but' instead of 'and,' or put in a few extra words. It does in Pinter, and it is excruciatingly difficult to get it completely accurate. But *when* you get it accurate, then the rhythm — and he has the most astonishing ability to write rhythms — begins to work. And you begin to feel the emotions underlying those rhythms.

There is a difference in Pinter between a pause and a silence and three dots. A pause is really a bridge where the audience think that you're this side of the river, then when you speak again, you're the other side. That's a pause. And it's alarming, often. It's a gap, which retrospectively gets filled in. It's not a dead stop — that's a silence, where the confrontation has become so extreme, there is nothing to be said until either the temperature has gone down, or the temperature has gone up, and then something quite new happens. Three dots is a very tiny hesitation, but it's there, and it's different from a semi-colon, which Pinter almost never uses, and it's different from a comma. A comma is something that you catch up on, you go through it. And a full stop's just a full stop. You stop.

What are the actors doing at this stage? How are you moving it?

They're going anywhere. I never mind where actors go before this. Not in Pinter. Though on the whole I would advise them to stay still, providing they don't find that staying still is inhibiting or tying them up. If they need to move, they move. But the reality of where they need to stand will not be evident until the melodrama has been investigated, and then the mask has been investigated. *Then* they'll begin to know where they can stand and where they can't stand, and where they can move and where they can't move. And who they need to look at and when.

But it is very much a matter of 'can' and 'can't' by that stage, as opposed to 'want?'

Well, yes, because by that stage what they want begins to be something necessary for what they're having to do as characters. All actors like to move too much in the early stages — it frees them, it's a means of getting away from the actual problem. Anybody can light a cigarette in order to feel natural, or go and get a drink: but in the highly-charged Pinter play, you don't do *anything* without it having some significance to the other characters. So the physical life comes quite late, and with that, I like to allow a total absorption, once it begins to grow, in the inner life. The actors should indulge their private emotions. At this later stage the actors should be encouraged to over-pause, to over-silence, to think very, very deeply, and feel very deeply what it is that they're hiding. They should take all the time in the world, in fact, so that the emotion becomes very full inside them. And at that point the play is obviously meaningless to an outside observer.

The next stage actually is to encourage the actors, if they see a chink in another character's armour, to challenge it. This gets things very tight and tense. If you really are feeling very heavy, it's almost axiomatic in Pinter that you play very light. But if you're revealing the heaviness, the other actor should say, 'I can see what you're feeling: you're vulnerable'. And this creates a terrific frisson.

You're setting up your own game to get at his game?

Exactly. Your own game. And this again is a very difficult stage of rehearsal, because often actors feel that those feelings, which they have so carefully nurtured, if they're going to be that evident, and that criticized, they're going to throw them away altogether, and start feeling like hollow shells with a mask on top. So it's all a matter of balance, of going from one extreme, then back to the other again. After that stage I have a very technical, shaping period of rehearsal which is equally horrible, because I shape what's been found — that is, I make certain quick bits quicker, slow up some slow bits, find motives to make this pause longer or that pause shorter. I did a whole rehearsal of the play in which the main thing is to see how quickly you can take the cues, if there isn't a pause or a silence. I orchestrate it, actually. But only from what has been reached. Shape what has been found.

By what time are you working on the actual stage, with the set?

Well, I would already like to be there, from about the third week. I'm usually not, but I would like to be there.

The third week out of how many weeks?

I think a Pinter play usually needs about five or six weeks. One of the reasons why it needs a long time is that a concentrated Pinter rehearsal is so exhausting for actors they can't take more than about four hours a day without actually cheating for the fifth or sixth, or just getting so taut that it doesn't work. Four to five hours a day is about the maximum they can take.

It sounds from the way you've understated it as though the moves almost happen by themselves. . .

Well, they do. And if a scene is not operating, it is sometimes because the physical life is not right, and you try other things. I once said that staging a Pinter play is not difficult: of course it *is*, but it isn't difficult if the actors are actually creating in the right way.

How important to all this is the set design?

The ideal way to work on a Pinter play would be to rehearse it for three weeks, and then design the set. Of course, we're never in that situation. I've only been able to do that once in my life, and that was for an Albee production. When it comes to sets, costumes, props, I think everything burns itself so strongly on the audience's mind in a Pinter play that the coffee cup really has to be very carefully considered. It sounds very fanciful, but the apples in *The Homecoming* had to be green — they could not be yellow or red, because they simply didn't disturb visually. The moment when Sam picks up the apple and eats it and says, 'Feeling a bit peckish' to the old man, is a kick in the crutch to him, and a soft yellow apple would not have had the effect. I sound obsessive, I am. The furniture, the costumes, are very, very carefully scrutinized and a lot of things change, until one builds up something where one can feel that each second is charged with something, and is right.

The artist that I have thought about visually for Pinter, ever since I read *The Birthday Party*, is Magritte — that hard-edged, very elegant, very precise style. Again, you see, you can't overstate. I remember in *Old Times* initially Vivien Merchant's Anna had a very elegant, rather warm reddish dress. It *wasn't* red, it was reddish, but it made a total statement of the Scarlet Woman as soon as she walked on to the stage, and it had to be changed for that reason. Pinter deals in masks in every sense, every person watching the play feels slightly different about it, and you shouldn't pre-empt anybody's solutions.

I remember having the impression of her being slightly old-fashioned, somehow.

That's correct, that was deliberate. She wore blue suede, in the end. Memory, and all that — for that first image of her standing there during the first scene, when you don't know whether she's actually there or what.

To what extent did you figure out whether she was there or not?

Well, she's not there, in actual naturalistic terms, but she is there, because she's been there for twenty years, in each of their heads. She's never left either of their heads, and she never will. She can't leave the room at the end. She tries to, it is impossible. Actually, the two of them would not stay married, they wouldn't stay related, they wouldn't almost exist, without the obsession of that third person in their heads, and the opening image illustrates that. It's a reaching towards a kind of imagery — an emblem in silence.

Getting back to the progress of rehearsals — have we got to the stage when it's 'fixed,' but very difficult to hold?

We're at the nit-picking stage. I've shaped it and orchestrated it, and it goes absolutely dead, and at this point you have to do some exercises about what's actually being felt all over again. You may even take the mask off in a couple of scenes, in order to revitalize the emotional levels. I've done that before now.

Does anybody panic?

Well, yes, people panic. I remember one very eminent actress panicking very badly at that stage, because she was being confronted with an intensity of emotional life which she didn't actually want to admit, certainly not on the stage, and certainly not in life. But she played it, she played a whole scene with tears running down her face, in actual agony, and the other actors wanted to stop it but didn't dare, because there was such a release going on. That is a measure of the intensity of feeling required. Once she'd got that, once we'd gone through that, it was all right. I don't believe in engineering rows in order to upset people, I think they're totally unproductive, but I think that complete immersion in the play can sometimes produce staggering emotional reactions, and they're of course very important.

So, at this stage I would say one is nit-picking about precise timings, precise inflections, precise patterns, precise orchestrations, which is all formalized and deadening. And at the other extreme, one is stoking up the fires of feeling all the time, so it's a crisis-ridden time. The other important point is that an actor's responsibility to his fellows in Pinter is absolutely critical. If an actor gives too much away or too little on a feed-line, it makes it absolutely impossible to play the answering line. So the actors must have developed — by now we're in the fifth week — a trust and an understanding of each other. At this point one is running the play probably once a day, or certainly once every two days, and doing exercises to make it more emotional on the one hand, and shaping it technically on the other.

And then the most difficult time of all comes when you meet the audience, because a Pinter actor has to control the audience in a quite deliberate way. It requires a degree of control in the actor, a degree of arrogance in the actor, towards the audience. For instance, you need to let an audience laugh in Pinter, so that at the precise moment when they have laughed themselves out, you can hit them hard with the actuality. The plays are constructed like that, and it has to do with that tenth part of the actor's mind, which has got nothing to do with truth, but with control and technique — the tenth of you standing outside and watching the whole thing. You have to be absolutely adroit.

You've described the creation of a very precisely-honed instrument, which is the finished production. . . how do you reconcile the precision of the thing on the one hand, and the erratic quality of audiences on the other?

Audiences are not that erratic for Pinter, actually. I think the precision is the instrument of control, and you can slightly increase the pause, or slightly increase the length of a laugh in order to grip a particular audience. Pinter audiences get off the hook and laugh at people as objects if you don't control them. You really have to make them listen, you really do have to hear that pin drop, and that takes a degree of expertise in the actor which is I think, pretty considerable. But all the time, the paradox remains, about this intensity of feeling. That has to be utterly true. Because I have seen my own production of Pinter, without the actors being aware of it, dry out in a fortnight or three weeks, so that the level of intensity underlying the masks has dropped, and actually what is being seen is a very chic series of patterns.

On the whole you've tended to talk about Pinter's work as if it were a unified entity — do the production problems actually not vary a lot from one play to another?

I've been talking very much about *The Homecoming,* actually, which I personally regard as his greatest and biggest play. I think that what happened in *Landscape* and *Silence* was a very exciting herald for the future, which hasn't yet quite developed, although I think the Proust filmscript he's recently done is well on the way. We've spoken a lot about hostility and jungle warfare and all the rest, but the other fascination, the obsession in

Pinter's world, is trying to pin down reality, trying to pin down memory, trying to pin down truth: which is why Proust is so important to him, and why he's managed to reduce those twelve novels to 212 pages of images, which actually do work. It's the most extraordinary thing to read. And *Silence*, particulary, was a beautiful heartbreaking evocation of the contradictions of memory. I would think that the problems of what is true, what is false, are going to go on being an obsession with him.

That particular theme was much more explicit in Old Times, *was it not?*

I think what is remarkable about *Old Times* is that Deeley's own sexual insecurities, personal inadequacies, actually make him invent relationships and happenings which were not, in my view, true at all. The play is not about two lesbians, in spite of Visconti. They are not lesbian.

I personally think *Landscape* is a little masterpiece. The problem of *Landscape* was not knowing, knowing and not knowing — a very fraught acting exercise. I rehearsed *Landscape* for about five weeks, I think — it was one of the most difficult things I've ever done, and it's not because of the physical life, because there isn't any. I think, again, you see, it's a fascinating theatrical image — a man talking to a woman, and she utters her thoughts and he doesn't hear them, and she apparently doesn't hear what *he* says. And then there was that set with the split in it — that was John Bury, who read the play instinctively and said, there you are. He's a very important figure in all this.

Perhaps the more important in that we don't seem to have mentioned him a great deal. . .?

Exactly. That's why I'm mentioning him now. And also, he is not a chatterer. He makes. He doesn't talk.

You mean you don't have long sessions with him discussing how the sets's going to be?

No. I give him an image. And we work from facts. From objects or models. I remember I had a piece of mirror, mirror-tile actually, from somewhere in my house, and I just put it up at an angle on the stage: and that was the *Silence* set. John made the set with a split in it for *Landscape* without any comment at all. We communicate with grunts and objects, really, not with theories. I really believe that in the theatre you shouldn't talk, you should do, and you should look at what you've done rather than talk about what you might do. It's certainly true in collaboration with a designer — it's much better to get an image going, and then look at it, and see what it does to the play, in model form, than it is to chat.

In *The Homecoming*, Harold envisaged that vast room. 'We knocked the wall down several years ago to make an open living area. My mother was dead.' Because of the big Aldwych stage John's first solution had a big iron beam across where they'd knocked the wall down. The iron was very evident, and I remember Harold saying, 'Now I think they would have put that big steel beam up, to keep the house up, that's right, and I like the whole proportion of it, but I don't want to see all that iron, that makes too much of a statement.' So we covered it with plaster. So you thought, well, maybe it's a big iron beam they've got there, but you weren't absolutely sure. That's an image, actually, of the whole process — the iron beam is there, but covered over.

I suppose that the other development I sensed in Landscape *and* Silence *was that whereas previously people were antagonistic towards each other, in conflict with one another, here were a couple and a trio whose lives almost couldn't have been lived without one another. . .*

Dependence on each other. . . yes, I think that's true. But equally I think one could make a case that in *The Caretaker* and in *The Homecoming* the hostility *is* the dependence. You must remember Pinter's Portuguese blood, I think. There is a kind of correctness, a pride, and a readiness for anger — in his writing, that is, I'm not speaking of him as a person!

And how important do you think the Jewishness is?

Very, in some areas — the extremity of family affection, the family unit being something which holds and encloses and makes everything possible, and yet also destroys everything. I don't say that is something which is special to the Jewish race, but it's something which they seem to have an extreme instinct for. But we all do it. Again, though, they are not 'Jewish' plays; to say that *The Homecoming* is about a Jewish family is already wrong. It isn't. And we went out of our way to make sure that they were not 'Jewish' actors.

Is there such a thing as a Pinter world-view?

Oh, Christ. Speaking personally, I get a very bleak, very uncompromising, very hostile view of life out of him. Counterbalanced by a longing for contact and relations and. . . not getting into a situation of deep regrets, which is very painful. Because all his characters do have regrets, do crucify themselves, and everybody else. But I think what is for me wonderful about Pinter is that in an unblinkingly hostile situation where everybody does go wrong in some way or another, there are little moments of light and tenderness which are cherished. He is a very pessimistic dramatist: but I don't really understand how anybody could honestly be writing in the 'sixties or 'seventies and be particularly sunny. People are always saying to me, 'Why don't you do happy plays, that are life-enhancing?' to which the answer is, 'Well, why don't people write them?' But I find the great thing about him is that his tenderness and his compassion are not sentimental, but absolutely unblinkingly accurate.

8

Howard Brenton

petrol bombs through the proscenium arch

Artistic and political developments overlapped as closely during the critical year of 1968 as they had in 1956. Then, the dying twitches of British imperialism in the Suez affair, and the realignment of political attitudes on the Left which followed the Soviet invasion of Hungary, were no less formative in shaping the new creative spirit in the theatre than the work of the English Stage Company or of Joan Littlewood's Theatre Workshop.

Similarly, as Howard Brenton points out in this interview, the 'events' of 1968 were 'crucial' — not only the student eruptions in Paris and throughout the western world, but the peak of protest against American involvement in Vietnam, and the outrage on the Left at the Soviet intervention in Czechoslovakia. Brenton felt that, although this watershed year 'disinherited my generation', it also 'gave me a desperation I still have': but for some, the feeling was one rather of exhilaration than desperation, at the apparent removal of barriers to revolutionary action. From both kinds of response came many new theatre voices — some entirely individual, but most, in the beginning, looking to collective ideals and inspiration.

For Howard Brenton — as for David Hare and Snoo Wilson, interviewed later in this volume — the itinerant Portable Theatre, of which with Tony Bicât they were the driving force, provided both the inspiration and the means of expression for their ideals. Not that these were always coherently defined, any more than was the political position of those curious, multiple-authorship plays so distinctive of their historical moment, Lay-by *and* England's Ireland *— which, like Portable itself, become recurrent motifs in the interviews from now on. For many theatre people of the time, political virginity was soon lost amidst a welter of permissive (and reactionary) ideals, and the years immediately following 1968 tend now to be recollected with a mixture of pride at real achievement and awareness of lost innocence.*

By the time Catherine Itzin and I talked with Howard Brenton in her south London home in September 1974, he was already aware of his own need to reach wider audiences, and to command the use of larger stages and theatrical resources. Soon afterwards, in 1976, his Weapons of Happiness *was seen at the National Theatre — an odd collision indeed between revolutionary play and well-heeled audiences. But four years later its impact seemed tame besides that of* The Romans in Britain, *when simulated (albeit unsuccessful) sodomy as a symbol of political conquest put the liberal tolerance of the National's mix of air-packaged tourists and middle-class trusties to an unusually severe test.*

As it happens, that play was presented in the National's open-stage Olivier Theatre, but the capacity for the outrageous it sustained seemed to justify the retention here of the title we gave the original Theatre Quarterly *interview. Brenton may no longer be offering recipes for practicable petrol bombs, as his anarchist 'hero' did in* Fruit, *but his formidable weaponry of flammable theatrical devices continues to warn audiences against those British concentration camps he foresaw in* The Churchill Play — *his most recent work to reach the stage at the time of this interview. Born in 1942, Brenton was the first 'war baby' among the dramatists in this volume, and found himself in an Anderson shelter within a few hours of his birth: but he had no personal recollections of the wartime years. Was his family's presence in Portsmouth during the war for military reasons, we asked?*

No, my father was a policeman. He left school at fourteen and came to London, where he was a warehouseman for a number of years. Then, when he got married, like many men of his generation he joined the police force for security. He was one of that generation of coppers from which the George Dixon myth came, the generation that's passed, in principle. Then, after twenty-five years, he left and joined the Methodist Church and is now a minister.

That must have been traumatic, your father suddenly changing from the beat to the pulpit.

It was a courageous act. It was like a renaissance in his middle age, which few people manage. I was nineteen when he left the police and joined the Methodist Church. But I remember him studying John Wesley and Thomas Aquinas at night when I was a little boy. My mother was the daughter of a Portsmouth docker, a wheelwright, and worked in the Co-op.

Did you have a religious family background?

My parents have always been, not fanatical Christians, but 'social' Christians. My father sees good works as the only principle, and a lot of doctrine as rubbish.

Did you spend the whole of your childhood in Portsmouth?

No, we moved all over the country. I was at grammar school, which I left to go north with them — against the school's advice. And then I taught for some time in Yorkshire. Yorkshire was my father's first post. I followed the family through Yorkshire and Wales: my father's now back in Wales where he's very happy.

You say you went to grammar school.

Yes. I was a state school kid. It was a very vicious school. I'm glad now that the grammar schools are going. I think they are as harmful, socially, as public schools.

Did you rebel against school?

I was always sullen and churlish, I think.

Did you go straight on to university?

No. There was a gap, which I was glad about because I saw some of the world. And then I got into Cambridge, sitting an exam. But I hated Cambridge passionately.

Had you had academic ambitions?

No. What happened was that at school I painted all the time, and I wanted to be an artist, a painter. I couldn't paint hands or heads, but I painted hundreds of abstracts, which I took to an art college in Bath called Corsham Court, and they accepted me. And then I decided to be a writer, and I thought, well, a writer must go to university and study English. So I dropped the art school and decided to get into Cambridge if I could.

Do you think you hated it because it was Cambridge, or because of the academic approach?

You had a lot of freedom. I soon gave up lectures and wrote all the time, and acted and ran a magazine — an appalling rag — for a while. I met a lot of fellow-writers, only one of whom — John Grillo — is still writing.

At what stage did the theatre start to interest you?

The interest was always there. Always. My father was a keen amateur director. I remember when I was nine, I wrote a play out of the Harris Tweed strip in the old *Eagle* comic, just copying my father.

You began by writing plays?

Oh yes. Also a lot of poems, and three novels, which taught me to type, but I was always stuck on plays. The first thing I discovered was that playwriting was like painting. You discover the skill to draw — like hands and heads — and then you can paint, or write, what you like. I discovered I had the ability to tell jokes and write gags, and for a time I was overwhelmed with the joy of entertaining. The real grasp of gag-writing doesn't really come, I don't think, until you're in your twenties, and that's when you can begin to write plays.

Were you affected by what was going on in the theatre in London — the Look Back in Anger *movement?*

Yes. I was in Bognor then, and very young — thirteen or fourteen — at the most. There was a rep on the end of the pier which did *Look Back in Anger* very soon after it was on at the Court. I said to my parents, 'I want to go and see this play.' And my father said, 'No son of mine is going to be seen going into a play like that.' So I went illicitly and I still remember it very vividly.

It was at Cambridge that your first plays actually saw the light of the stage?

The first one which was performed was *Ladder of Fools*, a huge, jokeless, joyless allegory. It was only much later — starting with a short farce I wrote soon after I left Cambridge, called *Winter Daddikins* — that I found I had a talent for writing gags. And then, with *Revenge*, I found I could get at the world, begin to create things which were public.

Winter Daddikins *was done in Dublin?*

Yes. And then I went and earned my living as a stage manager and bit actor in reps all over the country — most of them now, hopefully, dead, gladly dead. I was determined that I would earn my living from the theatre or go on the dole. I took many odd jobs, washing up and things like that, and bits of factory work and labouring, but I was determined to stay away from all the career jobs. I announced that I was a writer.

At what time did you begin to work with the other people who eventually became part of Portable?

It happened because of the Royal Court, really. *Revenge* was put on there in 1969 and I met David Hare, I didn't know him before. Because of *Revenge*, Portable, who were just forming, approached me, and I wrote *Christie in Love* for them. The encouragement of the Court was always there, because of Bill Gaskill. The Royal Court had seen my plays and contacted me. And although I'm not in the tradition of the Court — I'm not what you would call a humanist writer, not of the mainstream of the Court at all — they've always been good to me.

Was it before or after Revenge *that you were working with the Brighton Combination?*

Just before. I had a hard period of work. I worked in an office during the day and washed up at night, and saved like mad to have just a bit of money to go and work with the Combination. I saved up six months' money and lived on it down there in Brighton. When it was exhausted the Arts Council then gave me a grant.

How important was it to you that you should be making contact with an unconventional audience?

We didn't really know what we were doing at the Combination, we were feeling our way. But all the elements that are in the fringe, that have developed since, were there. There was the idea that theatre should be communicative work, socially and politically active. There was the idea of very aggressive theatrical experiment. And there was always the tension in the Combination — which has been resolved now that they are at Deptford

— between theatre and community work. They really are a socially active group now, not a theatre. I went the theatre way. Also, the idea of group work was there, the idea of instantly responding to events — street theatre, multi-media ideas . . . I did a collective show, and included a local painter who painted us — the actors and the whole theatre — for it. There was that kind of variety. Mixed film shows — it was all there, done very ignorantly and very quickly, and in terrible poverty. They also ran a restaurant, they tried to repair the roof. They had to get over difficulties, small difficulties like the box-office telephone being cut off because they didn't have the money to pay the bill. There were candlelight shows — always full — because there was no electricity . . .

But Phil, Greg, and Michele — the actors named in Plays for Public Places — *they weren't Combination actors, were they?*

No. They were at Bradford University. Chris Parr went to Bradford University, and started a very lively, very unpretentious, hard-working line in university theatre. The idea was to do all new work, which would just be a part of other entertainment. And those little plays that I wrote — *Gum and Goo, Heads,* and *The Education of Skinny Spew* — were all done after or during rock concerts given at the university.

Can you remember now why those little plays took the form they did — what the impulse was behind them?

Fear. Fear of the play not 'holding' in the rough circumstances, and not being 'held' by the good but elementary, straightforward performances you get from students. That fear was very creative — when playwrights lose it, they go otiose . . flabby.

Can you say something about Revenge? *How that archetypal early Brenton play started?*

It took three years to write, and was in a huge form at first, about five hours long. Politically I had no ideas, I was very immature. But I had an instinct that there was a conflict I wanted to get at, between public figures, between figures who meant something in public, like a criminal, an old lag from the East End of London, and a religious, almost ancestral, policeman from Scotland. And I was aware that there was a conflict and I wanted to give it expression, and out of that the play came.

It had very literary beginnings in that it was going to be a rewrite of *King Lear*, no less, and there still are the *Lear* elements there, in that the criminal has two daughters and he gives up his kingdom and tries to get it back and fails. And they never mention the mother, which is one of the oddly crucial things about *Lear*: Mrs. Lear is never present. And Mrs. Hepple is never present in *Revenge*: that's the only trace of its literary beginnings. It first had a formal scene with Hepple giving up his gangster kingdom and then going to gaol — that's how the play began.

But in Christie in Love *you were obviously homing in much more on the criminal. In the introduction you say the policemen aren't meant to be more than caricatures, and the audience is really supposed to concentrate on Christie.*

The development was that I could write gags, but I always wanted to write a kind of tragedy. What I did was to write comic scenes, comic situations, but stretch them intolerably by using massive pauses or bad jokes, which an actor has to try and tell so badly that an audience doesn't laugh, even at their being bad.

That was deliberate?

Absolutely deliberate, and is marked in the script, by hundreds of pauses and silences. I wrote it to find a way of expressing feelings of terror and horror and despair differently from in *Revenge*.

But you also say in the introduction to Christie in Love *that Christie himself is meant to be a naturalistic character, in the midst of this comic world.*

That was to try and get perspective. I mean, the search for something other than what Brecht was doing goes on endlessly amongst the writers of my generation, and it was in a sense an alienation device, because the surroundings are highly artificial. There was an attempt to look very hard at Christie, almost like a Bacon painting, where you have an absolutely hard edge, definite. Only a painter could invent that world, yet what's inside that world is a writhing live mess, and that's what I wanted for the play.

Fruit *presumably was written at the time of the General Election of 1970?*

Yes, it was written to tour during the campaign. It is about an osteopath who was a thalidomide child and grows up with a grudge against the government. And he moves into high circles and has as clients the Prime Minister and the leading members of the Opposition, who are Labour in the play — the government is Tory. He secures a tape of a drunken Labour leader confessing to homosexual relations with the Tory Prime Minister. When he confronts the Prime Minister with this tape, the Prime Minister says, 'So what?', more than confesses. The dogs are then unleashed on the osteopath, who goes on the run, and ends up in a warehouse in Covent Garden, confronted by an old man who's a syndicalist. And this old man teaches the audience, rather than the osteopath, how to make a petrol bomb, and how to really get at the world, if you want to. He ends up throwing a petrol bomb against the theatre wall, using a beautiful technique invented by David Hare.

We toured *Fruit* at the height of the Portable circuit, and visited about seventy cities in England, mostly for one performance only, but some for more. Then we toured it all round Holland. In Holland you can do anything in the theatre, you can kill yourself, you can nail yourself to the ceiling, you can kill cows . . . but the only thing you can't do is light a match, because they really go mad about it. So we were pursued round Holland by fire officers. It was aggro, pure aggro, the show.

Really your first political play?

I don't like the label 'political play'. But it resulted from feeling the public nature of the theatre. A better word for 'political' is 'public'.

What do you mean by 'public'?

With the plays that are not done on stages — like the Portable plays weren't plays for stages — the space between people defines the actual physical theatre, the space between the audience itself and the actors. And that space and relationship becomes an almost moral force in the writing and in the presentation — a sense of bodies and will and concentration, and laughter or abuse. From that feeling, you begin to want to write about how people conduct themselves in life as groups, as classes, as interests.

Having written in the way you've described for Portable, doesn't it make it very difficult to write in the vacuum, as it were, of conventional theatre?

I don't find that now. I know passionately what I want to write. I know the story, I know what it's about, and I want to get into bigger theatres, because they are, in a sense, more public. Until that happens you really can't have any worth as a playwright.

So now you are writing for a heterogeneous audience — anyone who happens to come into a theatre?

Yes, and it's a terrible tension. You can't reconcile it. The theatre is a bourgeois institution: you have to live and work against that.

It seems that your later, longer plays are much more dialectically balanced — almost more Shavian, in the way that people bounce ideas and arguments off each other . . .

On a performing — I was going to say proscenium — stage, the play has to have its own world, which must connect with the world outside, on the street. And therefore you have to write with greater clarity and force and dignity, and that's a good influence. The most amazing experience was finally having a play done at the Royal Court, on the performing stage. It's like getting hold of a Bechstein, hitting a really superb instrument, when all the time you have been shouting about a penny whistle, or a mouth-organ. You realize how powerful the instrument is, and varied, and how much fun.

That sounds as though you're saying the conventional theatre you've now broken into can do more, operate more effectively, than your fit-up, or fringe group?

I think the fringe has failed. Its failure was that of the whole dream of an 'alternative culture' — the notion that within society as it exists you can grow another way of life, which, like a beneficent and desirable cancer, will in the end grow throughout the western world, and change it. What happens is that the 'alternative society' gets hermetically sealed, and surrounded. A ghetto-like mentality develops. It is surrounded, and, in the end, strangled to death. Utopian generosity becomes paranoia as the world closes in. Naive gentleness goes to the wall, and Manson's murderousness replaces it. The drift from the loving drug scene in Amsterdam in the late 'sixties to the speed and wretchedness five years later illustrates the process. The truth is that there is only one society — that you can't escape the world you live in. Reality is remorseless. No one can leave. If you're going to change the world, well, there's only one set of tools, and they're bloody and stained but realistic. I mean communist tools. Not pleasant. If only the gentle, dreamy, alternative society *had* worked.

And, more specifically, the fringe as a theatrical phenomenon has also failed?

I think in that sense the fringe was a historical thing. Where it went wrong was when the audience became sophisticated. At a discussion or talk in the bar afterwards, they wouldn't say, 'I don't think you're right about the police, they do a wonderful job,' but something like 'Why don't you use acts like the Freehold, why do you still use words, why don't you use rock music?' The fringe circuit audiences became spuriously sophisticated. David Hare identified it quite rightly and that was when it was time to get out — it was becoming 'arty'.

Okay, why do *you still use words? You never felt impelled to move off in the sort of non-verbal directions some other groups were going?*

No, though I understand why there was a great reaction in the late 'sixties against words. My generation shares an idea that the theatre not only describes but actually shows new possibilities, that you can write so forcefully that a possibility of a new way of looking at the world, a new way of living, can actually be found through the theatre. And the search began quite analytically with the Freehold and Pip Simmons. They were onto the same thing — and, above all, there was the People Show, which is beyond doubt the greatest fringe group. They have for years tried to find new ways of behaviour, often by just going into a room and behaving, without script or structure or anything, by instinct. It's like a new renaissance feeling — that we may be the predecessors of an extraordinary end to this century. We may well discover — just as the renaissance discovered humanist egocentric thought, or the middle ages discovered romantic love — a new way of looking at man and his behaviour. This sounds very ambitious — but why not be ambitious? You can see this consciousness of a new renaissance in Snoo Wilson's work, and in the People Show. Wilson is a real voyager, inventing maps as he goes along. He's a writer of iron nerve and daring.

The visual devices are very important in your plays — the bouncing ball of the world in Scott of the Antarctic, *Brixton gaol in* Revenge . . .

Yes, but they're always predicated by something verbal. I like to know the theatre that I'm working for. Perhaps because I was going to be a painter, I fiercely imagine the characters, I can see them, I even draw them. I draw the look of a scene. Design is incredibly important, and it's a much abused trade at this moment.

But in the early plays you kept it very simple.

We designed them ourselves, really. I designed *Christie*, Snoo Wilson built it. The director placing the actors, or the actors placing themselves — that was the design. Or the spaces were the design — in *Wesley* and in *Scott of the Antarctic*. For *Wesley* we had a most magnificent, traditional, huge 900-seater Methodist Church. And the set, the design, for *Scott of the Antarctic* was an ice-rink. I actually want to write that one again, as a straight formal theatre piece, because Scott is incredibly interesting, and the reason for the expedition's breaking down is interesting.

How did you come to choose Wesley as a hero?

I'm very interested in people who could be called saints, perverse saints, who try to drive a straight line through very complex situations, and usually become honed down to the point of death. Scott was one of those. Scott's expedition failed because all the stores, all the teams and procedures, were planned for four people. At the last moment, just before they left all their support teams, Scott decided to take a fifth, because that fifth was a Petty Officer, not from the upper classes. And Scott wanted a working-class representative at the Pole. While they were remaking the sledge, Evans cut his hand and he didn't tell anyone. It grew septic, and in the end drove him mad. Their stores were completely confused because of it. But it was the act of a man trying to drive a straight line through the Antarctic, and of course he couldn't end that line. Jed in *Magnificence* has that sense of careering, headlong speed. And Violette Szabo in *Hitler Dances* was another one. Through the foul mess of the resistance the SOE, Special Operations Executive in France during the war, she drove a pure line of hatred for the nazis and all they stood for, and was in ignorance of the forces that propelled her, yet tried to keep a straight line.

Magnificence *appeared to attempt to combine different styles — the first act was naturalistic, while the rest was fragmented, collaged, almost surrealistic. Almost like two different plays.*

I wanted to establish different worlds very strongly in the play. I think one of the glories we've lost in the arsenal of the playwright is to use different styles completely. If I want to write about the old men who use a very elegant language, I go straight into it. I don't worry about the style of the play or anything, just aim to get the truth of those men speaking to each other. Then have a policeman and a bailiff — go into that. Don't worry about the world of style: write, and if it's truthful, they'll hold and act off each other. Just as the old playwrights had verse, rhyming verse, sonnets, broken blank verse, prose and songs. When it was fitting that someone spoke in prose, they went into it. And when it was fitting that a lover spoke in a sonnet — he went into it. I wanted with *Magificence* to claim that freedom. I wanted to write each world — there are three: the people who occupy a house, a bailiff and a policeman, and the old men — simply on the terms which those scenes demanded. With *The Churchill Play* I found that I could write with an immense variedness. If you found the place where it must all happen, you had the play. In the first draft, a lot of *The Churchill Play* was set outside the hangar, then I put it all in the hangar and suddenly I'd got the eye of the play right. There is a lot of difficulty with playwriting in an epic style, which is very important to develop. An epic style which has nothing to do with Brecht. Bond has gone the furthest.

How did Hitler Dances *come about?*

It came about in Holland. I've worked a lot in Holland, at the Mickery Theatre, which incidentally has really sustained the English fringe for years by giving them money. They offered to pay for me to go there for a month with the Traverse Workshop and write a show during rehearsals — which eventually became *Hitler Dances*.

Because evidences of Hitlerism are so much stronger over there?

As a result of talking to members of the resistance. Many of the theatre people in Holland who are middle-aged now were members of underground portable shows, travelling illegally in occupied Holland, usually doing Jewish songs and sketches. Incredibly brave people. And the idea of the show came out of what they told us about Europe, about the sense of debris which you still feel in Europe. The idea of the dead soldier who is resurrected, and years later wants to get home. It's not a thought-out show, it's a very emotional show.

The 'children playing' element seems to hark back to your early pieces.

I saw children in Eindhoven, which was flattened twice during the war, first by the Germans and then by the Allies, and is now the home of the world headquarters of the Philips Electrical Company. And at night in Eindhoven, the huge Philips sign, like a weird emblem, flashes everywhere in the sky. I saw a bomb-site there with children playing on it, while we were touring *Fruit*, and there the idea was lodged in my mind, because it was like children playing on this heap of rubble — history. And the idea of a German soldier coming out of the ground became meaningful.

How did The Churchill Play *happen?*

It was commissioned by Richard Eyre for the Nottingham Playhouse. I'd had an idea for a play about Churchill from when I was in the Combination, and I tried to write it first then. But I couldn't make it work. I had the idea of his coming out of the catafalque in Westminster Hall while he was lying in state, coming out and addressing the young soldiers around him. That idea was the beginning, and then there were more recent preoccupations, particularly the truth about Long Kesh. And I wrote a radio play about an internment camp in England in a few years' time. But they wouldn't do it on radio. And I was full of that idea, so I threw the radio play away and re-wrote the whole thing, framing the idea of Churchill in a camp called Churchill, somewhere in England ten years from now.

What came through in the play was a feeling of cause and effect — between what Churchill was saying then, and what is happening . . . well, now, and what will happen in the future.

Yes, it's about 'What is Freedom?' The idea that Churchill is universally admired by people who went through the war is not true, but what they always say, and what my parents say, is 'He gave us freedom.' And the question of freedom becomes paramount — you say, 'What freedom? What do we do with that freedom? What have we done with it?' And the answer at the moment is, we are in danger of throwing it away — and also that it's not freedom. That was the gut feeling behind the play. I also wanted, for the first time, not to write about one single person, but to write about a group of people, who are not particularly intelligent, who are not politically aware, who are not heroic, but together have an almost animal sense. Writing about the prisoners in the camp, that's how I approached them. I didn't want any of them to be saints, just trying to see it through, work it through.

At what stage did it become necessary that the prison doctor should take such a prominent role?

He was there from the beginning. I wanted to show everyone who ran the camp at their best. And not — to be blamed. There's a phrase that came to me to describe it — that 'there's a conspiracy of obedience' — and that's what a whole country can be involved in, very easily and very soon, and quite suddenly. There can be a conspiracy of obedience amongst everyone, and to say, '*He* is the villain', '*He* is the psychopathic fascist', '*He* is the man with the whip', is impossible.

It struck me that the wife of the prison doctor was a small but a very important character in the play — her vision of the house and garden in the South of England representing the silent majority and their acquiescing.

Yes. The pleasant roads in southern suburbs are as much of the wire in Long Kesh as the wire itself, and that was very important to register. The wife's 'Give me the garden where we grow the vegetables, where the children are brought up in peace' is a passionate thing. And yet that passion itself is part of the mechanism.

How prophetic do you regard The Churchill Play *in a real, warning sense?*

I think it could happen now. Hopefully the play will be absurd in ten years' time. I will be overjoyed if it is. But it's prophetic in that we are going towards that now. I wanted to subdue any science fiction angle . . . well, I couldn't resist putting Leeds in the Fourth Division, but, that was the most science fiction element in the play. *The Churchill Play* is really England now.

What is your method of writing? Do you have to wait for inspiration, or is it a much more arduous, conscious task?

I can't deliberately write half-heartedly. I find that you have to believe in it, word by word, so I write quite slowly, and with some pains. Then what I rewrite as the finished script becomes a draft. This always happens three times.

When you say 'always three drafts', do they take a particular shape?

Each one is complete. You always feel the first draft is the play, then a few weeks later you read it and you begin all over again.

All over again!

Yes, usually without reading it, you write it all again. And then a third time you rewrite it, after, perhaps, you've shown it to a close friend or an agent.

The third draft is more a polishing draft, then?

Yes. But there's a great change between the first and the third. Usually they're written over completely twice. I have in the past been faced with great pressure of delivery dates and written a good deal in rehearsal. That's invigorating, but dangerous. Now I'm writing without pressure and I like it much more, I can get further into it.

This would not seem to make you a likely candidate for the sort of collaborative work that you've done — Lay-by and England's Ireland?

It's not playwriting. It's like a long argument. It's like saying, 'there must be a show about this', particularly *England's Ireland*. As an English writer I was completely incapable of writing about Ireland, and that's why I joined the group, because together we could force a show onto the stage. But it was like an incredible argument. We all went away to the country, to Wales, and rented a cottage, and lived seven days and nights writing the show all together, in groups or individually — bits of paper stuck on the wall all over the place — with this passion to get that show done. And so it wasn't for any of us, I don't think, like writing at all.

Did the events of May 1968 have a very strong effect on you?

May 1968 was crucial. It was a great watershed and directly affected me. A lot of the ideas in *Magnificence* came straight out of the writing of that time in Paris, and the idea of official life being like a screen. There's a long speech in *Magnificence* about that. May 1968 disinherited my generation in two ways. First, it destroyed any remaining affection for the official culture. The situationists showed how all of them, the dead greats, are corpses on our backs — Goethe, Beethoven — how gigantic the fraud is. But it also, secondly, destroyed the notions of personal freedom. Freaking out and drug culture, anarchist notions of spontaneous freedom, anarchist political action: it all failed. It was defeated. A generation dreaming of a beautiful utopia was kicked — kicked awake and not dead. I've got to believe not kicked dead. May 1968 gave me a desperation I still have. It destroyed Jed in *Magnificence.*

So what are your feelings at the moment?

Feelings of revolutionary socialism.

An armchair revolutionary?

Yes. Though sitting in front of a typewriter.

You do think then, that there is some practical effect that theatre in particular, or art in general can have?

Yes, I do. I think it's crucial that, in public, truths be told. Also I dream of a play acting like a bushfire, smouldering into public consciousness. Or like hammering on the pipes being heard all through a tenement. No playwright of my generation has actually got into public, actually touched life outside the theatre. But it can be done. I don't think any of us have written well enough yet. I know I've not got anywhere near the real world.

Do you think that apart from, as it were, warning people with whose ideas you are in sympathy, you can reach, or convert, or at least influence others?

You don't write to convert. More — to stir things up. For people to make what they wish of it. When it comes to agitprop, I like the agit, the prop I'm very bad at. I'm not wise enough. Yet.

9

John McGrath

the process of finding a form

---

*Howard Brenton, like several others of his generation — David Hare and
David Edgar among them — graduated from the fit-up 'non-theatre spaces' of
the early 'seventies to the main stages of the national prestige companies. They
passed older playwrights, including John Arden and John McGrath, on the
way back, disillusioned and in search of their own alternatives.*

*Like David Mercer, John McGrath first found success as a dramatist on
television in the mid-'sixties, but after helping to mould such innovative
programmes of the time as the* Z Cars *series, he found himself out of sympathy
with the constraints of writing for television, and subsequently with the market
economy of working in film. So he returned to the more controllable world of
live theatre, and, after a brief but influential association with the Liverpool
Everyman, founded the touring company named enigmatically 7:84 — the
numerals signifying that tiny percentage of the population which owns so
massive a percentage of the nation's wealth. A second, Scottish 7:84 Company
followed.*

*It was during the early work of these companies that McGrath developed the
style of popular theatre in which he has since been working, mainly though not
exclusively with the two 7:84 groups. Among the shows which followed those
described in this interview were* Little Red Hen, *about the conflict between
traditional Scottish socialism and the new brand of nationalism;* Big Square
Fields, *dramatizing the rape of England during the Industrial Revolution;*
Trembling Giant, *a sort of pantomime-melodrama featuring English
capitalism personified;* Bitter Apples, *which picked up the threads of 1968 ten
years further on; and* Blood Red Roses, *tracing the hopes and despairs of the
post-war generation in the life of one person, from girlhood to her coming-to-
terms with divorce.*

*All these plays shared a strong musical element and a free-flowing sweep of
action, reflecting John McGrath's attempt to shape a 'popular' theatre in the
most precise sense — as described and analyzed in his recent book*
A Good Night Out, *where he defends his belief in small-scale theatres for
ordinary people as opposed to heavily-subsidized institutions for a social elite.
It was in the spring of 1975 that Catherine Itzin went to talk with John
McGrath in his Kensington home — a far cry from Birkenhead, where he was
born in 1935. We asked whether his background there had been working-class.*

Well, my father was from a working-class family, and had become a secondary school teacher. His father was a boilermaker in the yards. Both sides of the family were descended from Irish immigrant people who'd come over around the turn of the century, or just before, in search of potatoes . . . and gold . . . and pavements. Didn't find them. But my early background was weird, because we were evacuated from Birkenhead, bombed out, very early on, when I was four, and we went to live in a small town in North Wales. For various reasons, we stayed until 1951, when I was sixteen. Then we went back to Merseyside.

What was the political background of this Welsh childhood?

My family were Catholics — Irish Catholics. That's a political background. In the school I went to there were a lot of very good, fervent Welsh socialists, and the level of political debate in the school was very high. I used to get heavily involved in political arguments. So I was politically argumentative from an early age, which is perhaps distinct from politically conscious, in real terms.

You'd left school when you moved back to Merseyside?

I had another six or nine months at school, and used to commute back to Wales to the grammar school in Mold, just to finish off. Then I got into Oxford, but I had a year or a year and a half to fill before going in the army to do my National Service, because the university insisted on people doing their National Service first. Which I thought was great. I had a year working, most of it in a laundry — a big, steamy, sweaty laundry just outside Birkenhead. And then during the summer, I worked on a farm for a good six months, I suppose.

And without a second thought you went into National Service?

With a lot of second thoughts — but no option. I went into the army at eighteen, and did the statutory two year slog. But because I was going to Oxford, they reckoned that I was officer material, you see, so after I was sent to Germany, they sent me back to England before this . . . selection board. At that time my main objective was to get out of Germany, and the best way was to become an officer in the British army.

Surely you must have had to suppress a lot of your self and your feelings just to function?

Well, you find in the army that the suppression of any feeling — of all feeling— is ideal. I began keeping a diary in the army on the same basis as aircraftsman Ross, but found that, after a few days, to record feelings — or even *feel* feelings in order to record them — was not on, because it was torture. But I suppose I had a kind of philosophy from about oh, fifteen, when I started writing seriously, almost a kind of Zen feeling of acceptance of the world and the situations I found myself in — a kind of 'seeing eye' philosophy that absorbed all experience in a neutral way in order to build up a sort of bank of experience that could be used for writing. I was very consciously storing material for writing — not jotting things down in a notebook, but accumulating a whole range of thoughts and ideas and experiences.

After the Army, Oxford, to read English. Did you join in the spirit of 'being up at Oxford' too?

I wouldn't say I joined in the whole spirit of the army. I survived the army. With interest. And it was more or less the same at Oxford. I suppose that being an ignorant scouse grammar school boy in an officers' mess and then finding myself in an Oxford college full of twittish public school boys, at least in the college I was in, you begin to discover what the class structure of Britain is about. And it dawns on you in a very heavy sort of way. At home there was no such thing, we were all just part of the working class. My father taught, which made him kind of petty-bourgeois, I suppose, but our whole way of living and culture and ideology — and *backwardness* of ideology — and identification was entirely with the people with whom we lived. I didn't feel that we were middle-class because my father was a teacher, and I don't think anybody else did. He was teaching kids from the docks around Birkenhead, and it was like an extension of the docks, really.

How about the academic side at Oxford?

I took it seriously, the English literature. The system was such that you had to write one essay a week on one writer and it was good to have a lot of time just to read — Skelton, Wyatt, Surrey, Langland, Milton, Beaumont, Fletcher, all the Elizabethans. It was very good to chug slowly through English literature over the course of three years. The hang-up was, you had to read the critics as well, in order to write these essays, but the writing was great. And I've never ceased to be grateful for having to do Anglo-Saxon and Middle English. And Latin, obviously, and French. It just gives one a totally different attitude to the language that we use, and how it can be used, and where its roots are, and where it's at, and why it's changing. Particularly when you're writing verse, that tension inside the English language is good to know about. It becomes part of the whole feel of your writing.

And this was when you started writing plays?

It was just towards the end of my third year — about 1958. A girl called Colette King, who was very talented, but who has refused to work in professional theatre as far as I know, asked me to write a play, because I'd been writing stories and poems and stuff, so I said okay, and went off and wrote one. And it was put on.

This was A Man Has Two Fathers?

Right. *A Man Has Two Fathers* had everything in it. It was constructed like a poem with about five or six levels of meaning running through it. It was really, on different levels, about the struggle between America and Russia, between two kinds of imperialism. It was about psychological disorientation. It was also described — to my surprise — as theatre of the absurd. Which it certainly wasn't. Around this time I had also been doing some translating — Camus' *Caligula*, and huge chunks of Sartre, while I was at Oxford — just to get the idea of what writing a play was. I also translated *The Invasion* by Adamov, with a girl, which was done at Edinburgh.

Did you regard all this as apprentice work?

I regard everything as apprentice work. So far. But I'm personally still quite fond of *A Man Has Two Fathers*, because it managed to incorporate a whole lot of me in it. And it was quite entertaining. And because it was Oxford, Ken Tynan 'happened' to be swanning around that night, and somebody suggested that he come and see the show, which was put on the night before my finals — so much for my finals! Ken came and saw it, and liked it and gave it a very nice review in *The Observer* the following Sunday. *The Observer* being very influential theatrically, George Devine was made aware of me, and he asked me to come and work at the Court on some project that was going on there with a small group of actors and Anthony Page, who was a friend of mine anyway. So I went and worked there and did another short play that was done on a Sunday night at the Court with some others, all by this group.

Anthony Page had been working in America with a guy called Sanford Meisner, and Meisner had a specific rehearsal technique which was to do with working on an astringently truthful form of improvised relationship between actors, which was to be used outside the text completely. But in order to create the right feel, to give the actor the right feel for a relationship within a text. Now, what they wanted was not to improvise a play, but for me to get to know the actors and to write a text which they could use as a basis for working in this way. So I wrote two plays: one was called *The Tent*, the other was called *Tell Me*, and they worked on these using improvisational techniques. But they were very much 'written' plays — the interesting thing was working closely with the actors.

You were working at the Court in an extra-curricular way?

Yes. I did that during the summer, then went back to Oxford for another year. During that I did a production of James Joyce's *Ulysses*, and then a term's teaching practice. I'd met John Arden and Margaretta D'Arcy at the Court, and had stayed at their flat for this term in London, and had a pretty rough time teaching. But it was useful in some ways. That was probably the bleakest period, around then. And then I went back to Oxford to do a production of Aristophanes' *The Birds* in the garden, which I used a lot of music in, and which was, in many ways, like a lot of productions we're doing now.

Then you wrote Why the Chicken?

That was a kind of naturalistic, but not totally naturalistic drama. I've never written a totally naturalistic play after and apart from *The Tent. Why the Chicken?* was about a group of kids in a New Town with nothing to do, who go off to a farmhouse, which they make their own. And it's about the relationship between this group of kids, who've been dragged in from all over the place and a girl, who is a social worker and supposed to be providing some kind of richness in the lives of these kids. She comes out to the farmhouse to find them. The plot was ludicrous, which didn't matter very much — fortunately! It was a clash really between working-class consciousness and living and feeling . . . and Oxford consciousness. I never worked that out, never articulated it, but that's what it was. And the working-class kids, interestingly, end up smashing up the youth club. I suppose that was how I felt about the Oxford consciousness, actually. Anyway, it had a lot of nice writing in it — just saying what you mean to the audience in character, rather than going through a whole naturalistic scene.

George Devine came and saw the show, liked it very much, but had reservations. And decided that he'd rather get me to write another play than do this one, which was fair enough. John Dexter got the play through the Court, liked it very much, worked on it with me, helped me a helluva lot in the writing of it. He really is a great director in that sense, because he understands writing. I was very young, and he really helped me with the feel of a play. I was earning my living reading plays at the Court, and it was a pretty miserable existence. Finally John got the play set up with Lionel Bart and Michael Codron, who were going to go into management together to encourage new writers. It's a long story, and all I can say is that it discouraged me from writing for the theatre for another three years. I thought, well, fuck it, I'll go and write for television, and try to use the popular medium in my own way, and contribute through that to people's lives.

And what happened?'

A certain amount of script editing, then I went on a directors' course, because the only way you can learn about a medium as technical as television is to direct it — odds and ends, book programmes, bits of films, this, that and the other. I was working not so much in the Drama Department, more on the features, documentaries side, and I learned a helluva lot from people like Michael Elliott, who was a really good television director at that time, and Michael Peacock, when I used to hang around the *Panorama* studio, and then with Troy Kennedy-Martin. I shared a flat with him, and just talking about ways of making television work, we decided the form in which television could work best was the long-running series. So we decided we'd do a cops and robbers series — Troy was the writer and I was to be the director. Troy went off to Bootle, Crosby, and Kirkby to research a cops and robbers series which would not be . . .

Not be in the cowboys and Indians tradition?

Not in the cowboys and Indians tradition. What we wanted to do was to use a *Highway Patrol* format, but to use the cops as a key or a way of getting into a whole society. That was the original *Z Cars*. And it was very cleverly worked out, you know, the two kinds of communities these cops were going to work in. The first was called New Town, which was roughly based on Kirkby. The other was Seaport, which was based on the sort of Crosby-Waterloo waterfront. The series was going to be a kind of documentary about people's lives in these areas, and the cops were incidental — they were the means of finding out about people's lives.

And that, for six months, was what we did, but the pressures were on all the time, because after the cops kept appearing week after week, people began to fall in love with them, and they became stars. So the pressure was on to make them the subject, rather than the device. And when the BBC finally decided that's what they were going to do, then Troy and I decided we'd had enough. And we wrote a final episode which I directed. And at the end of it, as far as we were concerned, *Z Cars* was about to change. The series was very lucky, in that John Hopkins, who took over, actually managed to write about policemen in a way that was interesting — but we didn't want to write about policemen.

Nevertheless, in its early days, it was an innovation, even if it didn't innovate in the way you intended — it did change the nature of the cops and robbers series . . .

Well, that's what we wanted to do, to use a popular form and try and bang into it some reality. I was really fanatical about the ways cameras were used, the way a story was told, because up to that time, television had been a dreadful compromise between theatre and film. Now film concentrates on carrying a whole load of information, a complex of information through every frame — because it's a huge frame — independent of the content. But it also can carry a lot of content within one frame. Television is incapable of that. It's small. It cannot have a sensual relationship with the audience — what it conveys is a line of information, an accretion of information which can build to an emotional or dramatic point. And what I was trying to do with *Z Cars* was to use the cameras in such a way that you never did anything, never moved a camera, unless it was to file a new piece of information. No actor ever used a gesture or a line unless it was a new, fresh piece of information.

What was your relationship to the class world of television?

It was a much more subtle form of ideological penetration of the population — and a lot more effective. But I didn't come across any serious political or ideological confrontations at that time because that was a time of liberal influence, not the time of organized reaction which we now have. And because of that liberal atmosphere, I was able to work. But slowly, the bureaucracy grew, in part through technological advance, through the development of tape. At first *Z Cars* was done live, fifty minutes every week. You can't do that now, they won't let you, except for half an hour at midnight or something, it has to be taped, has to be reviewed constantly — from the idea to the synopsis to the script to the re-writes and the rehearsal script, then in rehearsal, in studio, after it's shot and before it goes out, it's reviewed by this elaborate machinery at the BBC. Now that was beginning to happen in 1964 and 1965, which was why I got out. Partly because television is such a demanding medium, it drags stuff out of you and gives you nothing back. And partly because that machinery was beginning to be really effective. I wrote a play during that period and it had one or two good songs in it, but that was about all.

That was Basement in Bangkok?

Yeah, it was done by some students in Bristol, I think. I didn't see it. Thank God. It was dreadful. It took me at least six months to a year just to recover from the television mentality — everything that glitters you grab, and put on the screen — which is totally inimical to being a writer. Then, after about a year, I wrote *Events While Guarding the Bofors Gun*, going back into my own experience to write it — and gave it to the Royal Court who sat on it for a year, and as far as I know, still have not read it.

But it finally went on at Hampstead?

Yeah, in 1966. I just got fed up waiting for the Royal Court to read it, and talked to Ronald Eyre, and he said he would be interested in directing it, so I showed it to James Roose-Evans at Hampstead, and Ron came along and did it very well. The real conflict in *Bofors Gun* was between the way I felt then, in 1966, and the way I felt when I was in Germany, in the army, in 1953 or 1954 — a kind of polarization. It's about . . . why people go on . . . about ambition, I suppose, and the protestant work ethic.

Having done that play, which was very successful, what was the next step?

Well, Peggy Ramsay has been my agent since I began writing, and has really done an enormous amount just to help me to keep going, and after she'd seen *Bofors Gun* she sent me a novel which she thought would interest me, called *The Danish Gambit*, by an American writer called William Butler, and I found it very exciting, because it was a kind of continuation of the last duologue in *Bofors Gun*. The circumstances were totally different, but it was about a priest who was trying to convince a man in a death cell that he should live. I really was very excited by it, and adapted it, as a play. I called it *Bakke's Night of Fame* and again it was done by Ron Eyre at Hampstead. I liked that play. Butler's metaphysical gymnastics are amazing, and I liked being able to get those going in the theatre. Also the character of Bakke is an amazing creation — Butler's, not mine. It did well and it's been done in Germany endlessly. Been very useful as a way of keeping alive, though I was doing movies around that time as well. When I was in television I knew Ken Russell, and worked with him on some of his films, and he rang me up one day and asked me, would I like to do a spy film. By that time I was completely broke and heavily in debt, and the idea of doing a spy film anyway appealed to me. And working with Ken. So I had a go at this one, which was *Billion Dollar Brain*. And that opened up yet another world of amazing people — but this time getting into the whole American film market machine.

Yet another area to soak up?

And be banged on the head by, eventually. But I really enjoyed it. And during those years — oh, 1967 to 1972 — I worked with and learned a lot from quite a lot of people — Fred Zimmermann, Carl Foreman, Saltzman.

How does this period of movie work relate to the beginnings of your own discovery of a new form?

Financially. Getting enough to buy a van, work for two years without wages for the 7:84 Company — to have the sort of confidence that I could stay alive for two years and help it financially. Having gone through the commerical theatre bit, and having gone through television and come out the other end, and then having gone through movies, I finally came to the conclusion that the mass media, at the moment, are so penetrated by the ruling-class ideology, that to try to dedicate your whole life — as distinct from occasional forays and skirmishes — to fighting within them is going to drive you mad.

This was when you wrote Random Happenings in the Hebrides? *Before starting the 7:84 Company?*

Yes, that was a play for the Lyceum in Edinburgh, a kind of intermediate stage in what I was doing. Up till then, all the plays I'd written took place within a small group of people, all in the course of a day or even less. *Bofors, Why the Chicken?, The Tent, Bakke* — they were all to do with cloistered groups of people, working out their destinies within a short period of time. I felt the need to write more of a chronicle sort of play. And *Random Happenings,* although it takes place all on one set, actually spans quite a number of years, about a decade.

How much of you was in that play? I mean emotionally, autobiographically?

It's hard to say. The danger when you say, there's a lot of me in a play, is that people think, aha, that character is *him.*

Well, it is about the political awakening of a young man, Jimmy, who was 'educated' out of the working class and who realized he had to find a way to reroot himself, if he was going to be politically effective . . .

Yes. The interesting thing about that play was that I began to write it in April 1968, and in May 1968 things started happening in Paris. And I went over and spent some time there, until they started exporting foreigners. And the importance of the thinking around that whole time, the excitement of that whole complex set of attitudes to life which that para-revolutionary situation threw up, was incredible — the thinking about ordinary life, the freshness of the approach, the urgency and the beauty of the ideas was amazing. *But* what didn't happen was organization. For a lot of reasons. A lot connected with the French Communist Party, a lot connected with the fact that the rest of the Left was split and disorganized, and with the fact that much of the student leadership was middle-class and not dedicated to social revolution, and with the power of De Gaulle and his wilyness as a politician. I came back and left the play, actually, for about six months to a year, and then I finished it. But it was changed by that whole experience. Apparently it had nothing to do with Paris and people throwing paving stones, but that experience went into it. That conflict.

And 7:84 started soon after this?

Right. I came back from a couple of weeks' holiday, loaded with energy, and not much else, and decided to put on a play that I had in my head, at the Edinburgh Festival. That play was called *Trees in the Wind* and it first went on in 1971, for three weeks during the Festival. A lot of very good, very important work had been done by Portable Theatre and Pip Simmons and those people — assisted by the Arts Council — creating a fringe circuit, and people said, come and play to us here, there and everywhere. So I just rang up a lot of people and said, can we do the show? And they said, yup, and I went to Sue Timothy at the Arts Council, and said, will you give us some money to help us? And she said yes. So we got a bit of money there, we got a bit of money from the gigs, and shot off, and did *Trees in the Wind*. We played Aberdeen Arts Centre, Stirling, Lancaster. A lot of gigs like that which were quite good, with young audiences.

How much did the meaning and aims and identity of 7:84 evolve out of that, and how much did you have in your head as a goal?

At the beginning I had a lot of ideas about it. I decided that for the first year it would have to be a sort of benevolent dictatorship, and ran it that way with growing consultation with members of the company as it grew. We did a second tour in the spring of 1972 and then another two plays following that, in the late spring and early summer of 1972. All those plays were by me, but then we did *Occupations* by Trevor Griffiths, along with *Underneath* which was mine. Which was about . . . building bridges, in a very broad sense, and also specifically. It's about two people who both claim they build bridges.

One is a designer, with a very elitist attitude, who designs an experimental type of bridge which is very likely to collapse. And his attitude is that if progress is going to be made, it's going to have to be at the expense of a few human lives, maybe — though he's a very kind, gentle, wonderful man, who does make progress in the construction business. The other is a man who actually works on the bridges, and gets killed on one. The link between the two is the designer's son, who grows from being a kind of upper-class dropout. He works with the man who is killed on the bridge, sees him killed and goes through a politicization as a result. It's about a conflict of ideology again. And about the value of human life.

We got together *Underneath* and *Occupations* from May to July of 1972, after which came into rehearsal *The Ballygombeen Bequest*, which John Arden and Margaretta D'Arcy had written. I'd known John and Margaretta since 1958, and when we started the company I asked them, would they write us a show? They said, well, they were writing a show which would be right for us, but had been commissioned by Charles Marowitz for the Open Space. But Marowitz had wanted certain cuts made — basically all the politics — and they weren't prepared to make them, so they'd rather we did the show. And after various hassles, we did.

Did you work with them on the production?

Yes. I wanted to talk with John and Margaretta about the play and about another idea that John had had, which was that I could update *Musgrave* into being a para-sergeant coming back from Derry after Bloody Sunday. And I had a very strong feeling that *The Ballygombeen Bequest* needed an actor to direct it. Gavin Richards had never directed before, but he is an amazing actor, very intelligent and highly organized, though wilfully self-disorganizing: I asked Gavin, would he like to do it? And he did it very well. It was a really smashing show. And with that company we also did *Sergeant Musgrave Dances On*, which Richard Eyre directed. We toured the two of them together for . . . far too long — oh, about sixteen weeks — a really knackering tour. But at last we'd got a company who could take over the running — so that was the end of the benevolent dictatorship.

Was this when the Scottish venture was starting up?

Yes. I was thinking in terms of this company being autonomous, and me being able to go up to Scotland to work with another group there, which would also become autonomous. Unfortunately it ended in a certain amount of confusion because the English company didn't stay together — they were lured away to Nottingham and the Royal Court, places like that. So there was a slight disintegration, and it became a question of the people who stayed working as a collective. And that's how it's been run.

It must have been around this time that you were also writing Fish in the Sea *for the Liverpool Everyman?*

Yes. But in fact this whole bout of writing, from 1971 onwards, began with the Everyman. I wandered in there one night and saw a show about Bessie Braddock by Stephen Fagin. That was good and interesting and right, but playing to rows of empty seats. I was excited by the kind of actors Alan Dosser had put together, the way he was using the theatre, and above all by the fact that here was someone trying to reach an audience that I knew and loved: the ordinary people of Merseyside. I wrote a set of short plays, mostly set in Liverpool, called *Unruly Elements*, that began to break new ground for me in style, and to open up whole areas of my life that I had been wanting to write about for years. They got quite good audiences, and Alan and the company and I began to work well together.

But still the Everyman was not getting the audience it deserved. So I sat down and wrote *Soft or a Girl?*, a Liverpool play with loads of songs and lots of comedy, lots of local involvement and a serious theme. The form was nearer to a concert with scenes than anything else. Happily, it worked. The theatre was packed with the people we wanted to see in it — and we had to run it again. This was overlapping with the beginning of 7:84, and for the next two years, as well as working with 7:84, I worked a lot for the Everyman — adapted *Chalk Circle* for Liverpool, adapted a Peter Terson play, and finally wrote *Fish in the Sea* early in 1973. For that I took the form of *Soft or a Girl?* and really pushed it near to its limits: it's a very ambitious play, and I would not have believed it would work if I hadn't learnt a great deal from the Everyman audience. It's a big play, springing from a family situation into all kinds of areas.

A central situation built around a family is typical of a number of your plays.

Well, the Liverpool plays, yes.

And music . . .

Yes, pop music, rock music — I was trying to write lyrics which would relate to the scene, and do things in the course of the play. They were slightly like pop lyrics, but different — obviously in meaning, but also in style . . . just a little bit off the pop idiom, slightly more articulate, more literary than the pop idiom. Because they were to be listened to.

There's a strong entertainment element, in using popular themes — like romantic love?

Romantic love — and jokes. That whole thing. I loved that anyway, being from Merseyside — it was the kind of show I'd always wanted to see.

How conscious have you been from the beginning of trying to find the right theatrical methods of communicating with an audience which is not the normal theatregoing audience?

It's been very much a process of finding the form. For example, working in the Highlands, there's a form of entertainment which is not unique to the Highlands, but is very common there, called the ceilidh, where everybody goes along, sings a song, tells a story, plays a piece of music, and so on. We used that form to create a historical play — *The Cheviot, the Stag and the Black Black Oil* — again with lots of variety in it, lots of jokes. And the role of the ceilidh in the nineteenth century was very much a double one — of reinforcing the Gaelic culture, which we were also trying to do, and of a political getting-together. The ceilidh became a way of people getting together about what was going on, and this is very much what's in *The Cheviot* as well — people are talking about what's going on, what went on, and keeping the folk memory alive.

Soft or a Girl?, Fish in the Sea, *and* The Cheviot *also have a very strong narrative element* . . .

Well, there are two different kinds of stories. In *Soft or a Girl?* and *Fish in the Sea* there's a plot, a story, a family situation, or a group situation, which develops, with twists and turns and events of a personal nature which relate to the meaning of the whole thing. In *The Cheviot* and in *Boom,* which was another Scottish show, and in *Lay Off* which is the current English show, the plot *is* the element. The plot is history, the plot is the events. And they are different kinds of shows altogether, using a different kind of theatrical technique — variety, music, acting, singing — to relate more or less directly a series of events without the intervention of a fictional device. I like both forms, but I think now and again — or often — you have to say what you mean, directly. And if the contact between the audience's experience and what you're saying is real, then the play works. But if you're doing a show about industry and people being made redundant, about the growth of large corporations, ripping off the workers by dividing and ruling, but are doing it for an audience which is not really involved in all that, then you find that the audience is saying, oh, what happened to *Fish in the Sea,* that lovely family story? But if you do it for an audience of people who are working in industry, then the contact is real, and the dynamics of the play work through the relationship between the meaning and the audience. The audience is coming back at you the whole time.

Literally?

Not shouting back, but, yes, reacting — recognizing, applauding, booing the villains, laughing in such a way that you know it's a recognition thing. You know that their heads are right into the story and it becomes a different kind of plot. So a fictional story is one way of doing it, and this direct way is another way. In the direct way, you find that people use words like 'didactic' when they're not actually involved in the meaning of it. The people who *are* actually involved in the meaning of it don't think of it as didactic. They think of it as self-evident — truths being stated publicly, socially, in an entertaining way, and that is very much what theatre is about, uncovering and giving expression to what is there, and to the realities of people's lives.

10
David Hare

commanding the style of presentation

Another writer who began as a 'Portable playwright', David Hare quickly broke into the commercial theatre after his three-woman play Slag *reached the fashionable Hampstead Theatre Club in 1970. He has continued somewhat disarmingly to straddle the fence which conventionally divides 'alternative' theatre from the institutional variety.*

Thus, while the left Hare's foot made a memorable imprint with the production of Fanshen *by the Joint Stock company (of which he was a founding member), the right landed firmly back in Hampstead, where* The Great Exhibition *duly confirmed its audience's worst suspicions about the political and sexual deviancy of Labour politicians. And while he took a leading role in creating those collaborative sports,* Lay-by *and* England's Ireland, *and with Howard Brenton also co-authored* Brassneck, *an impressive study of provincial political life, for* Knuckle *he again found a commercial stage best suited to a fast-moving parody-thriller with a Spillane-type hero-cum-commentator.*

Hare hoped also to break into Shaftesbury Avenue with Teeth'n'Smiles, *a musical variation on the breakdown of the values of the late-'sixties, as experienced by the female leader of a touring rock group. But, as he explains in this interview,* Knuckle *lost money for its West End management, and it was at the Royal Court that* Teeth'n'Smiles *eventually reached the stage. David Hare wryly went on to accuse us of not believing him when he claimed that for all these plays it was the content, not the anticipated venue or audience, which determined the form: there had, he went on, 'never been any bar on ideas, even in the West End'.*

It was in the Lyttelton auditorium of the National Theatre that David Hare's next stage play, Plenty, *was presented in 1978. Using chronological cross-cutting to contrast the experiences of an Englishwoman involved in the French resistance with her peacetime life, the play impressively confirmed Hare's ability, demonstrated as early as* Slag, *to present female characters without condescension or the usual veneer of male presumption: more important, it showed a capacity for compassion — sustained in his television play,* Dreams of Living, *in 1980 — whereas the contempt more usual in his earlier work had sometimes palled in its very insistence.*

Catherine Itzin and I talked to David Hare in his south London home in November 1975, shortly after the production of Teeth'n'Smiles. *He told us that his childhood had been spent in seaside Sussex, mainly in Bexhill — 'an extremely geriatric sort of place where people go to retire'. Here, he had been 'forced up through the class system'.*

I went to Lancing, a public school, and I enjoyed it a great deal. It was . . . eventful. I boarded from the age of thirteen. It was a liberal, arty public school, then. Very decadent and art-oriented. My parents saved up a lot of money and went without themselves in order to send me to a good school.

Did you have to do things like joining the cadet force at school?

Yes, but I did write a letter of complaint to *Peace News* — which they printed like a shot — complaining because I wasn't allowed to wear my CND badge. The headmaster was very angry about it. He said that I could, if I wanted to, set fire to the school, but I had to exercise self-control — neither set fire to the school, nor write to *Peace News*, which was like burning down the school . . .

Had you started writing seriously?

No, not till after I went to Cambridge. When I was twenty-two. I enjoyed school a lot more than university, though. I thought the university was very narcissistic — very ingrown and self-conscious. And because it was so small, and because of the sexual imbalance, I suppose — nine thousand men to about six hundred women.

Why had you wanted to go to Cambridge?

I had been studying English at school, and I wanted to be taught by a Marxist — that was my ambition. But as it turned out the man concerned had rather lost his enthusiasm for teaching.

And you weren't writing?

No, I would have been too self-conscious. It was impossible to do anything at Cambridge without a view to the effect you were creating. The writers were writers in order to be thought of as writers, not because they had anything to say.

So, where did you go from there?

I went to work for A.B. Pathé, who made Pathé Pictorials. They were making a series of films on sex education, but you had to make the films out of Pathé stock material. So I saw almost the whole run of Pathé Pictorials . . .

This was with the idea of getting into films?

Yes. I can't remember exactly how it happened, but I'd been to Elstree and seen the people who were running that — it was part of the ABC set-up at the time. And they sent me on to Pathé.

And from there, somehow, into Portable Theatre?

Yes, straight into Portable Theatre, with Tony Bicât. As I remember, it was mostly his idea — it was certainly his idea calling it Portable Theatre. It came out of a long series of conversations about the theatre, in which he was very interested, and in which I became interested.

Through him?

Yes. He was a lot more cogent about what he wanted to do. What happened was, we were both directors and we didn't have any writers. It's very difficult, because in retrospect people say it was a writers' theatre. That's how it fell out, but we began with Kafka and Genet. Once we were even going to do Lawrence Durrell. Neither of us were writers, and the Kafka show was a literary thing, really — not very different from Emlyn Williams reading Dickens, as four square as that.

What was the original philosophy behind Portable?

The idea was to take theatre to places where it normally didn't go. We weren't to see that a variety of arts centres and groups would spring up to accommodate that. But when we started we played more army camps and bare floors than we were playing by the end.

Were you aware of the other itinerant theatre groups that were beginning to happen about that time?

That is what is odd, actually. La Mama happened at the same time, we had never heard of La Mama. And similarly, when after the first Portable production two of the actors started saying it would be much more interesting to use our bodies rather than these dull words, we were actually bemused. We couldn't think what they were talking about. So they went off and founded the Freehold . . .

How did Portable develop from those literary beginnings?

Through Howard Brenton, really. One night Howard came and was literally the only person in the audience, so we said, would you like to go to the pub? And that's how we met, and when we wanted to do new writers Brenton's *Christie in Love* was certainly the best play that came our way. But we had also started working with John Grillo.

And the first play you wrote on your own was How Brophy Made Good?

Yes. That was because we were waiting for a play from Snoo Wilson — for reasons which I can't really remember, except that Tony had met Snoo somewhere and asked him to write a play for us in two weeks, which he'd rashly promised to do, but failed to deliver. So *Brophy* was written to fill that hole, very fast. I can say almost nothing about it now. I didn't like it very much when I saw it, and I don't think it's a particularly interesting piece of work. I haven't read it for a very long time.

Yet there must have been a moment when you recognized that you had somehow become a writer?

I think it actually happened after *Brophy*, because for some reason people actually came to see it, and I got an agent. And then I got a job at the Royal Court as Literary Manager — that was mostly through Christopher Hampton, who was the Resident Dramatist there. And he had been persuading me to try and write a play for a long time, on the basis that I was so voluble about the plays that I had to read, I ought to try and do better.

What was the job of Literary Manager like?

It was just the sheer grind of reading through umpteen scrips. But it financed the work that was important to me, and left me some time as well.

It was while you were at the Court that you wrote What Happened to Blake?

Yes, because Portable needed a play. And, though it's hard to believe it now, we were interested in literary biographies, in trying to represent the lives of writers. That was through Tony's influence: he was interested in artists. Blake was a man I had wanted to write about, and it also meant I could develop a line of work that Portable was doing, a kind of stripping down of stagecraft. Though I think *Blake* came out like an imitation of a La Mama play, like a Paul Foster play. I admired Blake, and loved his poems. But I found his madness useless. I don't think artists going bananas are very interesting, it's their job to stay sane. That contradiction in my attitude to him blew the play apart, I couldn't handle it. The most successful passages in the play are about Mrs. Blake, for whom I have a great deal of time.

Was Slag *originally conceived for Portable?*

No, for Michael Codron, like virtually everything else I've written since. He had read *Brophy*, and asked me to do a play for him.

It's very odd, really, that this first big success should have been about three women exclusively — after a public school and Cambridge background such as you've described . . .

The subject matter came from a zealotry about women, I suppose. It was written at a time when I was deeply impressed, delighted with women. It's written as a play in praise of women. I always protest when people claim it's a misogynistic play. It is schematic, but that is a vice of plays which have three characters and happen in an enclosed space. You inevitably polarize in a way that in a large-scale play you don't. And the point is that it's really a play about institutions, not about women at all. Only that I thought it was delightful to see three women on the stage. It's about every institution I had known — school, Cambridge, Pathé, and so on. They are all the same. That is how institutions perpetuate themselves. With rituals that go on inside them — ever more baroque discussions about ever dwindling subjects. But it happens to be peopled with women, partly because it was the sort of play that I thought I would enjoy going to see — women on the stage, represented as I thought more roundly and comprehensively than was then usual.

Writing for Michael Codron, did you find yourself thinking in terms of a 'commercial' audience?

No, I don't really think of the audience when I write. Certainly not in the case of *Slag* — though this again was partly through ignorance, because I had no idea of what 'writing for Michael Codron' entailed. I know what it entails now — one set and three characters! But I have been very happy with Codron, enjoyed writing for him.

How important was it to you to continue to succeed in the commercial theatre, after the work with Portable?

I think that if you can possibly survive in the commercial theatre you should, because otherwise you're just blocking up the subsidized theatres for new writers. But what happened, of course, was that as soon as I'd adjusted to this, *Knuckle* lost money, so that it became impossible to present *Teeth'n'Smiles* in the commercial theatre.

Were you making a living from playwriting in the Portable days?

I really don't know how I did live. We had no money from Portable, and I was getting seven to ten pounds a week from the Court.

Was Slag *the great watershed, then?*

That was what I was determined not to make it. After it did well, I was determined to keep my nose down — which was why I wrote *Blake*. There was something flukey about *Slag*, in the sense that it was a subject about which I was very clear in my own mind — about institutions. But when I came to write *Blake*, it was a great deal more complex, a mixture of my own approval and disapproval that I just couldn't handle. Although it's shorter, it's much more formally demanding.

Because you knew Portable could meet the demands?

Exactly. But it was arrogance which made me think I could just toss a play off. To write a play at all you have to work extremely hard on what you believe about the subject — and the writing process is finding out the truth or otherwise of what you believe by testing it on the stage. So you're just not conscious at the time of where you are going to sell it.

Yet you have had to write for two distinct kinds of audiences — even now, with Fanshen *for the sort of audiences who go to see* Joint Stock, *with* Teeth'n'Smiles *for commercial audiences . . .*

I don't accept the implication. The writing ambience of those two plays was identical. When I'd finished them I showed them to the same people. There was the same seriousness in their presentation, the same production techniques were employed. There's absolutely no difference — except that you want as many people as possible to see them, and not to clog up the subsidized theatres. There's absolutely no justification for Pinter being done in the subsidized theatre now. It is a waste of the taxpayers' money.

How were your own political feelings developing at this time?

As I've said, I was very pissed off with life while I was at university, and very disillusioned about the activities of the Left. It's really only as a writer that I've begun to think myself straight, work out for myself the answers to political questions. It's a rigorous discipline, playwriting, in the sense that you need to answer questions which are never answered by polemic or journalism or propaganda.

It's as conscious a process as that when you're writing?

I think it's become more and more so. Playwriting is a ruthlessly truthful medium, and I've come to believe in it much more as I've gone on working. I think that the judgements the audience make show up insincerity, reveal the superficial, and more and more I have trouble writing until I've worked out in the greatest possible detail what I think myself about some subject or other, whatever I'm writing about.

Does this apply to the 'craft' aspect of the work? Does your work go through many drafts?

More and more as I go on. Looking back, I don't know how on earth I ever wrote a play in ten days.

Take The Great Exhibition: *how long did that take to write, all told?*

About a year. I have trouble now remembering what the original idea behind the play was. I think it was to do with Labour and politics generally in the 'sixties. The only political experience I had had was believing passionately in the Labour Government of 1964, and watching that government sell everything down the river. So the play was about a disillusioned Labour MP

But the disillusionment is witnessed at a very private level. Like in Slag, *about institutions . . .*

Yes, I think that's a mistake, I wouldn't do it now. Because I think people have expectations of plays which have one set and a limited number of characters, and I think those expectations are impossible to resist. And although *The Great Exhibition* starts in a room, and then deliberately explodes and opens out to try and confound the audience, I don't think it really succeeded in that. There is something about the ritual of a play in which there is this guy at the centre of the stage with all the best lines, who's being witty at everybody's expense, and whose uniquely subtle psychology we're going to explore during the course of the evening, which is limiting, which is dead. Because it stops the audience thinking — or rather, they imagine they're there to find out what this man on the stage thinks. They're not: they're there to find out what *they* think.

I felt that The Great Exhibition *was much more about the rather tortuous interdependence of this particular couple than about the failures of the Labour Government of 1964.*

The thing is, Hammett feels himself to be an exhibitionist both in his public life and in his private life. He feels conscious that he's performing in parliament, and conscious that he's performing in front of his wife.

You actually contributed to Lay-by *before writing* The Great Exhibition, *didn't you — while you were still working at the Court?*

Yes, just before. *Lay-by* came out of a writers' conference where, having discussed all day what was wrong with the situation of writers, I suggested that anyone who wanted should try writing a play collectively, given the guarantee that it would be presented at the Royal Court on a Sunday night. In fact, the Court let us down on the guarantee. But we went off and wrote, seven of us together, based on a clipping that appeared in the paper that day and which Trevor Griffiths happened to have — an extremely prurient description of an alleged rape on a motorway, and the trial. We started work the following Wednesday with wallpaper and crayons. An experiment in public writing.

And how do you think it worked?

I think there's something totally distinctive about the play. It touches on an area that has never been treated in that way. It has got the authentic stink of pornography, which I have never experienced except from pornography itself, and I think that was an achievement: there's something about the ugliness and perverse excitement of pornography in the play, something about the battering of the minds of working-class people. That said, it is also sporty, and of course it shows off.

Your own work as a director had been going on simultaneously with all the writing, and for that matter preceded it. Do you see these as separate activities in separate compartments?

No, not at all. It has now become a deliberate pattern, going backwards and forwards, from desk to rehearsal room. I try to keep that up.

When you're directing somebody else's play does your writing instinct tempt you into trying to rewrite somebody else's work?

When it's my own work it's difficult — just physically. But certainly as a director I'm extremely keen on rewriting, and nearly every play I've done is unrecognizable from the script that was delivered to me. Trevor Griffiths's *The Party* changed quite considerably, and Snoo Wilson's *The Pleasure Principle* was unrecognizable. Howard Brenton and I rewrote *Brassneck* over a weekend. I think it's useful that as I writer I am somehow able to ask for quite radical rewrites — it's something that most directors in England don't seem self-confident enough to undertake, yet's it's one of the director's jobs, to get the best out of a play and a writer.

Is this reciprocal — when other directors want revisions from you?

Oh yes. In fact often I want to rewrite and the director doesn't. And we end up in the ludicrous situation of me saying, please can we have rewrites, and the director saying, no, no, it's fine as it is.

Your career somehow seems to have become more ad hoc since you left Portable . . .

But you see, I don't think of it as a career. I just think of it as following my nose, from one subject to another. It's the subject matter that dictates everything. It's true that I've never had a 'home', theatrically — never had a theatre that regularly did my work — since Portable. But I think most writers enjoy whoring around, actually, much as they pretend to need a home.

From the number of Portable writers who have become important figures in their own right, what was it that was special about that company?

What we had in common was that we thought we were living through a period of extreme decadence, both socially and theatrically. We just couldn't believe that the official culture was incapable of seeing the extreme state of crisis that we thought the country was in. Now that sort of doom talk is the fashion of the day, of course.

Yet while some of the then established dramatists, like John Arden, have opted out of the 'official' culture, Howard Brenton and yourself seem actually to have come closer to it . . .

That's because I don't think either Howard or myself were ever technically innovative writers. We can now command the standards we want, the style of presentation that we want, there's never any argument about how the plays are to be done, where five or six years ago there would have been. It's always the content of the work that determines everything — which I say over and over again, and I know you don't believe me, but it's true! And where can ideas be most clearly presented? There has never been any bar on ideas, even in the West End.

One gets the feeling from what you've said about your plays that once they're written and staged you regard them as almost . . . disposable.

I think so. I think if I were honest, which I'm not, I would stop them being done after a period of time.

Is that something that will continue, or is there going to come a time when you will be able to say, yes, that's mine, and still worth doing?

I don't think *Knuckle* or *Teeth'n'Smiles* have been superseded as plays either by what I now think, or by what other people have written after me. They stand. The rest of my work I'm happy to consign to oblivion.

Yet your own vision seems to have changed from the destructive one permeating Knuckle *to the constructive one underlying* Fanshen . . .

Oh, *Knuckle* is an almost obscenely constructive play! It says something about it being impossible to live within this system without doing yourself moral damage. That's a huge claim.

And a destructive one . . .

I don't agree with that at all. It's a play about knowing, about the fact that there are no excuses, and the fact that people who are damaged by the system know themselves to have been damaged, and are not ignorant of what they've done to themselves. And that is a large claim, because how you feel about capitalists — whether you believe them to be knaves or fools — determines everything you believe and think politically. I felt that in *The Great Exhibition* I'd written a play that was only intelligible to the politically minded, to anybody who cared about the future of the Left in this country. If you don't care about that, the play's just a farce or satire — forgettable. So with *Knuckle* I particularly wanted to write a play which was available to everybody — it's about people for whom political rhetoric is no part of their lives. The characters aren't political — or intellectual — at all.

Is that why you used the sort of Spillane element?

Yes, and partly because there was a character in the play who saw himself as a Spillane character. But the reason I don't find the play pessimistic is because it also contains the most admirable person I've ever drawn, this girl who is meant to be a good person. The whole play deals with moral values, and concludes that there *is* such a thing as moral value. That seems to me quite cheerful.

Yet not enough to make the play a financial success. The truths maybe still weren't digestible enough for a West End audience.

That proved to be true. Yet now the discussion of the decline of our society has become fashionable, and society discusses itself obsessively, and uses terms that it hasn't used before. The word 'capitalism' was never used before 1970 to describe their system by the capitalists: they called their system 'life', and then there was something else called communism. Now our decline is voraciously discussed; but the means of discussion are failing us. That's to say, journalism, however intelligent, will always fail you. It is glib by nature. Words can *only* be tested by being spoken. Ideas can *only* be worked in real situations. That is why the theatre is the best court society has.

Did this have anything to do with the way Fanshen *happened in quite a different theatrical set-up?*

I think like everybody I was sick to death with writing about England — with writing about this decadent corner of the globe. The excitement of *Fanshen* was to write about a society and to cover a period of time in which one felt that people's lives were being materially and spiritually improved, in a culture that was completely different to anything we knew about. We wanted to write a positive work using positive material.

Though you've said that Fanshen *originated like your other plays, as an independent idea of your own . . .*

It was complicated, because the play I wrote originally had as its fulcrum an idea that is not in the book by William Hinton. Now that, at the time, was very important to me. Since I've talked to Hinton and since we've done the revival at Hampstead, a lot of that has been removed, and I don't think to the play's detriment. There was a running idea in the text that people need justice — talking of morality again, that is something I believe, that people have a sense of justice, and that they need justice, and need to believe a society is just. A large claim, but I have found it to be true. Hinton, as it happens, doesn't believe that: he feels justice is a bourgeois concept. Whose justice? And justice in what terms? So he asked me to remove most of the references to justice in the play, which I've done. Also I had deliberately written a text that was as resonant of Europe as was possible, so that people might make their own analogies, about political leadership and so on. And at the very first performance, somebody did come out of the play and say, 'Wouldn't it be marvellous to get Reginald Maudling at a meeting like that, and quiz him?' But that was not what Hinton had intended in the book.

How did the relationship with Joint Stock evolve?

We did a five or six week workshop period, during which we explored different ways of approaching the work. The actors mostly dealt with the question of 'how do I play Chinese?' Which to me was a non-question, but to them was very important, and they satisfied themselves with their answers. The way we eventually dealt with it I worked out on my own, and then with Bill Gaskill and Max Stafford-Clark. And the story I found is one of, oh, a hundred and fifty possible narrative paths through that book.

Do you find it ironic that Knuckle *failed to break through to the wider audience you intended, yet the apparently less accessible* Fanshen *has now reached a television audience of millions?*

Yes I do, though I wish I didn't. But I do feel that people who have seen it on television haven't really seen the play. It was the intensity of the thought that to me was remarkable about audiences watching the play. I remember in Sheffield, particularly, the silences were the most profound silences I've heard in the theatre — it was very gratifying, twenty minutes going by without a sound from the audience. Everyone was thinking: and I can't honestly believe that happened with the television version.

Was it only the 'justice' element that was altered before the Hampstead production?

No, I'd also misunderstood a long passage in the book which Hinton explained to me — which was why egalitarianism would have endangered the revolution. When the Secretary says, 'You must go back and tell them the policy has changed,' he thought that I'd slanted it to make the Secretary unsympathetic, because I'd not explained his real reasons for the policy change. In fact, I'd misunderstood them.

There did seem to be a real element of brutality and ruthlessness at the end. Was that why?

Partly that. And partly I think it has to do with the endless question, which Hinton refuses to admit, of how do people know whether their democracy is a good democracy — how can you genuinely scan the party, make sure you're not being manipulated? In the second draft I tried to explain why the Chairman thought that if everyone was given equal shares it would simply set worker against worker, that within three weeks the shares would no longer be equal anyway, and that egalitarianism is the worst form of socialism.

You mean there is no point in giving people equal shares in a system that still allows personal property at all?

Yes, until you can collectivize. What he says is that you must be 'bold in concept, gentle in execution'. Having analyzed your situation and objective, be bold in concept, but don't then do anything which, however excellent in intention, will in effect be destructive. So that change of policy was necessary. They had to say, that's it, that's the fanshen, that's complete. Until the land could be collectivized, there would be no further redistribution.

Do you intend to continue to seek that sort of writing situation, with a company like Joint Stock?

It certainly was very exciting, and I enjoyed it very much, but, again, the main attraction was the subject matter. Also, the need to do without the things that English playwrights usually rely on — irony, sarcasm, innuendo, all the shadings that make playwriting easy. There aren't many things that make playwriting easy, but the fluency of the English language is a tremendous help. Now if you choose to write in Ur Chinese, you haven't got that, you've only got the meaning of what is being said. And that was bracing, after years of tweedling around with words.

11
Trevor Griffiths
transforming the husk of capitalism

While David Jones was artistic director of the RSC's Aldwych Theatre in 1970, he decided to mount a nine-week experimental season at The Place, a small dance studio off the Euston Road. For the opening production, he chose a play that had been sent to him by the agent of a writer previously unknown in London, Trevor Griffiths — and, to stage it, a director also virtually unknown in the capital, Buzz Goodbody.

Although the two were never again to work together, their brief conjunction was of some moment in the development of contemporary British theatre. Within four years, Goodbody had persuaded the RSC management to open The Other Place in Stratford under her direction. Although her own main contribution to its work was in shaping the company's 'studio style' for Shakespeare (a healthy corrective to certain ossifying tendencies one detected, as the company approached that ten-year danger period defined by Peter Hall), the opening of The Other Place led, three years later, to the creation of a London studio theatre for the RSC, The Warehouse, with an emphasis on work by new writers. Tragically, Buzz Goodbody's own life had by then been cut short by suicide.

Trevor Griffiths, believing — with an acknowledged innocence of the London theatre set-up — that the RSC and the National were part of 'one job lot', found himself commissioned to write his next play for both companies. Eventually, The Party *was staged at the National — although, like* Occupations, *it later went on tour, in a new and more satisfactory production by David Hare.* Comedians *also came to the National, from Nottingham, in 1975, before transferring to the West End.*

By this time, Charles Marowitz's Open Space Theatre had staged Griffiths's early, autobiographical Sam Sam, *and he was busy writing an eleven-part television series about a Labour MP, the eponymous* Bill Brand. *Now, most of Griffiths's work is for television — though he did collaborate with Howard Brenton, Ken Campbell, and David Hare on* Deeds, *seen in Nottingham in 1978. In contrast to John McGrath, he strongly defends both the influence and the integrity of the medium — at least so far as his own work is concerned, as a socialist playwright wishing to reach the widest possible audience.*

It was in the offices of Griffiths's agent, the late and much lamented Clive Goodwin, that Catherine Itzin and I talked with Trevor Griffiths in the spring of 1976. Conscious that it had taken Griffiths, born in Manchester in 1935, rather longer than many of his contemporaries to break into theatre, we asked about the influences on his formative years. Had he any childhood memories of Manchester during the depression?

I can remember very clearly when I was two. We didn't have a house, right, so the family was split up. We were living in the extended family, spreadeagled across Manchester. I was billetted with my gran, who was Irish, and by that time half blind and gangrenous and kept falling down the stairs. I lived with her from two to five. She was a witch really. She made the most marvellous Irish stew out of lettuce . . . anything. And she believed in Indian brandy for stomach ache. She had flag floors in the kitchen, and you could peel the dirt between — little bits of moss grew there. It's very vivid, very concrete, very immediate, that life. And the priest was always around, because I was a Catholic: she was a devout, totally unthinking, wild Irish Catholic.

The whole family?

No, my father wasn't, my father was Welsh, son of a Welsh miner. And in so far as they were anything, and I don't think they were, I suppose he was Chapel. There was a big conflict about that, right through the early life, very much centred on me. Because by a very curious and unique contract between my parents, the first child was non-Catholic, and the second child was Catholic. I went to school when I was three and a half, simply because my grandmother liked to lie down in the middle of the day, because she was quite old. So they had to get me into a Catholic school because that was where she had some pull, with Father Malone as he was called, or Father Riprap as we referred to him.

So it was an exciting very early childhood, and, because of the extended family, a secure one?

Very secure, yes. There's really nothing like it. Once we go into the nuclear family, as we did after that — well I didn't like it very much. From five onwards it seemed to me to be very inhibiting to be totally dimensioned by four other people. My grandmother helped out by getting gangrene in the other leg and coming to live with us permanently, setting up extended wars between her and my father which she loved. And so that was another complication. The principle fights then were about money. My father was an extraordinarily decent, tidy, hard-working, fair-day's pay, just-look-after-yourself kind of guy, and my mother was wild, a bit like her mum, and also in an odd way aspirant, slightly excited by the possibilities already existing in post-war Britain for self-advancement.

Did you carry on at Catholic school?

Yes, I went on to a Catholic grammar school. And my brother went to a non-Catholic state school and then to a technical school — at fifteen.

Did you notice school particularly?

Oh yeah. Historically it was interesting to be in a Catholic school, because Catholic schools were very much fighting for their survival as distinct separate educational entities. And they thought that the way to do it, as indeed it was, was to join the meritocratic rat-race, and therefore to get as many people through the eleven-plus as possible. So there was very intensive combing and sifting. From seven, I found myself placed apart from slower children and all the rest of it. Their words, not mine.

You got through the eleven-plus?

Yes. Because I had gone to school when I was three, I was actually quite lively when I was four and a half and the new school I went to recognized fairly early that I could read very fluently and that I was fairly bright and all the rest of it. So I was always a year younger than my peers, than my class-group, and I passed my eleven-plus when I was nine and went to this St. Bede's College which was a grammar school, with a lot of Jesuits teaching, when I was ten.

Still very firmly Catholic.

Yes, in some ways more so, because one was so much more aware of Catholicism. Then I had the 'culture slump,' from about eleven to fourteen and a half, when the whole impact of the middle-classness of education began to really nail me, hammer me to the ground. I got very small, very frightened. I worked things out in terms of my own individual psychology for a long time, because I wasn't in any way related to anybody else, I was isolated. I was very frustrated when I was an adolescent.

Sexually or in every way?

Certainly sexually, no question of that. Catholics have a heavy time anyway, because the whole notion of touching one's body is outside the allowable; yet it's wholly improbable that one could survive for very long without doing it. So terrific crises used to develop. Then I was pretty small, and they used to call me Shrimp — that was difficult. I was also very aggressive, but I couldn't ever win fights, because guys were always a year older than me and maybe a stone heavier. I used to fight, but I used to get hammered. So I developed a kind of verbal acidity, which you had to learn with delicacy, because if a guy knew you were getting at him, he'd get you. So that was all problematic.

But you had a sort of pick-up at fourteen or fifteen?

Well, I couldn't leave school at fifteen, or rather you had to be fifteen in the year you took the new certificate, the GCE. So they did this con job on my parents, because my father was very keen for me to leave and start earning, and I stayed an extra year in order to get a leaving certificate, by which time

I'd suddenly begun to taste independent academic work. As there was nowhere to work at home I used to go into the Central Ref. — the library in Manchester — and work there, and I suddenly got very excited by it and began to score again quite heavily.

Were you writing anything then?

Yeah, though not writing for a living or writing for any other people. But when I was thirteen I wrote two short westerns, then when I was fourteen I wrote my mother a poem. An attempt to buy some love, you know, because it was pretty thin on the ground, and I really snatched almost all of it from a book I had on English literature, which had a photo-copy of Christina Rosetti's poem to her mother called *To My Mother on Her Natal Date*. It's a birthday poem — a terrible poem — and I lifted half of it. My mother thought it was terrific and for three days she talked about it, so it served its purpose. So I did do little pieces like that. Then at fifteen I started doing more poems, and from seventeen to twenty I suppose I wrote about two hundred poems.

You had to face the prospect of National Service?

Yeah. I went to Manchester University when I was seventeen, left when I was twenty with an upper second in English.

Were you still living at home?

Well, I lived at home for the first year, and then I left home and lived with a third-year student — I was second-year — then I went back home, but that was tough. I was not relating to anybody at home then, not even my brother. My brother went into the army and did his National Service in Kenya, coming back with extraordinary, 'gentle' stories of torture and horror, which maybe was the first real politicization I had — to see somebody come back from engagements with the Mau Mau, and to hear the way they handled people who were out after curfew. And he told it as simply and naturally as he might have discussed what they had for breakfast. Stringing guys up by their thumbs, leaving them up all night, and if they didn't talk, they'd be dead. He didn't boast about it, there was no sadism, it was just what they did — 'that's what we do, you see?' It was terrible. I went into the army when I was twenty — again it was a very northern working-class thing.

Could you have been a conscientious objector?

No, I could have said I wasn't fit with my flat feet. But being a conscientious objector — that possibility was just not inside my mental horizons at all.

What did you do in the army?

I was an infantryman in the Manchester Regiment. It's a very Manchester life you see. Born in Manchester, schooled in Manchester, university in Manchester, the army in Manchester. I didn't even leave Manchester in the army, apart from doing one 'prisoner escort' to Germany. I came out at 22, bronzed, beautifully fit, alive, a real man . . . Absolutely. And had my first really Giant Sexual Affair. Up to that time I had had a romance, which lasted two and a half years — all these you can find in the plays, they litter them like tombstones. That one was not exactly pre-sexual: it was fumble and grope and excitement and breathlessness, but it was not penetration, it was not mature. But this one really was big time. This girl was 29. She was the adjutant's secretary, and she was engaged to Henry Cockburn who played right half for Manchester United and England, and she was terrific.

You seem to have needed a time-lag to catch up . . .

Yeah, the really important awareness time was around 24, when, through meeting another girl, who was a sociology student, and who I later married, I suddenly became aware of a whole new way of looking at the world, of describing and accounting for reality. She introduced me to the whole social and academic network, which was full of community medicine people, social and preventative medicine people, sociologists, anthropologists, people who have now got Chairs here and what-have-you's there. It was really coming into that world that I first began to discover some cultural humility and to see that I had a lot to learn.

For a Marxist playwright it was a remarkably un-Marxist background . . .

Yes, I think that's good. And for a playwright, I've had an untheatrical life as well.

You'd had nothing to do with theatre?

Nothing at all. I don't think I've been to the theatre to see a show more than fifty times in my life, and I'm forty now. Certainly not more than fifty, and I could probably list the shows that I've seen. I've read a fantastic amount, but I've actually seen very little. I've never seen any Ibsen in the theatre. Though radio is another thing. The first play I ever heard performed, that I ever experienced as a performance, was Strindberg's *Easter*. That was on the radio. A wonderful production as well. That was when I was thirteen or fourteen, so that would have been in 1948 or something like that. About the time my father used to come home from the dogs and turn it off . . .

Was it when you were teaching and meeting this crowd that you started becoming politically conscious?

Yeah. Very much so. You see this period we're talking about is the beginning of CND, the Committee of 100, the late 'fifties and the early 'sixties. We're talking about the emergence of the British Left: Edward Thompson, Peter Worsley, John Rex, Stuart Hall, Alexander McIntyre, the *New Reasoner* and the *Universities Review*, which became the *New Left*

Review. By about 1960 I was chairman of the Manchester Left Club, and about a year later I was acting editor of Labour's *Northern Voice* and all those 'Voice' papers, with Frank Allaun as managing editor and chief censor. It began to increase experientially my preoccupation with politics, and my understanding of it to some extent.

Was the Osborne theatre 'revolution' of 1956 impinging on you at all?

Yes it was, although mediated through things like reviews. What I began to do in the mid-'fifties, the late-'fifties, was to read the arts pages. All my teachers had been Leavisites, so the place you didn't go to learn anything was an arts page of *The Times* or *The Sunday Times*, because that was all part of mass culture and so on. But I began to read the arts columns, and especially *The Observer*, and suddenly I sensed something else around which was radical, which was challenging, and it made you feel good that it was there. I didn't come to London, I didn't see the plays. Though I did see a key production, maybe at the end of 1960, maybe around the time of an Aldermaston March, and that was Wesker's *The Kitchen,* which John Dexter directed, which I thought was amazing. Just amazing. It was a play about work, it was a play about people I knew. It had — apart from the ending, which, anyway, was bad in the text, I think — no self-regarding sonorities. It was just itself, it was good. And I thought, yes, yes, yes, yes!

When was it you got interested in writing for the theatre?

Much later.

Motivated by what?

I don't know. I'd stopped writing poetry in 1961, and then for a number of years I did this unpaid job of political journalism if you like, and big organizational jobs as well. I was teaching full time. And I just had a lot of sap that wasn't being used, that just presented itself as a dialogue. I mean, I've always thought in terms of dialogue, or dialectically if you want to enhance that a bit. I've always thought about opposites, about the possibility of opposites for ideas. And after a couple of years of writing this political journalism I suppose I just wanted to say something that was other than that. So I wrote two fairly dreadful plays, which I've lost, and a third one which I thought was quite good, called *The Daft Un*, which was about — surprise surprise — my brother and me, or people rather like my brother and me. Anyway I've lost that as well now.

So there were three plays — one about the army, one about a homosexual, one about me and our kid. Then in 1967 I wrote another play, after meeting Tony Garnett, and by this time I was working for the BBC as a further education officer — in Leeds now, working from Leeds, but travelling all over the north of England, Scotland, and Northern Ireland. I met Garnett in late 1967, and he said, 'I hear you've written some plays, or would like to.'

And I said, 'Yeah', and he said, 'What do you want to write about?' And I said, 'I want to write about a big factory,' and he said, 'When did you work in a big factory?' I said, 'Never.' He said, 'Why do you want to write about a big factory? Where *have* you worked?' And I said, 'I've been teaching.' So he said, 'Why don't you write a play about teaching?' Which is just the way Tony works. Whatever you know, write it. Bloody important lesson.

So I wrote a play called *Love Maniac* which is about a guy who really tries to love kids in the teaching of them, and the problems he has. I set it in a brand new, purpose-built comprehensive school. And Tony bought it for his new company, Kestrel Productions. It was going to be produced, but they couldn't get a 90-minute slot, so it never was. It reverted to me, and was done subsequently on radio. But that was the first time I'd actually got money for work. And it was clearly an important moment. That was 1967 or 1968.

Between the time Tony Garnett got, commissioned, and didn't do this first play, did you write any more, or was it a matter of waiting till the play got done?

Looking back, I think I spent most of my time on the phone asking whether it was going to be done. I mean *that* seemed to be the most exciting thing to be happening, apart from when I was actually 'doing' my life. And I didn't write anything till maybe about nine months later, and then I think the next thing I wrote was an exercise play called *The Wages of Thin*, which was picked up by the Stables Theatre in Manchester and put on for three performances as a late-night. Actually, I might have started *Sam Sam* before I wrote *Wages of Thin*, but I know that *Wages of Thin* was on before I finished *Sam Sam*. And I may well have started *Occupations* as well before I finished *Sam Sam*. *Sam Sam*'s a two-acter, and I know I wrote the first half a good year before the second half.

Sam Sam was presumably a much more felt play, less an exercise play.

Oh yeah. It's also a favourite play. I care for it a lot.

How did its 'split-personality' structure happen? Did you set out to write two complementary halves about two different people, or two different plays, or what?

I'm not sure how it happened. I didn't know I was going to write two halves like that. I think I chickened a bit, when I'd written the first half, which was really my brother — I was really writing me in my brother in the first half. And then to write me in me in the second half was a bit too much, and I pulled away from it, I think. I held it up and dithered. And then thought that the right shape was heightened naturalism for the second half, whereas the first had been a kind of bravura attempt to go beyond that and use a real space, with interactions with the audience, and tricks and tropes and all the rest of it.

You were thinking in those terms, of how things interrelated to an audience?

Yes, it was certainly the first theatre play I wrote, because *Wages of Thin* was a play for voices, much more a radio thing. *Sam Sam* was the first one where I really thought in terms of a space, and of people being co-present with the work. I don't really know why I did that, because I started the play before The Stables opened. The Stables was the first theatre I ever related to, in any way.

Did you have much to do with the Open Space production of Sam Sam?

I'd never heard of the Open Space when I wrote it. And I'd certainly never visited it. The first time I visited the Open Space was when Charles Marowitz sent me a card from a boat on his way to Denmark, I think it was, saying, 'I've just read your play *Sam Sam*, and I hope that we can do it.' And then he mentioned Strindberg, and my heart leapt, and he talked about the fractured relationships, and the very best of this and the something of that, and I was amazed, because what I'd read about Charles Marowitz in the papers suggested that he was a fairly dry, screwed-up New Yorker, with no feeling for English sociography or anything. Yet here he was, really keen on it, and indicating in a few lines that he knew to some extent what the play was about, what it was saying.

What was it you wanted to 'say' in Sam Sam?

There was an eagerness for, an awareness of the whole world of sociology and sociological enquiry. Which came out of having taught as well as having been taught. Sam is a teacher, the second Sam. The first Sam is a bricklayer — and that's pretty close to what my brother and I were. There's a line in one of the *Bill Brand* scripts that we're actually rehearsing now, which says that this guy used to go to Manchester Reference Library and sit down and be studying the metaphysical poets and would see a tramp at the other end sheltering from the rain and pretending to read. And he talked to him once, one guy, who asked him for a cup of tea, and the guy said, 'I've been to China, and now I'm back,' and Brand thought, 'Why him him, me me?' So it comes out of that — what is changeable in the individual psyche which is not to do with genes but with environment, background, the shaping and moulding which goes on inside a society? You take two kids from the same womb, and they have very different experiences. It's not an easy metaphor: it's a metaphor that needs testing against the evidence again and again.

It's extraordinary how the play was received, I mean with no understanding of what it was about. I can remember one review that talked about the drive of one guy, the torpor of the other — as though that was any way to relate to the play. It's very interesting how drama critics and others in society want to relate to life. That's the way they want to think — in terms of winners and losers. I think the play is much more difficult than that. It doesn't allow those easy conclusions to be drawn. But this is the problem, say, about putting a play on at the National. Putting a play on at all is braving a lot of ignorance, a lot of ignorance of history, a lot of ignorance of society. Most of the people who are responding to a play know fuck-all about the society they live in. They know much more about the plays that are part of the selective tradition of the society. They know nothing about the society itself. What the experience of *Sam* was based on was the 1944 Education Act and the sudden controlled liberation of a certain quotient within society needed for other things. People who were never born proletarian, and who were never invited or pushed or harried into becoming some kind of middle-class professional, really don't know what it's all about.

Occupations which went on at the Stables and then The Place . . . an unusual play for a very northern-based dramatist to write — suddenly your setting is Turin, and historical. What was the impulse behind that change of direction and locality?

I'm aware of no changes in fact. *Sam Sam* was dealing with a particular set of circumstances in my own life, and I suspect in the lives of a large number of other people as well, to do with social mobility and pressures to conform on various levels on the spiral upwards, as it's called. *Occupations*, I think, was an advance politically and ideologically. That is to say it bears all the evidence of a man who has suddenly had a large part of his own life and the lives of those around him eliminated by theory. And the crucial theory I think, was Gramsci's own, which I had encountered and later confronted through works like *The Modern Prince* and other essays, in the late 'fifties and early 'sixties.

Turin isn't that different from Manchester. Before I wrote the play I stayed a fortnight in Italy, spent a lot of time wandering round the perimeter wall of Fiat Centro, Lingotto, and all the other places, talking to people, going to the Gramsci Study Centre, which has got all the photographs of Gramsci, of the occupations, and so on. I didn't feel a stranger in Turin at all, although I didn't speak Italian very well. And if you look at *Occupations* in terms of its significations, rather than in terms of its loci, it's also a play about two men, like *Sam Sam*, and about different developments of those people, different stances, different ideological perspectives, or political perspectives from the ideological base. It's not funny — that's maybe what finally makes it very different from the earlier plays. It's not so much distempered, it's contemptuous of diversion, it's a really grave piece of development, and it has a lot of curious, singularly 'me' things about it, like the character of Kabak.

You're a Marxist. And to that extent part of a political movement. What do you feel the relationship to be between that political commitment and what you're doing in the theatre?

I don't feel proud of the fact that I get enjoyment out of writing for the theatre and yet can't lock into what is particularly efficacious about it. And I can't at all. Because I'm northern, working-class and puritan — by origin anyway, and development to some extent — I feel rather guilty and I'm quite happy to keep my inventions in the theatre down to one every two years, or whatever it is. Most of my working life is spent in TV. I don't have an overview, because to have an overview is to know where one's going, and I certainly don't know where I'm going in the theatre at all.

You can, though, present much more complex arguments, say in Occupations, *than you could possibly do on television. At least, isn't part of the television process inevitably simplified, in that you just can't assume the same degree of concentration?*

I hope that my work has challenged these sort of assumptions every time it's been presented. I've never written, I've never delivered, a simple play. A play I've just written for *The Fall of Eagles* series received no attention whatsoever, but I know it had an audience of several millions. It's about the formation of the Bolshevik split — it's like *The Party* in 1903, the London Martov Second Party Congress, and so on. And it deals I think very fertilely and properly with Martov and Lenin and the confrontations and conflicts that developed between their particular ideological positions. It also presents the 23-year old opportunist Trotsky as what he was — a very brilliant opportunist. It is a play that is as dense and as difficult as anything I've written, I think. And that was presented, and there was no uproar, either way.

Occupations has been presented on TV, and the great limitation there was not in the material, but simply that we were only offered 78 minutes, which is a 90-minute slot on ITV. So the material came across as being as difficult as it was in the theatre — in a sense as more difficult, because there was less of it. It was leaned and thinned and pruned. Nothing was taken out on the grounds that it was difficult, but simply on the grounds that it took a lot of time to say it. So while overall it wasn't totally successful as a production, it was an enormously brave attempt to get that play's essence down a tube to very large numbers of people. *The Party* will be done on TV and I hope in much the same way with much the same effect.

Can you say how you broke into the rather incestuous London theatre scene, taking large strides from the Open Space to the Royal Shakespeare to the National?

It went slightly differently from that, as a matter of fact. It went from the Stables to *Lay-by*, and when I was working on *Lay-by* I heard that David Jones wanted Buzz Goodbody to do *Occupations* at The Place, and it was put on there before *Sam Sam* was put on at the Open Space. So *Sam Sam*, which had been written earlier, was actually presented later, and came after the quasi-success of *Occupations* at The Place. And then *Occupations* went on a 7:84 tour, around England and Scotland. But *Occupations* at the Stables, or the notices for that, attracted the interest of Ken Tynan towards the end of his career at the National Theatre. In a note he sent to me 'care of' the Stables, he said this was something like the sort of play they should be doing at the National, and could he have a copy and would I like to meet him? Two years later came *The Party* — no hurry on my part, because I was writing for TV and doing other things, leaving a secure job and running into crisis with my marriage, other relationships.

That was the point at which you became a full-time writer?

Yes. Not in any way honoured by this attention, nor contemptuous of it. I admired Tynan's work from the 'fifties and thought he made a very positive response to *Occupations*.

What was the genesis, where did it start?

It started with a number of images, really. It started with 1968, in France. And the American universities, the Blacks in Detroit, Watts. It started with the experience of the Friday night meetings at Tony Garnett's, where sixty or seventy people would cram into a room, and the whole sense, the aching need to . . . to do more, to get it right, to be correct, to read the situation as a first step towards changing it utterly. All of that was there. And with it all, the faint sense of . . . not silliness exactly, but lack of candour that people offered, for example in relating their life-roles to their abstracted revolutionary role — the lack of connection between what they did day-by-day and what they did night-by-night. That was very much there, but not in any satiric way. Not at all. That was the great problem with the National production: English actors have to be restrained, preferably with reins and a bit, from commenting on a character, on the text. And we weren't wholly successful in that production. But the play certainly succeeded potently and savagely in the second touring production by David Hare, for which I did a lot of pruning and rewriting, and restructured the play to a certain extent.

Would you regard The Party *as a Shavian play?*

I don't know. I've always been suspicious of Shaw because it seems to me that he takes more pleasure out of the forms of the argument than out of the substance. He doesn't seem to have any particular passion *about* the issues he raises or *for* the issues, or for the solution to the issues.

Isn't that, in a way, the situation you were criticizing in The Party?

No. I tried to present people who were deeply rooted in their arguments. Though the rooting was different in each case. You could never say Tagg was in any way a satirized or a parodic figure — he was absolutely what he was. That thing on stage was Tagg, and I had no intention whatsoever of satirizing Ford, the *New Left Review* guy, though in the production it did go through as a satiric invention, praised by some people — social democrats — as precisely that.

A play we haven't talked about yet, Comedians, *seems to deal with social democracy at one level . . .*

Yes. It's basically about two traditions — the social-democratic and the revolutionary tradition. It's about a tradition in culture that, say, Richard Hoggart represents, which is the persuasive, the rational, the humane tradition — arguing, educating for good, trying to change through education, through example. Set against that, there is a younger tradition, very violent, very angry, very disturbed, that says, 'No, that isn't the way. That way we can look back down through history and see the objective compromises that emerge, stem necessarily from that tradition. We've got to restate in our terms what the world is like, what the world can be like.' Basically, that is the confrontation. The play has been read as being about humour, as a play about comedians. At another level, it is probably that, too.

You did choose that particular image.

Everything comes from how I've lived, and what I've lived. *Comedians* is about a teacher. I was a teacher. It's about an old man. I feel that. It's about a young man. I feel twelve. It's about a classroom. I've spent a lot of my working life in classrooms. It's about Manchester, which is my town. It's about staying put, which I did. It's about moving on, which I did. It's about saying, 'Yes,' which I did. It's about saying, 'No,' which I did. It's about being seduced by success, it's about trimming, which I've done. I mean, it's the stuff of everything which all of us live out day by day in this fucking rock-heap of a society. The real, usable past, in Gwynn Williams's phrase, hasn't been reclaimed for use by revolutionaries or by people who want a transformation. We've got to do the work. So I wanted to write a play that wasn't overtly scratching and scarring the revolutionary theory. I wanted a play removed from that, and therefore I wanted it to be like some of my television plays, more immediately accessible to people who haven't had a background in revolutionary theory or revolutionary history or whatever.

Also I'm passionately interested in stand-up comedy. I can't tell a joke to save my life, so there was some excitement about writing that. I sensed that, although I don't really know about it, the comedian now had become, or was about to become, something quite different. His social role was somehow slightly different to what it had been in the past. I wasn't quite sure about this, but there was something about the Granada series, *The Comedians*, which changed stand-up comedy, rather as the Beatles changed popular music. They brought a heightened realism, and a heightened cynicism and a heightened bitterness into the common colloquy in ways that hadn't been there before — or at least that had been suppressed. We weren't aware of it in quite that way in the 'forties, 'fifties, and 'sixties as we were in the early 'seventies.

How does your method of writing differ when you're writing for the theatre from when you're writing for television?

It's the same process. It's grappling with the material and handling the evidence: it's finding the metaphors and the structures within which they can operate, out of which come people. Physically, and geographically, it's always the same: it's in a room, in the dark, except for an anglepoise, on lined paper with either a biro or a pentel. And it's in long-hand, it's always at night — I do rewriting during the day. I can't bear to be doing anything else during the day except rehearsal, or whatever the days are for. But night is for writing. And that actually seeps in, in a curious way, as a signification. If anybody did a semiotic analysis of the plays they'd find a hell of a lot of scenes taking place at night. I think that's because I write at night, and I also write atmospherically, and so I'm aware of the night.

It sounds as though you find the philosophical problems of the play more difficult to solve than the actual problems of structure.

Yeah, I think so, because to some extent we're all prisoners of some socio-cultural formation or other. In my case, I feel very responsible to the Left, to the history of Left thought and Left action — socialist, communist, revolutionary — whatever. So, at the same time as wanting to interpret the stuff, one wants to be interpreted onself. And I've simply learned to live with the fact that isn't going to happen, or it isn't going to happen very easily. You know, I get tons of shit lowered on the plays quite regularly by *Workers Press* or *Socialist Worker* or *Tribune* or whatever, and it's difficult to know why, because I feel myself to be the very opposite of a political opportunist. I feel myself to be patient, painstaking, obstinate and all those kind of tortoise-like qualities, whereas I'm seen to be fly-by-night, gipsy, uncommitted, a floater. What was it Corin Redgrave said? Oh yes, he described me as 'paddling in the shallows of revolutionary practice'.

In Occupations *you seemed to be saying, 'Well, capitalism has got through that one.' Is that the way you're feeling now, that capitalism will get through this one?*

No. What I would argue, though, is that people don't write off capitalism too soon. And I don't mean in the value sense. I think, morally, capitalism was exhausted fifty to one hundred years ago, certainly fifty years ago. The way that people ought to organize their lives is not within capitalist structures, that's what I'm saying. And that's why my plays are never about the battle between socialism and capitalism. I take that as being decisively won by socialism. What I'm really seeking is the way forward. How do we transform this husk of capitalist meaning into the reality of socialist enterprise? The socialist future!

12
Kenneth Tynan
on the moral neutrality of Peter Brook

The figure of Peter Brook stalks post-war British theatre like an absent-minded guru, pausing to bestow an occasional aphorism on an audience of generally uncritical acolytes. My own feelings about Brook had by the 'seventies become equivocal: too young to have seen the rediscoveries of 'minor' Shakespearian masterpieces or the string of theatricalist successes with lightweight new plays which had established his reputation as a leading director by the mid-'fifties, I'd first known his work through the galloping musical Irma La Douce *and the markedly more sedentary play by Friedrich Dürrenmatt which opened London's Royalty Theatre,* The Visit.

After joining Peter Hall's team at the Royal Shakespeare Company in 1960, Brook directed a King Lear *in the light and the dark of Beckett's* Endgame. *For many, the production demonstrated that Brook could, after all, scale the heights as well as show off in the shallows of Shakespeare's genius: but it left me with an uncomfortable awareness that in the process the play had been twisted to fit Brook's and Beckett's bleak view of humanity, rather than expressing Shakespeare's arguably redemptive but certainly more complex vision.*

My worries were reinforced by Brook's production in 1964 of Peter Weiss's Marat-Sade. *True though this was to the tenets of Antonin Artaud — whose theories Brook had recently been exploring in an experimental* Theatre of Cruelty *programme with Charles Marowitz — it made little attempt to sustain the dialectic balance of Weiss's text. And by the time Brook first shrugged off the need for an original script in the collectively conceived and created* US *in 1966, I was second only to Kenneth Tynan in defying the ranks of accusing actors at the end of the show, and storming from my seat in rejection of the complicity Brook appeared to feel his audience should share over American involvement in Vietnam. There were surely limits to the luxury of liberal masochism.*

Brook proceeded to tantalize us with a Stratford production of A Midsummer Night's Dream *which, though short on intellectual challenges, was visually and emotionally a stirring experience. He then left England to create his International Centre for Theatre Research in Paris — the base from which came* Orghast, *seen at the Shiraz Festival under the Shah's regime in 1971, and from which* Timon of Athens, The Ik, *and* Ubu *later emerged. When* The Ik *was received with almost universal rapture during its visit to the Roundhouse in 1976, I felt that we should attempt in TQ at least a corrective discussion of the nature of Peter Brook's theatre. Knowing that Ken Tynan, though no longer writing criticism, shared many of my own doubts, I asked him to talk with us to try to analyze our worries, and the discussion with Catherine Itzin and myself took place in his Kensington home in the autumn of 1976. We didn't want to let Brook's undoubted qualities of genius as a director be 'taken as read' in our anxiety to pin down the deficiencies we sensed in his theatrical world-view: so we began by asking Ken Tynan whether Brook's early productions at the end of the war were indeed as brilliant as report had it.*

Peter is several years older than I am, and he preceded me at Oxford, but I saw the first of his work as a protegé of Sir Barry Jackson at Birmingham Rep, when he did *King John* and *Man and Superman* with Paul Scofield. I was a schoolboy then, in Birmingham, and I was enormously impressed. A sort of crisp, attacking clarity was replacing the general woolliness of Shaw and Shakespeare productions of the time, and there was a very precise attention to inflection and to sudden, surprising detail in Brook's productions which quite astonished me. From Birmingham, he went to Stratford in 1946 and did a remarkable production in Watteau costumes of *Love's Labour's Lost* — with Scofield as Armado. And again one was knocked out. It was the first time that one had seen — not an *intellectual* work on Shakespeare, because I don't think Peter was or is an intellectual — but an incredible, leaping, visual imagination and a very precise sense of startling intonation.

Following that he did a less widely praised *Romeo and Juliet*, in 1947. But I responded to that, too, because he made it a young person's play of extraordinary violence and passion which at that time was quite new. It was not a sort of soft-centred romance: it was extremely tough and vivid and it was voraciously passionate in a way that one was quite unused to in Shakespeare. I was immediately won over by him, as was all my Oxford generation after the war. Then in London he continued with extraordinarily realistic productions — of Sartre's *Huis Clos*, and of a play by Howard Richardson about rural superstition in the United States called *Dark of the Moon*, at the Lyric, Hammersmith, which had a revivalist meeting. That was one of the most exciting events I had ever witnessed on the stage. When he went on to Shaftesbury Avenue, he took with him this decadent but exquisite sense of visual effectiveness in productions like *Ring Round the Moon* and even a boulevard comedy like *The Little Hut*. He got designs from Oliver Messel for those two productions which I think are the best things that Messel ever did. Brook's sense of stage trickery, of a sheer magician's box of theatre, is quite unrivalled.

I think what ultimately convinced not only my generation but the older generation that Brook was a master was the famous production in 1951 of *Measure for Measure* with John Gielgud as Angelo. It was the first one for which he did the sets as well, and it still remains in my mind as the most unified Shakespeare I've seen — with every costume, every shoe, every piece of décor, every side-effect, contributing to a total vision of the play. It gave Gielgud's career a second lease of life, because it was a much more restrained, realistic, unromantic performance than he had ever given before.

How would you describe that 'total vision'?

Sort of like Hieronymus Bosch. Brook saw the *Zeitgeist* of Vienna as the dark underside of the Elizabethan world — and, indeed, of our world. It was the time of *The Third Man* and films like that, so the squalor of contemporary Vienna kept crossing one's mind as you saw Peter's *Measure* — the whorehouses and the corruption. The approach had a certain grimy realism that again we had not seen in Shakespeare. The characters were not played for low comedy, or farouche laughs: they were played bitterly, straight, and with incisiveness and split-second timing — and as always with Brook, there were the unexpected inflections, the unexpected images. There's the speech, for example, where Lucio reels out a list of all the people who are in the Viennese jail. Peter made this a procession of people being introduced by Lucio — a really scabrous parade of deformities. The procession ended with 'Wild Half-Can who stabbed pots', and this extraordinary tattered, barefooted, baldheaded figure strutted on his heels, almost like a premonition of the maniacs that were later to inhabit the *Marat-Sade*.

Up to that time there was no doubt in anyone's mind that Peter Brook was the leading Shakespeare director of the post-war era. And he continued to go from strength to strength. There was a feeling in the back of one's mind that he was a reclaimer of the secondary plays rather than interpreter of the major plays, that he was a great man for taking a neglected text and imposing on it his own image. He had done this with plays which were regarded as less than the top rank of Shakespeare — *Love's Labour's Lost, Measure for Measure,* and later *Titus Andronicus.* But when he took on *Hamlet,* with Paul Scofield, it was a great disappointment: he had nothing to bring to a masterpiece, as if the masterpiece were a self-sustaining monument, and Peter, instead of reconstructing it to fit his own vision, was rather dwarfed by it. He just chipped away at the edges.

Wrongly, did you feel?

I felt he regarded plays, then, as adversaries to be overwhelmed, and the masterpieces simply defeated him. But that is not to run down his extraordinary achievements in elevating previously under-rated plays to the status of masterpieces. It's very hard to realize, now, that until that time *Love's Labour's Lost* and *Measure for Measure* were not regarded as Shakespeare plays that anyone in their right minds would do.

Now, at that time, he became a great friend of Edward Gordon Craig, and saw a good deal of him. I met Craig about that period and I know that he was very impressed with Brook. And I suddenly began to see Craig's influence in what Brook said, and later in his work — like Craig's idea that the playwright was a destructive intruder in the theatre, and was detracting from the person who really ought to be in charge, the director.

Brook seems to have had more success working with real live actors than Craig . . .

Yes — he was one of the few directors of that time who was obsessed with working with actors. He bridged the gap between what was then fringe theatre and commercial theatre. He could work with actors who were established on Shaftesbury Avenue, or who were at Stratford, or who were working at little theatres like the Torch or the Chanticleer, where he did things like *Dr. Faustus* and *The Infernal Machine*.

But he did exert almost a confidence trickery over actors . . .?

Oh, yes. But in *King Lear* I think he began to get a philosophical background on which to build. Quite soon after that he launched his *Theatre of Cruelty* season at LAMDA, and in this he was clearly beginning to regard the omnipotent playwright as someone who had to be cut down to size, as a figure who should not become indispensible. Now nobody wants the omnipotent author or the omnipotent anything, but by the late 'fifties and early 'sixties Peter had achieved an eminence which allowed him *carte blanche* to do virtually what he liked in any country in the world. Being multilingual, of course, helped. For a brief period he even took on the colossus of Covent Garden as artistic director: he brought in Salvador Dali to do the sets for *Salome*, and outraged a lot of the omnipotent opera stars there.

He was always pretty much — even when he was more active as a director of the RSC — a loner. You couldn't really associate him with any particular 'school' of theatre.

Nor could you accuse him of imitating anybody. He was one of the few English directors of my time whose career was, in a sense, a search for antecedents: he found one in Craig, and found one in Artaud, but he was already established by then — until that time, his ideas were spun out of his own intuition.

He did very pragmatic work on individual productions, but he doesn't seem to have found his theoretical base until he had also found those mentors . . .

From them he did get a basis in dramatic theory: but what he didn't have was a world view, as you might say. That is, a view of the world outside theatre. And as he began to acquire that, his work changed, and not for the good. To my mind, his last two really successful pieces of work were the Scofield *Lear* in 1962 and his *Dream* in 1970. In the *Dream* he had a sense of what you might call 'sport' in his work. It seems to have come out of a fascination with circus — I think he might have read of a Paris production in the 'twenties, a production of the *Dream* done in the form of a Chinese circus. I came across a description of this in a biography of Cocteau, and I think Peter probably read the same bit. But that was an exception, and the end of *Dream*, when the actors extended hands to the audience and joined hands with them, was as close as Peter has ever come, I think, to establishing an emotional communion with that part of society which is not on the stage. One really felt a desire on his part to make the play flow emotionally over the footlights, and to celebrate something shared with the audience rather than to impose something upon it by sheer technical brilliance.

Lear, which very much impressed me at the time, was, of course, based very much on Jan Kott's view of the play, and its connection with Beckett and *Endgame*. I think the connection with Beckett, and the philosophy behind him, gave Peter a justification for the world view which was later to become dominant in his work. Now, if I could sum up that world view, it would be this: that human beings, left to themselves, stripped of social restraints, are animals, and are inherently rotten, and destructive. You might almost call it a ritualistic misanthropy: and it has been the driving force behind Brook's work from the early 'sixties onwards.

Now let me explain what I mean by this, because you can trace it back to some of his early productions, starting with the *Theatre of Cruelty* season. The point there was to demonstrate how much suffering a human being could undergo without splitting under the pressure. Now *Titus Andronicus*, of all Shakespeare's plays, is the most deeply pessimistic in its view of what human beings are like in a society without moral restraint: and in *Marat-Sade* Brook deliberately tilted the entire production to stress Sade's nihilistic view of human beings as opposed to that of the social reformer and revolutionist, Marat. I gather that Peter Weiss was not altogether happy with this shift of emphasis, but it certainly reflected something important to Brook.

You got the same deeply felt bleakness of vision in *Lear*. That's why he cut out the moment of compassion when the servant protests against the blinding of Gloucester and sacrifices his own life. That was very much in character: cutting that scene indicated to me something, perhaps, in Peter's own nature, and it didn't surprise me when we invited him to go to the National Theatre in the 'sixties to do Seneca's *Oedipus*, as opposed to Sophocles' *Oedipus*, that he accepted immediately, and said he would love to. Now just as *Titus Andronicus* is the grimmest of Shakespeare's Roman plays, so Seneca's *Oedipus* is Sophocles without the redeeming philosophical graces. It is the naked thing itself, and in it Jocasta doesn't hang herself, she impales herself on a sword in her womb, because that's where the sin began, the birth of Oedipus.

In *Timon of Athens*, which Brook chose to do in Paris, and which I didn't see, it was again significant that he should choose another deeply misanthropic play which further demonstrates and underlines this view of human nature which begins to dominate his work. And then there was also, during this period, the film *Lord of the Flies*. When one begins to ponder it, this immediately falls into place, as part of the pattern, because *Lord of the Flies* is pre-eminently a parable about what happens to human nature outside a quasi-civilized society: it becomes brutal, sadistic, and cannibalistic in the end.

I noted all these developments, but I didn't react with open hostility until his *US* in 1966, at the Aldwych. While that was in rehearsal Peter had consulted me, because I was pretty vocal at that time about the Vietnam War, and we had several long talks about it in which I gave him books to read, reports to read, and fed him fairly consistently with my own attitude towards the war and the total lack of justification for United States intervention. I took him step by step through the history of the war from the Kennedy involvement onwards. I'm sure he'd done a lot of this independently, but I spent several luncheons expressing my point of view. But the point of view that he eventually expressd in the show was simple — the Viet Cong reprisals, the American bombing, there was nothing to choose morally between them. That was the attitude Peter fed out: one of moral neutrality. Which served his purpose. Again, the purpose of demonstrating the fundamental depravity of all humans.

Not only blaming the Americans or Viet Cong in Vietnam, but also the impotent audience in the theatre.

Absolutely. It seemed to me he was using the war to get at the Hampstead intellectuals — that, in a sense, he was exploiting the brutalizing and destruction of a country, as if the only purpose of the war was to prove how hypocritical intellectuals are!

I think what he was saying was that human beings are basically amoral. The Viet Cong pretend to have moral and social justification for what they do: the Americans pretend exactly the same. In terms of what they do, there is nothing to choose between them. So Peter's attitude was, you could say, a moral one. It would be theologically described as a Manichaean one — the Manichaean heresy being that evil was created at the same time as good, and is probably winning the battle against it. And evil is the dominant factor in the human psyche. William Golding's *The Lord of the Flies* also illustrates this, after all — another piece which has an unfailing appeal to facile pessimists. And it certainly chimed perfectly with Peter's general opinions.

In US, *of course, this philosophy was brought into an overtly political arena . . .*

Quite. And I think in the political arena Peter is something of a child, in that he has always led a very isolated, theatrical kind of life, always working behind closed doors with actors, among whom he has been the unquestioned leader and inspiration. I think he'd argue with you if you said, 'Surely if you're going to pronounce on Vietnam you've got to make a close and really exhaustive study of the politics involved?" He would probably say that a group of actors working on their own in a little room could create — out of their own psyches, perhaps, and out of their own collective subconscious — images of any possible political, social, intellectual conflict, that it could all be done in a hermetically sealed-off room, that you don't have to go out in to the field and test your theories against reality. And then when he founded his International Centre for Theatre Research in Paris, his first effort was to try to by-pass language altogether. He got Ted Hughes to construct this non- language of Orghast, made up of sounds that had no relation to any existing language.

That was one of the prime motivations of the Centre in the beginning . . .

Absolutely. He talked about his disbelief in the power of communication through words. If you are going to put over an essentially emotional view of nihilism, words are your enemy, because words are the bearers of rational thought. If you're going to put over those ideas, you need to get reason out of the way completely; the first thing you have to do is to abolish words. So he tried this experiment. I didn't see any of the performances, I can only go by the response of the audiences and certain of the actors, but I suspect that Peter would now say that it was an interesting exercise, but that it did not work, theatrically, with the audiences it was addressed to.

The first end product that I saw of this experiment was, of course, *The Ik.* I went to it after hearing so many years of rumours, secondhand opinions, and hearsay, that I wanted to form my own opinions. And my reaction was one of great, baffled sorrow. It seemed to me that he had discarded all the immense technical skills that he had used previously to dazzle, startle, amaze, and stun audiences by appealing to their sensibilities, which I think was his great power. He had abandoned the strength of language, and he seemed to me to be doing a surprisingly conventional documentary dramatization of Colin Turnbull's book about an African tribe forcibly removed from its hunting grounds and declining into a state of brutalized amorality — in which the mere possession of food (by whatever means, including taking it out of the mouths of babies and ageing parents) was the only criterion of virtue. In other words, Peter was harking back to his earlier preoccupations — saying, if you remove the necessities of life, remove the social conventions, people will behave appallingly.

Now you would have thought this was something of a truism: but Peter was presenting it gravely, as a horrific revelation. And the analogy that came to my mind was, if you close down all the traffic lights at crossroads, and remove the brakes from all the cars, there is the possibility that collisions will occur — that it is not the part of an intelligent man to be too surprised at this, nor should one conclude from it that those who drive cars are innately homicidal. But this seemed to be the sort of conclusion that Peter was inviting us to share. He probably seized on the book because it supported the thesis which increasingly has dominated his work.

The quality of acting and the style in the performances certainly proved that he can make actors transform themselves into African tribesmen with considerable skill. But throughout the evening I couldn't help reflecting how much more effectively a BBC2 film documentary could have done exactly the same job — not just a parallel job, but the same job, done better. There seemed to be no specifically theatrical excitement in the show — it was just a series of short, realistic scenes linked by straight 'voice-over' narration. And that whole production seemed curiously detached about the present fate of the Ik tribe: the book was written some years ago, and in the programme it just said 'as far as anyone knows, the Ik still exist'. *As far as anyone knows?* I mean, here we were, invited to feel compassion and horror at their plight, but nobody in the production had even bothered to find out whether they still existed!

I was also deeply disappointed by the lack of the pure theatrical inventiveness on which we had been able to count in the past from Peter, and what I can only call, with real regret, the intellectual shallowness of it. And I thought, while Peter's been away in Paris, and elsewhere, our fringe theatre had somehow overtaken him in intelligence and passion. If we're going to do theatrical documentaries, and I think we should, David Hare's *Fanshen* with the Joint Stock Company seemed to me to be an infinitely more compelling — theatrically compelling — and socially informative piece of work, conceived in terms that made it a purely theatrical work and not a film *manqué*.

I had a sort of fantasy — I invented a documentary of my own that began to take shape as my attention wandered from *The Ik*. This would be a documentary designed to prove that if you deprived a theatre audience of food, drink, tobacco, theatrical stimulation, and intellectual sustenance, they will slowly go mad with boiling rage and begin to contemplate acts of violence on the cast and on its director, and may even revert to conditions of savage anarchy, culminating in the terrible ceremony of 'demanding one's money back.'

This may sound cruel, but I wish this immensely talented man would stop tackling vast philosophical problems and return to the things he did better than any other English director — things less ambitious, but more theatrically viable. I mean, I don't want to hear Peter on anthropology, any more than I would have wanted to hear Houdini talk about spiritualism. It's almost as if Peter has come to despise his own real gifts and regard them as superficial, whereas, in fact, the sort of effect he was capable of creating set up vibrations that linger in my mind still, and that taught me things about human behaviour. Details from which I could draw my own conclusions, not from which he drew conclusions and then imposed a pattern upon me.

Just as I can't forget the details of any of his earlier work up to *Lear*, the theories that are implicit in his later work dissolve in my mind like snowballs in hell. I couldn't help thinking, after *The Ik*, of that famous exchange between Max Beerbohm and Henry James when they attended together one of William Poël's exercises in Elizabethan stagecraft. After it was over, Beerbohm said to James, 'It's all done with great economy of means, wouldn't you say?' And Henry James said, 'And of effect, too.' That's what I felt about *The Ik*. I want Peter to embark on a voyage of rediscovery, almost of regression.

A return to the kind of theatre you suggest he's best at would suggest a return to a fairly conventional theatre structure . . .?

Yes, I think he works best within that structure. I think he may go down in history as the last real master-director of the proscenium stage. And since we have a lot of those stages left, and a lot of plays written for them, there's a lot he could be exercising himself on. I suppose he got bored with his own brilliance, felt he had to take on the role of the philosopher.

There's a seeming paradox in what you have said about Brook's best work being done with minor masterpieces, since his Lear *was generally considered a major masterpiece.*

Lear was a mountainous achievement. I think it's the only case where he's taken a serious masterpiece of the first rank, met it head on, made a comment on it, and not been dwarfed by it. What he did to it was to approach it from a standpoint of strict moral neutrality, in that he showed what was obnoxious about Lear, that there might have been some justification for Regan's and Goneril's behaviour. He may have been influenced in this by R.D. Laing — in the view that Lear is perhaps most sane in the dissociated images, the schizophrenic images of his madness, that there was more sanity in the madness than in the earlier scenes. I think there he had a genuine insight which made the play seem greater, did not diminish it. It's perfectly reasonable to be susceptible to outside influences: and I think that Brook was perfectly capable of assimilating Kott and Laing. They served him rather than dominated him. They simply gave him springboards. But since then, in this country anyway, he's shown little interest in working with established texts.

To me, the irony is that he has successfully contemporized the past, through Shakespeare, but failed to make anything of contemporary issues.

He did Genet's *The Screens*. I saw a rehearsed version of it. It was quite suitable that he should be drawn to Genet at that time, for Genet's view of mankind can be accommodated to Peter's easily enough. Why that production was never completed I do not know. But I do know that when he attempted in the early 'sixties to do a play which, whatever you may think of it, ends with an extraordinarily benevolent view of human nature — *The Tempest* — he failed almost completely, because he could not possibly share that view.

Another thing that interests me about him is that he's never been closely associated with a particular contemporary author — that essential thing for a great director. He's never had a continuing relationship in the same way as Stanislavsky and Chekhov, or Brecht and Brecht, or Jouvet and Giraudoux did. And you've got to do that, if you want to establish yourself as a director in the great tradition. You have to attract into your company one or more young playwrights of real merit, just as in his early days Dexter had Wesker. Peter's never done it — whether it's because playwrights feel his personality is too strong for them, I don't know. Or whether it's because he hasn't wanted it himself. Maybe he's resisted it because of this idea inherited from Craig, that the playwright is somehow the enemy of the theatre.

From the early years one associates him with plays or playwrights whose theatricalism as distinct from theatricality enabled him to run rings around the writers.

Yes, but he also could take a deeply pessimistic play like Sartre's *Huis Clos* and interpret rather than exploit it. He has never been a wrecker of plays; he has never taken a play and contorted it out of all recognition.

Not the Marat-Sade?

That was slanting. And you must remember that Peter Weiss never publicly complained about the production. Brook didn't take the play, rewrite it, reshuffle it. It's interesting, though, that when he came to do the Seneca at the National, we had a translation prepared, which I thought was rather good, and which stuck fairly closely to Seneca. That was because I simply wanted to rediscover Seneca for English audiences as one of the great influences on Elizabethan theatre, and therefore on the Enlgish theatre as a whole. But Peter insisted on having Ted Hughes rewrite the whole play. And what Ted Hughes did was virtually to write a new play, with long, long speeches which weren't in the original, but which echoed Hughes's view of life as expressed in his *Crow* poems, which came very close to Peter's brand of despondent nihilism. That's the only time I can think of when a play has been really radically reconstructed by Peter.

What is worrying is that, by and large, the critical response and the audience response has been highly favourable, even eulogistic and idolatrous, not recognizing the nihilism and the intellectual shallowness. Why do people follow Brook now, unquestioningly?

There has been so little questioning of his work since the *Dream*. No one seems to have reacted with the same amount of confusion and dismay that I have, and yet I can't believe that I'm a unique member of the audience. I think it's partly that so little of his work has been seen in this country since *Dream*. And when an experimenter is working behind closed doors — it's as if we're all waiting for the atom bomb to explode. We don't feel we should rock the boat by questioning the value of the experiment until we see the explosion. If *The Ik* is the explosion, one must say that the experiments have been misguided and must be radically rethought, reconsidered, revalued. And yet those who went to Paris and saw *Timon of Athens* seem to have reacted with extremely eulogistic reviews.

Is it partly because Brook's views accord with the present fashionable world view, which is nihilistic and pessimistic?

Quite. I think it's an extremely fatalistic view of life, that all human efforts are doomed to eventual failure, and all we can do is record with a compassionate smirk the degree of failure or disaster. I think Peter should leave the job of analyzing the predicament of our times to people who are actually more involved in it than he is. I think he would be horrified to be called merely a stylistic experimenter. But style has always been his trademark, and the Brook style was as emphatically present in *Huis Clos* and *The Brothers Karamazov* as it was in *Lear* and *Dream*. But it was always an envelope, a shining envelope for another man's play. The envelope was marvellous.

Part of my point in talking about this is that I don't think we should ever run down the achievements of the pure stylist, which Brook was — a pure master of theatrical gesture. There are very few of those in the English theatre. We've had many plodding, earnest directors. We've had many boring, socially-conscious ones. But we've produced very few masters of the theatrical conjuring trick. And that's a very important part of theatre: it can be put to extremely useful service. I wonder, too, if in talking about the influences on him, we haven't failed to mention Grotowski. Because he was certainly a great admirer of Grotowski. I don't know how much work he saw, but he certainly wrote and spoke passionately about Grotowski's theatre — another theatre, as it were, for the few, sealed off behind closed doors, a violent experiment on the actor's psyche, a sort of surgical operation, which the audience were invited to watch and share.

But where Grotowski would accept that definition as an elitist director, Brook has, at least ostensibly, been proclaiming a much broader world view.

Yes. And if he were working with a playwright of the stature of Brecht, in tandem with a writer who could supply his deficiencies, then we might be witnessing one of the great theatrical collaborations. Is it just that that writer doesn't exist, or is it that Peter doesn't want him, if he does exist? That's the question that will only be answered in the next few years of his career.

13
Arnold Wesker
a sense of what should follow

Back in 1967, Charles Marowitz and I put together a collection of interviews and production casebooks entitled Theatre at Work, *to which many of the leading dramatists from the late 'fifties contributed. These included John Arden, Harold Pinter — and Arnold Wesker, who alone reappears here among the 'new theatre voices' of the 'seventies.*

This is in part because the British theatre has (almost conspiratorially, it must at times seem to him) done its best to quell Wesker's voice in the decade just past. In Theatre at Work *I had discussed with Wesker the early plays by which he remains best known —* The Kitchen, *and the 'Wesker Trilogy' of* Chicken Soup with Barley, Roots, *and* I'm Talking about Jerusalem — *together with the transitional pieces written after his period of involvement with the Centre Fortytwo movement in the earlier 'sixties,* Their Very Own and Golden City *and* The Four Seasons. *In this interview, we therefore picked up the threads of his career with* The Friends — *that major, greatly misunderstood play to which, in 1971, we had devoted the second production casebook in* Theatre Quarterly. *It had been accompanied by a lengthy piece from Wesker himself, in which he analyzed the often obtuse critical responses to his own Roundhouse production.*

Around the same time, The Journalists *was scheduled for staging at the Aldwych, and* The Old Ones *for the National: due to a combination of theatre politics, personality conflicts, and palace coups, neither production took place. Wesker's latest work at the time this interview took place, his complete reworking of Shakespeare's play as* The Merchant, *was due to go into rehearsal for a prestigious Broadway production with Zero Mostel as Shylock. Mostel died during the pre-Broadway tryouts.*

Wesker seems fated to such misfortunes — yet one notes again and again the regard in which his dramatic work is held by fellow theatre workers, even those who dismiss his 'arts for the people' campaign with Centre Fortytwo as paternalistic. Wesker has himself written widely about that campaign and the cultural issues it raised — as also about the broader, social and critical issues raised by the plays themselves. We thought it important therefore, to concentrate in this interview rather on their conception and crafting: and it was because Wesker, as a largely instinctive writer, finds these aspects of his work less easy to discuss that the interview was, in the event, knitted together from two separate conversations, for both of which Catherine Itzin and myself were joined by Glenda Leeming, author of the only full-length study of Wesker's plays.

At our first meeting in February 1977 we talked in the top-floor workroom of Wesker's Highgate home, cluttered with books, pictures, and memorabilia. The second interview took place that June in my own study, down in the rural wilds of Kent. On both occasions, as so often in the plays, a meal played a catalytic role. But we began by asking Wesker how it felt to be writing still so much in the shadow of his earliest work.

One part of me feels . . . fulfilled? Perhaps not quite the right word — what's the word that describes what one should be feeling looking back at a body of work? Not satisfied, because that suggests smugness, and to refer to myself as 'consummated' would raise eyebrows. I look back and do have a sense of achievement, and yet, because there is this sense of bare toleration, and a feeling that the work is not taken seriously in this country, I feel a sense of uncertainty, and lack of confidence.

Certainly in my later career I feel an enormous debt of gratitude to foreign countries — especially to Scandinavia, Germany, France, Japan, Latin America. Their faith in the plays has reassured me — to put it in simple, crude terms — that my works do 'speak'. But it is very strange, in England, to have this struggle to get the work on, when at the same time there's an educational system using my plays as required reading. It's a disorienting paradox, yes.

Can you account for the break which comes in your work around Chips with Everything *where, from being the Royal Court dramatist everyone was talking about, you became a writer who was quite difficult to get put on in Britain? Was it something about the audiences . . .*

The audiences didn't get the chance to pass judgement! I'd like to think that if the later plays only had a chance, the audiences would slowly come to accept them. Perhaps I shouldn't be talking about this, but it seems as if the personality of the man has got in the way of the work. For reasons which I really don't think I understand, I do seem to arouse hostilities and irritations.

Do you personally see a division between the early work and the later work?

Not a division, but, I think, a progression. I would like to think that the values the early work was communicating are still being communicated, but set against a much more complex re-creation of experience. *The Friends* can be seen, on analysis, to have many of the same preoccupations as *Roots*.

And instead of having Beatie talking about roots as 'the things you come from, the things that feed you', you have Esther talking about being a revolutionary because she sees the past as 'rich with human suffering and achievement and not to be dismissed'.

Yes, and instead of Ronnie reassuringly saying, 'You can't learn how to live overnight', there's Manfred terrified at how much knowledge he doesn't possess. But *The Friends* is a much more complex play, more intricately developed. I suppose that's what they call maturing — that's what I would like to think has happened.

But surely The Friends *wasn't just a step in a progression. Wasn't it also some kind of watershed, in that there was something special you had to confront in that play?*

The only thing I can consciously remember having to confront was the knowledge of death — and though I say 'only', that was clearly a major confrontation. Not only death, but a sense of one's mistakes. I suppose at that time I considered all the plays before then not to be of any great value or importance. I was very conscious of the failure to make Centre Fortytwo work. And all this came together at a time when death seemed much more a reality.

And you were, indeed, continuing to draw very directly on your own experience.

It seems to me that there are two ways in which an artist can approach his work. One, for want of a better word, is an intellectual approach — that is to say, to begin with a concept, with a theme, an idea which the artist wants to explore in a play or a novel, and then to look round for situations or characters to flesh it out. Other artists begin with experience. At the climax of a certain kind of experience, they suddenly burst and feel that they must organize it in the form of a play, a poem, or a novel. Both of these approaches have produced very great works of art, but I would hazard a guess that the very greatest works of literature are those which spring from experience — they have the quality of guts and urgency and inevitability. You feel this inexorable drive of experience in the work — it couldn't be any other way. Which is not to say that my plays are great works of art, but to describe the way I work.

Was The Friends *a difficult play to write, in terms of how long it took, how many drafts it went through?*

The first sheet of notes is dated 12 June 1966. It's headed *The Friends*, and it goes on to say: 'Six friends. One brother and sister and friend, male, both men love the sister. One man who is discovering unbelieved sexual needs within himself, another who more and more loses the patience to listen to himself. He doesn't despise himself, he simply has lost the spark of curiosity for his and other men's thoughts. The woman who despises other people. She grows gradually to see only their pettiness, inhumanity, weakness, but she cannot, at the same time, stop being good-natured. The result is not cynicism, her acts are genuine, but confusion, bewilderment: she can't reconcile these contradictory things in her. "I retain the trick of sweetness, but in my mouth the taste is sour".' And so the notes go on, in that form.

The Friends *has a very unified, Aristotelian kind of structure, whereas the later plays are much more complex in structure, and in scenic demands* — The Journalists *with its different rooms on different levels, and* The Old Ones *also accommodating various different but quite specific settings. How conscious are you of the physical demands of a play as you write?*

It never occurs to me that the notes I'm making suggest that this has got to be in three acts over twenty-four hours, or in fifty scenes over fifty years. I think that the shape comes, almost instinctively, with the material. When I knew I wanted to write *The Four Seasons*, I didn't say, ah, now I must divide this into four acts. It could have been in some other form, but the way in which it was eventually written just emerged from the material.

Once you've got the first draft, which is presumably a beginning-to-end draft in longhand, how substantial are the changes from one draft to the others?

Well, *The Friends* was written over a period of three years. The successive drafts don't usually affect the structure, but are more in the way of polishing. Though part of the polishing takes in, I suspect, some of the structure. *The Friends*, though, always took place in one twenty-four hour period — it was never a week condensed into twenty-four hours. And *The Kitchen* was always conceived as 'a day in the life of' — whereas it could have been three mornings. *Chips* was always the eight weeks of the square-bashing period. *Golden City* was always from 1928 to 1990. And so on. I might rearrange scenes, but I regard that as part of the polishing. And I might have given the wrong dialogue to the wrong characters. Or have got the rhythm wrong. And getting things like those right is all part of the act of polishing, but it couldn't be called changing the overall shape.

The Friends was a very unfashionable play to write at a time when the tendency was to treat very serious subjects in a rather flip manner. Do you think this affected the critics' response?

I really don't know. There is obviously a blind spot in either me or them. It seemed to me a perfectly valid, inevitable, and natural kind of play to write. It had all the elements that the theatre requires: it had rhythm, it had dialogue, it had drama, it had people who were different at the end from what they were at the beginning. So I really don't know what it was that drew such anger from them.

You wrote an unproduced play entitled simply The New Play, *which apparently exists only in one draft — and was about your not being able to write a play about old people.*

I was trying to write *The Old Ones*, and I had an old-fashioned blockage. And accompanying this blockage was this urge not to write plays in the old way. I was tired of the ordinary stage, with actors coming on and off and sets being changed, and with inventing slightly different characters with different names. So I decided to let it all hang out, as they say. Everybody in that play is called by their real name. There is a character called Arnold, there is a character called Leah, who is my mother, there are characters who are my mother's friends, there are characters of Jennie Lee, Robert Maxwell, Harold Lever — people who were involved in Centre Fortytwo — and my wife Dusty, and so on. Because they all seemed to come together and form a part of my experience which was blocking me. I was paralysed, crippled. So in terms of character and name, everyone was who they were.

Did it clear the blockage for The Old Ones?

It seemed to have done, yes. But it's an entirely dissimilar play, except that there are certain characters in it who are also in *The Old Ones*. There may also be bits and pieces of dialogue that have been lifted out of *The New Play*.

But you still needed to write this play about old people, after having written a play about not being able to write a play about old people . . .

I suppose it's as simple as that I had an enormous admiration for my mother and her cronies, her band of extraordinary old ladies. Sarah is the still centre, surrounded by these extraordinary old people who find all sorts of ways to survive and carry on. A retreat into eccentricity — for example, the woman who writes a lot of books in *The Old Ones*, translating this Polish poetess. In reality she is a woman who writes books, which she pays to have printed herself. I don't think I can say any more except that I'm full of admiration for all the relatives, aunts and uncles, who are mixed into that play — a very extraordinary collection of tough personalities who were good and vivid, and seemed to make significant patterns.

But compared with The Friends, The Old Ones *is more comedic — in fact, a very funny play at several points, although not formally a comedy in the way that* The Wedding Feast *is. But humorous, almost in the Jonsonian sense —in the recurrent theme of the quotation contest, for example.*

Well, this raises an interesting question, to which I have a reply, but I'm not sure whether it's *the* reply. You can imagine that all the old ones in all the plays are the same people. Obviously, I could have spent twenty years writing a novel in twenty parts which would have dealt with all the different aspects of those same old people that the different plays deal with. But I didn't: I handled them as they came up, as the relationships touched what was concerning me at a particular moment. Now in *The Old Ones* I was concerned with survival, and to have had the old ones in that play preoccupied with death would somehow not have allowed time to concentrate on how they were surviving. I think it's also psychologically true that because they are so near death, they don't actually talk about it — they do other things, in order to carry on living.

What is the importance of the young ones to The Old Ones?

It's a question of colours. You know more about how old a person is, or in which way a person is old, if alongside there are young people — and you can see the ways in which values are handed on and how personalities of parents and children react. The young thugs were different — they aren't there to 'represent' youth in any way: they are there because I sensed violence in the air.

You went back to the Royal Court with The Old Ones. *Why was that?*

The play had been contracted by the National Theatre, and Dexter was going to direct it there. Then he went on holiday, and I went on holiday — it is on holidays that all the coups take place. Whatever the reasons, it was withdrawn from the repertory. I was furious, threatened legal action, and they gave us a new date. But Dexter himself was incensed and offended at this cavalier treatment by a theatre to which he had given so much, and the Court expressed interest in the play, so Dexter said we'd take it there.

Obviously, The Journalists *marked a radical new departure for you. How did the central theme emerge?*

I had met a number of journalists, and I had one particular friend who was a journalist — in fact, that same lady to whom the play is dedicated. I wanted to make sure that I didn't perpetuate any clichés about journalists and the atmosphere in which they work, but I didn't want to write a play about journalism as such. I wanted to explore what I called the Lilliputian mentality, a kind of mentality with which I've been obsessed for a long time — since school, in fact, where there was a boy who wanted me to suck at his liquorice stick and I didn't want to. He was very distressed about this, which I couldn't understand, and he beat me up. This provoked a very powerful image which has stayed with me. I think also that I inherited from my parents a contempt for a certain kind of mentality which is petty, lumpen, one that diminishes or minimalizes. I've encountered it in my air force experience, in work, in my schooldays — and, especially, with journalists. And so it seemed to me that journalism was an area in which I could explore this Lilliputian mentality. In addition, there seemed to me to be a very disturbing relationship between the rise of the Lilliputian mentality and democracy.

What is Lilliputian specifically about journalists?

Like most people I'm very ambivalent about journalism. There are many aspects of society that journalists investigate and reveal as corrupt, in need of attention — and yet at the same time trivialize. The tendency seems to me to be to diminish achievement, to concentrate on blemishes, to assume that success is accompanied by smugness and complacency.

Would you compare your treatment of the characters in The Journalists *with your treatment of the characters in* The Kitchen?

The work situation is central in both of them. One could have written a play exploring the minimalizing theme in the way that, say, *The Front Page* worked — in just one room. I think the structure of *The Journalists* prevents one from going any deeper psychologically into those characters, but what might have happened, and I really can't judge this, is that my tuning-in to people has been sharpened, and so one has selected that which reveals personality more succinctly than at the time I was writing *The Kitchen*.

Is it perhaps true that your plays tend not to be about political structures, but about the way political structures shape and influence people? In The Journalists, *the political structure is very implicit.*

The play is concerned with politics at a different level. I'm concerned with the way in which politics and everything else are trivialized by a certain kind of mentality which often manages to gain power and credence at all levels.

You went to the National with The Old Ones, *and ended up at the Royal Court. You went to the RSC with* The Journalists, *and ended up . . . in the law court. Would you agree that at the moment you don't somehow fit into the established structure of the English theatre? And do you feel this might have been different if Centre Fortytwo had succeeded?*

If one pretends that Centre Fortytwo had succeeded — that it had actually become the sort of organization we envisaged, with a permanent company at the Roundhouse — I can easily imagine having said, okay, I've done my work, here it is, the ship is launched, and having gone back to writing, offered *The Journalists* to the artistic director of the Roundhouse — and for it to have been turned down by them too. Which confirms, I suppose, that I *don't* fit anywhere at the moment — in the English theatre.

Do you feel deeply this lack of a continuing relationship with a theatre or a company now?

Very much, but I've felt this for a long time. My relationship with the Royal Court is extraordinary, because they did turn down all the plays — remember it was the Belgrade, Coventry, who did the *Trilogy* first, and then the Court. I did feel very much at home there, though, and I feel they should have done all the plays. They are so clearly Royal Court plays, in the sense that they have a limited life for a limited audience.

You've said in relation to The Wedding Feast *that at last you knew you could write a comedy. Yet there are many very funny moments in your earlier plays. Were you implying rather a more formal distinction, a more primary intention?*

Yes. I think that I'm slightly bludgeoned by the image of being humourlessly serious, pompous, and so on. So I tend to forget that all the plays have comic moments, and that, indeed, when Bernard Levin was desperately trying to keep *Roots* on in the West End, he said 'Above all, this is the funniest play in town'. But I think that what I meant was the discovery of being capable of writing a formal comedy. I have a sense of humour, yes, and I find lots of things funny and I'm always giggling, but this is the first time I've got it all together in one play. What I would wish critics would do is allow each new play to make them think again about the previous plays, so that a play like *The Wedding Feast* should remind them of what comedy there was in the others, and *The Four Seasons* should remind them of what lyricism there is in the works, and *The Friends* of the psychological truths of other characters.

You don't want to work in a collaborative relationship, and yet in a kind of way that's what you were doing in The Wedding Feast, *because you had the model of Dostoevsky to take off from.*

Let's remember that it was originally a film script — I tend to forget that, too. There are only two films I've ever agreed to script, and in both cases it was because they were about things that interested me. The first, *Madame Solario*, because it was about an incestuous relationship, and incest has always fascinated me. And the Dostoevsky because, obviously, here is an ironic look at the worker-employer relationship. Now because that relationship particularly preoccupies me I could bring a great deal more to it than I could to *Madame Solario*, because I've never been involved in an incestuous relationship, and if I had I wouldn't be telling! Even though the original film script was about an Italian, because Anthony Quinn was an Italian, the man was actually so Jewish that when I finally made it into a play it was inevitable that I should make him Jewish, not Italian.

The Wedding Feast *is a play in which there are some very interesting formal innovations — notably the use of the narrator in the first act . . .*

They result from resolving problems of moving from film script to stage. You'll find when you see the final script that there is now no narrator. It struck me that it was a red herring and that critics would talk about 'the narrator in the first act who disappears in the second and third acts'. So now he's just Stephen Bullock, who happens to come forward and narrate.

It's a very gradual process, the way the narrative slowly becomes 'dramatic'. A development from pure 'telling', to illustrating the action, to being totally caught up in it.

I think so. Doris Lessing observed once that you can do anything in a novel — you can compose it of exchanges of dialogue laid out like a play, or in exchanges of letters, or using poetry, or all those things mixed up together, providing there is *something* which makes it add up to a whole. I can see no reason why a play shouldn't have its own 'introduction', as it were, or why a narrator shouldn't fade into a character. It would be intrusive only if the mood or the texture of the language was different, but in *The Wedding Feast* it isn't. Put in another way: without that first act, you couldn't have the wedding feast happen as it does, for two reasons. One: you'd have to spend a lot of time filling in all the background, so that the rhythm would be lost. Two: because those first scenes set out the personality of Litvanov in such a way that you're dying to know what happens to him in that situation.

There's one entirely consistent element in The Wedding Feast — *that same climactic feeling of what one might call 'optimistic pessimism', a feeling that, although somebody has experienced a defeat, in this case a humiliation, yet a kind of dignity is maintained — in this case a comic dignity.*

I wouldn't object to the phrase 'comic dignity'. I suppose I would identify with Litvanov: he's not me, but I do identify with him. He's warm, attractive, and he not only wants to behave justly but actually does do so. Yet he's caught up in a situation that will inevitably humiliate him.

You have said that one of the focal points in the play is at the end, where Kate says to the unconscious Louis, 'Don't try to be too nice, or how are we going to hit you when the time comes?' Did you think of that 'moral' first?

I don't think that I had the image of the shoe game and the beating. But the point I was trying to make — and which the critics have missed — is that anybody who comes from a working-class background, but who through fame or accident or whatever is brought into contact with industrialists or politicians or the aristocracy, will obviously discover that many of these people are not evil monsters. So the critics might have said, 'This exemplifies Wesker's dilemma. He's going to have problems, when the barricades are up, shooting them.'

Where do you stand at the moment, relative to the barricades?

I don't know. I can only tell you simple things. Like it seems to me that what I've always been is a simple, old-fashioned humanist. At the moment I'm writing a story about a middle-aged couple who visit a younger couple, old friends, after a long period. It's just an idyllic Whitsun together — they eat together, they ride bicycles, they sunbathe, talk, listen to music. And there's a moment when one of them reaches out for a tape to put on, which is marked Corelli. They're all waiting for Corelli to come on, and instead they hear the voice of an eastern European giving a lecture on classical Marxism. It is a lecture by Isaac Deutscher which one of them has recorded and put in the wrong box. It's like a voice from their pasts. And Deutscher reaches a crescendo, in which he says that the whole of Marx's work was directed to pointing to the conflict between the social character of work and the anti-social nature of property. The result must be conflict, revolution. But when this marvellous old voice finishes, the friends realize that something is wrong, something is missing. And it strikes one of them that it's natural to look for the contradictions of capitalism, because it has been around a long time: but suppose socialism has its contradictions, too? And they discuss whether these may not lie in the conflict between the social nature of co-operation in a socialist society, and the anti-social nature of state control. My position, I think, is that I *know* there is a conflict within a capitalist society: but I *suspect* that there is this other conflict within a socialist society.

Compared with the works immediately preceding it, Love Letters on Blue Paper *seems a very much smaller-scale work, perhaps because it is based on a short story. I must admit I hadn't gathered that it was based on the character of Vic Feather, the former general secretary of the TUC — and presumably on Vic Feather's death.*

No. I had no idea that Vic Feather was dying of leukaemia — that was a rather macabre coincidence. The original story was written long before I heard that news. But the *character* was certainly based on Vic Feather — hence the use of the same name. There were other key points, too. I had the whole of that last letter already, in note form — it just came, 'in a blinding flash', or however it goes. And there was the image that I had always had of Vic Feather's wife. As a personality he always appealed to me, but one never knew his wife, and he never talked about her. On occasions I would drop him off on a roundabout near his house, but we'd never go to the house. So I never saw his house, or his wife.

The other ingredient was the personality of an old friend of mine called Robert Copping. I first came across him when I was sixteen, and had just left school, and heard the news that he was trying to form a schoolboys' union. I wrote to him and offered my services, and I became a district organizer for him for about six months. But I remained a close friend of his. He ran a free school up in the north, but this was closed down because he had an affair with a sixteen-year-old pupil, and then he went off to South America with a woman whom he married, and disappeared for many years. And one day he came back, dying of leukaemia. I watched him for some days in Guy's Hospital, dying. And his wife Valerie showed me some letters, written to a friend of his, a psychiatrist, and they contained these two incredible passages — one describing how he first was told that he had leukaemia, and the other telling how, after the initial shock, he began to think that 'Karl Marx is dead, Freud is dead . . .' The letters were very impressive, and touched me. And somewhere in the play is my relationship with Dusty, too. All those things came together to give me the idea.

This is another play of yours which contains detailed instructions for the preparation of food in an appendix. There is something specially significant about food in your plays . . .

Food is essential to all human activity. When you go to visit someone in hospital sometimes you take flowers, but more often fruit. I've been taking my aunt smoked salmon sandwiches. When you invite people as guests, you touch them through food. And in the preparation of food there is a kind of ceremony, isn't there?

To you it's very obvious — yet how many dramatists who might regard a ceremonial element as important in their work would achieve that element through the preparation of food? And it's there again, of course, in that very important, very ceremonial meal in The Merchant — *which must be quite unique among your plays in developing, essentially, from your own response to another man's play. Was it a particular production which set you thinking?*

Oh, yes. It was the Jonathan Miller production of Shakespeare's *The Merchant of Venice*, which I didn't like, and I certainly detested Olivier's 'oi, oi, oi' sort of Jew. When Portia suddenly gets to the bit about having a pound of flesh but no blood, it flashed on me that the kind of Jew I know would stand up and say, 'Thank God!' My first thought was that perhaps one day I would be able to do a production of Shakespeare's *Merchant* in which that's the way it would happen, and I discussed this with Ewan Hooper one day. He said, 'That's very interesting, but you'd have to do a lot of rewriting'. I thought about it, and realized it would be simpler to write a new play.

How did the student from Colorado, to whom the play is dedicated, help?

Well, I was at Boulder teaching a course on the 'History of Contemporary British Drama', and after about two weeks I confessed to the students that I felt very fraudulent, because I didn't really want to talk about my contemporaries. I just wanted to talk about this new play I was going to write, and perhaps that might tell them more about the new British drama than anything I might say about other writers. So I involved them in all the background research that I would otherwise be doing, and some of the students wrote papers. And one student in particular wrote a very long and, I thought, brilliant paper, in which she gave me one of the pillars on which my case rested, about how you couldn't have dealings with a Jew except through a contract.

Which really became the focal point for your rewriting — the motivation of Shylock's insistence on the bond, which in Shakespeare's play he reiterates against all sense.

Yes, but there was also the issue of why he entered into the contract in the first place. If the 'real' Shylock would have thanked God for the getout Portia gave him, one had to work out how he had got himself involved in a contract which he clearly didn't want, and this meant a close study of the history of the Jews in Venice. And because of the need for all dealings with Jews to be contractual, it is in fact Antonio who insists on the bond, in order to save Shylock from breaking the law, respect for which was so crucial to the Jewish community's existence in Venice.

You ditched Gobbo and found a good reason for the bond — but you retained a third 'hump' in Shakespeare's play, the business of the caskets. Why?

That fitted in very well with Portia coming from a ruined background, because the same father who had allowed the estate to go to rack and ruin would also be the sort of man to produce this lunatic idea of the daughter choosing the right husband through virtuous interpretation of the caskets.

In the relationship between Shylock and Jessica, you've kept close to the surface of what happens in Shakespeare — yet whereas Shakespeare's Jessica betrays her father for no good reason, here there is a genuine, love-hate relationship between Shylock and his daughter which is strongly rooted in the nature of their ages and relationship. How far were you looking for 'real' reasons for what happens in Shakespeare, how far did you rewrite to make what happens real?

I started knowing that Shylock entered into a contract he didn't want to enter, that he and Antonio were friends. I had distinct images of Portia, Lorenzo, Bassanio, and Graziano. And I had this very concrete image of the play ending with a broken Shylock, and Antonio and Portia and Jessica — this triangular shape, with the three lovers celebrating in the middle. I knew that Shylock was going to be a bibliophile. I suppose I read about twenty books about the history of the Jews, and in the process of reading I discovered the meat to put on this framework. The Venetians hated having the Jews in Venice, and they kept throwing them out and giving over the dealings to the monks, who either made a complete mess of things, or else were so successful that the poor were thoroughly abused. The only people who knew how to do it well and with sufficient humanity were the Jews, but the Venetians didn't want them in the city, so they found this plot of land just outside Venice called the New Iron Foundry — or *ghetto nuevo*, the original ghetto, which became the Jewish quarter.

It does seem that you find it much easier to talk about the themes, the characters, the personal tangents in your plays than about their structure and about technical matters. Looking at The Merchant, *there is so clearly a balance being preserved — between kinds of scene, tones of voice, setting, emphases — that one feels this must have involved a more conscious process of shaping than you usually acknowledge.*

A sense of what should follow something else is surely a very basic sense in any playwright's make-up. But, for me, yes, it is still very much a *sense*, an instinct. When I move from one scene to another, obviously something is saying to me, that is logically or psychologically correct. When I deny any conscious technical prowess, what I mean is: no writer sits down and says, right, this play has got to start off at a temperature of twenty degrees, and then it's right and proper that it should go up to fifty degrees, then down to thirty-five, and up to a climax of seventy. You know that you're telling a story, and what event is to follow after what other has to meet a number of criteria: it must be in the right place from the point of view of the narrative, it must be musically correct, it must be poetically correct, and so on. But you don't work it out in advance. You just . . . feel it.

14
David Edgar
a drama of dynamic ambiguities

Possibly the most prolific and surely one of the most successful among the generation of dramatists which emerged after 1968, David Edgar chose a theatrical career with more deliberation than many of his contemporaries — even to the extent of studying (mistakenly, as he now thinks) in a university department of drama. Here he found himself in 1968, when, as he puts it, 'bliss was it in that dawn to be alive, but to be in full-time higher education was very heaven'.

Following a brief apprenticeship in journalism, he came into theatre through Chris Parr's pioneering scheme to encourage young writers at Bradford University, and was one of the multiple collaborators on England's Ireland: *but most of his early work was with the General Will, an itinerant agitprop company for which he wrote almost instant plays on topical themes — though seldom without the scrupulous background research which has always been a characteristic of his working method, whether into the history of Concorde or the social fabric of Dickensian London.*

While not disowning his 'agitprop period', Edgar found he wanted to deal with subjects the form could not contain, and, like Howard Brenton, began to feel the need for the facilities offered by larger companies and stages. After a somewhat protracted period of gestation, his anti-nazi play Destiny *finally reached the main stage of the Aldwych in 1977, via a studio production at The Other Place — and, while he continued to extend the range of his writing with* Mary Barnes *and* Teendreams, *it was for the RSC that Edgar wrote both* The Jail Diary of Albie Sachs, *seen at The Warehouse in 1978, and the blockbusting, two-part, nine-hour Aldwych adaptation of* Nicholas Nickleby, *which carried off virtually every available award of the 1980 season.*

Many mainstream theatregoers thus know Edgar as the author of just three plays — from an output to date of over forty. While a number of these were only intended to be topical — almost disposable — pieces, many others retain intrinsic interest, and when TQ associate editor Clive Barker and myself talked with David Edgar in his Birmingham home in October 1978, we were concerned to discuss these as well as the better-known plays. But first we asked David Edgar about the influence of his educational background — which sounded, in its due sequence of prep-school, public school, and university, almost dauntingly conventional.

Yes, fairly conventional, more or less upper middle-class, except that both my parents and three of my grandparents, an aunt, and various other slightly more distant relatives were involved in the theatre. I think that had a fairly strong influence, and I probably saw rather more plays at a young age than most middle-class children, even from culturally aware backgrounds. I suppose I would have seen almost all of Shakespeare's plays by the age of fifteen, and in the Easter holidays I would go to everything that was available, which was then three Stratford openings, three plays at the Birmingham Rep, and three at the Alex — the Alexandra Theatre — which meant I had a comprehensive knowledge of Agatha Christie, and the sort of plays one would never go to now. That was advantageous in terms of my picking up a number of techniques, and disadvantageous in that I think I spent rather longer than I might in forging an individual style, shaking off that almost osmotically communicated 'forties or 'fifties sense of the dramatic which obviously does fall over into my early non-documentary drama.

Was it a conscious vocational choice, to read drama at Manchester?

Yes. I think it was a mistake, in that it meant that I ploughed through a lot of criticism that I probably would not otherwise have read, and a lot of plays that if I hadn't read already I would have read anyway, or seen. I've always felt the lack of a discipline, really *any* discipline, like history or economics or even, God forbid, chemistry — a system of looking at the world. The discipline which I did develop, which has had advantages and disadvantages, came through being a journalist. I think that three-year period in my life was much more important, really.

So it was not university that bred in you the habit of going to the extraordinary lengths of research that you've felt necessary for some of your plays?

No. I think at university the most important things that happened were nothing to do with the drama department or academic life at all. They were to do with being at a university in 1968 — you know, bliss was it in that dawn to be alive, but to be in full-time higher education was very heaven. Editing a student newspaper, and being involved in the political life of the union, and then going into journalism gave me a talent, which has had mixed benefits, for getting inside a subject very quickly and quite precisely.

It's what I call a colander effect — you do actually find that your mind gets trained to letting the bits that are not immediately useful disappear through. That's splendid for a piece like *The Case of the Workers' Plane*, the play I wrote about the Concorde in Bristol, which I researched in about a month, actually on the ground, getting a fairly comprehensive knowledge of all that was necessary to write that play. But there were all kinds of . . . tensions which actually went through the colander. So that one is aware in retrospect that actually the journalistic mind loses all sorts of things.

Could you say a little more about 1968, which obviously was crucially important — the fact that you were at university in that year.

I think I got into left-wing politics on a kind of rhetorical level, really. There's a kind of mythology on the left that middle-class people become revolutionary socialists because they wake up one morning, look in the mirror, and suddenly realize that there is an inevitable tendency for capitalism to collapse, and that all history is the history of the class struggle, that all value emanates from labour, and bang, there we are. But I think many middle-class people become revolutionaries simply through an *instinct* against social injustice. And, obviously, there is also simply the entertainment value of being revolutionary at a particular time, which is one of the reasons why more students were revolutionary in 1968 than are now.

As a journalist you specialized in the theatre and in education, though I know you were also involved in the first exposé of the Poulson scandals. Had it not been for Chris Parr happening to have been in Bradford at that time, do you think you might have gone on to a journalistic career?

Well, it's very difficult to say. I think I was never a hundred per cent committed, waiting-eight-hours-in-the-car-across-the-street, every-time-you-hear-a-siren-leap-in-your-car-and-follow-it type journalist. I'm very proud of being involved with the Poulson story, though if I look back on my limited contribution to it, I do remember quite frequently thinking, oh God, have I got to go to Pontefract *again,* to follow up some ludicrous little lead. The only type of journalism I would really have wanted to make a career of would have been that sort of investigative journalism, and I don't think I was really cut out for that.

How did you become involved with Chris Parr?

What happened was that Chris Parr had this extraordinary (though it seems to me very obvious) policy, which very few other universities have taken up, of getting students to do new plays specifically commissioned for them by up-and-coming writers — who could still use being paid between twenty and fifty quid per play. And that was the bargain. He did three of Howard Brenton's plays, and a number of John Grillo's. He also developed a number of new people, including myself and Richard Crane. I had gone to a lot of his productions, and covered one or two of them as a journalist, and got to know the people socially very well. And I had the idea of writing a play about the Springbok tour — which was the first but by no means the last occasion when I've been overtaken by events, because the tour was cancelled. Chris didn't like the play at all, but even before the tour was cancelled he commissioned another one for two actresses (who were very good, and he felt needed something rather larger than was available for them to get their teeth into), so I wrote *Two Kinds of Angel* for those two student performers. After that Chris did *Acid, The End, A Truer Shade of Blue,* and a number of other works. And then I had two offers. One was to participate in writing *England's Ireland*, and the other was to do a project with Max Stafford-Clark at the Traverse Theatre Workshop. And I couldn't have taken those up and stayed in journalism. By that stage, *Two Kinds of Angel* had been done in London, and various other things were beginning to get done elsewhere, and I thought I'd make the jump.

As a first play, Two Kinds of Angel *is not very characteristic of a lot of the work that came immediately afterwards. . . .*

No, that's right. It's a highly melodramatic piece, which I can't look at any more, relying on a series of fairly obvious effects culled from watching the wrong sorts of plays at an impressionable age. But at least one had got that assurance, actually to be able to write a one-hour play for two women which jumped about in space and time. I don't think I thought stylistically about how to do it at all.

You don't seem to have gone through a 'realistic phase' at all.

I don't know, but that may have to do with the fact that I've always been quite good at parody, which again has advantages and disadvantages. And so a lot of my early non-agitprop stuff was imitative — which in a sense I don't mind. I teach a playwriting course at Birmingham, and the three things I tell the students are: you are going to be melodramatic, you are going to be autobiographical, and you're going to plagiarize. Don't worry. Start worrying if you're still doing it in two terms' time.

But I did take a conscious decision not to write a play about a sensitive young man coming down from university and having sex problems, with a big scene with a tart with a heart of gold at the end of the first act. I think I was very pleased that my first play was about two women. And I've only really recently begun to be sure enough to be able to start writing plays in which my own life features at all.

Does it make any sense to try and distinguish between the plays you wrote for Bradford University, and the work which you then did with the General Will? These different relationships made for very different kinds of play, didn't they?

Yes, I think so. For Bradford I wrote five or six plays of very different kinds. *A Truer Shade of Blue* was a small farce about sex. *Two Kinds of Angel* was a semi-naturalistic two-hander. *The End* was a vast spectacular. *Acid* was a sort of social-realist piece about terrorism — though I did in fact also base some of it very loosely on *The Bacchae*. Kind of jumping in and out, plus a great deal of rhetoric: it wasn't a happy amalgam, although I think there was some quite fine individual stuff in it. But its ending, which has the daughter basically giving the line of the piece to these three Charles Manson-type monsters, I now find embarrassing.

It happened to be a coincidence that I originally wrote *The National Interest* for Bradford, as a documentary on the first year of the Conservative government. It happened that a group of people wanted to set up a new theatre company arising out of Bradford, and this became the General Will: but the first performances of *The National Interest* were under the auspices of Bradford University. And really the whole series of work for the General Will came out of that coincidence. It might have been that a group interested in another sort of work might have done another kind of play of mine, and that would have been the line of development.

Would you agree that of all the Bradford plays, The End *was the one closest to the kind of work you went on to do with the General Will?*

Yes, in a way. Chris Parr had this project for doing a series of spectacular events geared to specific environments, which included Howard Brenton's *Wesley,* which was done in a Methodist hall, and *Scott of the Antarctic,* which was done in an ice rink, and *David, King of the Jews,* which Richard Crane wrote for Bradford Cathedral. *The End* was written for a university with a computer in it, and was very much designed for that environment — so the sequences set in a Polaris submarine were geared to the fact that there was a stage with a fire curtain which went up to reveal the Polaris, and a huge hall which you could take the seats out of, which was the main acting area, and there was room for the computer console as well. So it was very much an environmental piece. Having said that, the techniques it used of fairly rapid, brisk, multi-doubling, and the cartoon-storytelling style were clearly features that carried over into the General Will. And I think that the most finished technique that came out of Bradford was for anecdotal storytelling — sliding very quickly from different images which would tell a consistent story through any number of different settings or images.

What was your relationship as a writer to the group?

The National Interest I wrote completely by myself. We then developed a system of writing which is really the way, broadly speaking, I've written with collective companies ever since — that is, I write the words, but the process of deciding what each scene is to say (and, indeed, the way it is to be said) is a collective process. Though it must be said that the writer contributes more to the process than most other people. *The Rupert Show* I wrote more or less by myself. With *State of Emergency* we developed a technique whereby I would bring in a great pile of cuttings, and people would look at different areas and report back. That was quite easy in the sense that it was a chronology play, so we knew we had to do Upper Clyde Shipbuilders, we had to do the 1972 miners' strike, we had to do the railwaymen. So we'd talk and we'd range around ways of doing something, and get an idea, then I'd go away and write the scene and bring it back the next day.

Rent was perhaps the classic example — it was written in a week. That was at the time when I'd finally given up journalism, and I had an extraordinary baptism of fire. I left journalism on Thursday; on Friday evening I was sitting down in Pembrokeshire with Howard Brenton and Snoo Wilson and David Hare and the others to write *England's Ireland*. Then a week later I was back at Bradford to write *Rent* in a week, two scenes a day, which included six songs. I really don't know how it happened.

How did the audiences relate to the work?

Well, every group has its story, and ours is the Bangor NUPE story. We did a gig for the National Union of Public Employees in Bangor, and we started with eighty people and ended up with two. After that, whenever I suggested a line which included a word of more than three syllables, people would say, how would that go down in Bangor? I think we did become much more conscious of the need to relate to real working-class audiences, as opposed to the sort of wonderful Aristotelian creatures we'd got in our minds.

So it's quite paradoxical that *The National Interest*, although it was the first of those plays, perhaps went down better because its objectives were quite simple. But *Rent* was the most successful agitprop play I've ever done, because it actually got to exactly the audiences it wanted and was intended for. We got a link-up with the Child Poverty Action Group, who were campaigning vigorously against the Housing Finance Act, and the play was a series of scenes from Victorian melodrama, putting the Harddoneby family through a series of situations — in a squat, in a rented house, in various sorts of council housing. It was a very mechanical piece, but it did actually explain a complicated Act of Parliament in reasonably simple terms. It played to thirty tenants' groups, and it got its audience.

When we got to *The Dunkirk Spirit*, we *were* attempting, much more ambitiously, to explain the currency of capitalism, and that I suppose is the agitprop play with which I am most pleased, because in two hours you actually get through the most massive amount of extremely complex material: but judged in terms of its audiences, it was not nearly so successful. And I was wanting to say things which agitprop couldn't say. It can't, I think, put across emotional optimism — or, indeed, any kind of emotion. And so when you do try to put across emotions it can get very embarrassing and tacky.

How was your own political thinking developing during this period?

I think a lot of people of my generation of the late 'sixties went through a kind of counter-cultural experience, based politically very much on the assumption that working-class revolution in the west was dead, and that one had to look elsewhere — the Marcusian line. Then, in Britain, working-class militancy showed this sudden and unexpected revival in the early 'seventies. That led to a rejection of the cultural revolution, particularly in the International Socialism group which I was close to at the time: that was one of the reasons feminism took so long to escape scorn in this country.

The Rupert Show is a bit of an odd one out among those General Will plays —
much more of a frolic, almost. Was that how you conceived it?

Yes. Really, it was an attempt to deal with a subject — sex and pornography
— and the Mary Whitehouse, Oz Trial backlash, in an agitprop way, which
I think made it rather less satisfactory than some of my other work at that
time. Again, because the form wasn't frightfully suitable, though I think it
was quite a good thing to do a journalistic hatchet job on the anti-
pornography campaigners. At the end, there was a kind of demonstration
with riot police and two hippies being beaten up by them, which was meant
to suggest the inadequacy of the counter-culture, and was an implied
criticism of the Oz Three, whose trial was still viewed by some people as
being somehow a great and important revolutionary event. That critique,
theatrically, was interestingly presented. But of all the plays I did for the
General Will, *Rupert* was the least successful.

In talking to Howard Brenton now, in his puritanical phase, he seems to have a
sort of nostalgic regret about leaving the alternative culture, whereas it seems you
were always fairly clear-sighted and objective about it.

Yes. But remember, my first play was written eighteen days before Edward
Heath was elected Prime Minister. So that although a lot of my work and a
lot of me is about the late-'sixties, all my plays were written in the 'seventies.
And I think that's quite important, in that they're all plays about a now
rather embarrassing feeling of the late-'sixties generation being the Peter Pan
generation. Almost everything I've written relates to that, either by saying it
was nonsense anyway, and we always knew it was — which I think a lot of
the early plays do — or by looking at it in a more distanced and I hope
positive way, as I'm trying to do now.

I do think that when Poliakoff says that anybody who is writing now has to
relate to the late 'sixties, although it's a piece of shorthand, it's quite
accurate, at least for anybody who was between fifteen and thirty then. All
components of the culture were affected. Yet almost everything academic
that came out of the late 'sixties has been undermined. Laing has been
undermined, since it is now much clearer that there is a chemical causative
effect to schizophrenia. Chomsky has been undermined. Marcuse's theories
have been shown just not to have been true, and the Black Power Movement
has withered on the vine. The generation that was never going to be
assimilated *has* been assimilated.

What in a sense I was trying to do in *Mary Barnes*, without being
ambiguous for the sake of it, was to look again at these apparently rather silly
looking people, who really did think that the world was going to change by
some process of radiation out from the East End of London, but who,
nonetheless, helped to cure this woman — quite inappropriately, not a young
left-winger, like Clarissa in *Family Life*, but a 42-year-old, fervent Catholic,
who got better without drugs or electric shocks. The play presents a kind of

counterpoint, I hope, so that the audience get amused and perhaps irritated by the psychiatrist, but are confronted with their own emotional response to Mary's story, to a point that I call a dynamic ambiguity — an ambiguity which will hopefully lead to people's attempting to resolve it in their own minds, as opposed to an unpositive ambiguity, which tends to be vaguely comforting in its confirmation that there really is very little that can be done about life, so you may as well just enjoy your little bit of it.

Concurrent with your developing relationship with the General Will, you were also doing various one-off pieces for other groups — Still Life *and* Tedderella *for the Pool up at Edinburgh, and* Gangsters *at Soho Poly, all rather more light-hearted pieces. Is that the way you approached them — as slight relaxations?*

Yes. I've always done that. I like writing comedies, and I do actually enjoy the sensation of sitting down at a desk without having read piles of cuttings. So it would be quite accurate to describe all of those pieces as plays which I wrote to wind down, or something like that. But *Tedderella* was also an attempt to create a more popular and less factually-based form of political theatre. It turned out to be a very good spoof, and it gave me confidence in writing large-scale parody — whereas before, we'd do, say, a terribly good Chicago gangsters parody for five minutes, and then go on to something else. It was good to be able to sustain a parody form, albeit as imitable a form as the pantomime. I'd done *Still Life* for the Pool, and they said, why don't you do something about the Common Market? And at that stage, when people said, why don't you do something about something, I usually did. I don't do that so much now.

Was that the case with Excuses, Excuses *at the Belgrade?*

That was slightly different. *Excuses* was the first play that I'd had commissioned by a theatre proper, and there were two things I wanted to do. One was to write a play about doing a play, because I'd tried that out with *Bloody Rosa*, which, though I'm quite fond of it, was a very unsatisfactory epic about Rosa Luxemburg. That was my first attempt to set a play within a play, and it was rather mechanical — you know, there was the usual planted noisy man in the audience, that sort of thing. The other element in *Excuses* was the story I happened to have picked up from a paper about this guy who'd burned down a mill, because half the work force had been made redundant — the interesting thing being that he wasn't *in* the half that was made redundant. And I suppose the third element was a sort of constant anger at the way in which people said, I behave like this because I believe in that, and other people said, no you don't you do it because you weren't breast-fed or because you're in social group E, or because you're educationally sub-normal. Hence the central wheeze of the play: to have the curtain call, and then to have the guy saying, you've wasted two hours, ladies and gentlemen, listening to all these clever explanations of my arson, the reason I gave at the beginning is the reason I did it. I think that was actually a gut play — there was a kind of anger at psychologism, an anger at the view of human behaviour which attributes everything to internalized memory or your ego or your id.

Was O Fair Jerusalem *also a gut play?*

Yes. That was a kind of attack on . . . fashionable despair. The point of the play was to say: no, it is not true that we live in an eternal cycle of ghastliness and that there is no way out. I think if I was to connect it with another play, it would be *Death Story* — the idea of a Black Death in one, of a modern *Romeo and Juliet* in the other. And both were attempts to point morals allegorically, perhaps in a kind of over-reaction against the real, gritty contemporaneity of the agitprop work, a search for the freedom to be able to create one's own world again, without being surrounded by press cuttings.

I think what happened with *Death Story*, and its simple moral that love does not conquer all, was that there was quite a lot of talk in the papers that problems in Northern Ireland could all be solved if people just got a little friendly with one another. And the play was trying to make the point that life doesn't work like that. The rather melodramatic qualities about the play have made it extremely popular with young performers, but people who are older than I was when I wrote it don't find it satisfactory.

Why do you think there is this recurrent parodistic element in your work?

It's always dangerous to theorize, partly because the way one's work develops does not necessarily look like that in retrospect. But I think it would be true to say that I've only recently had sufficient confidence in the validity of myself as a writer, and the validity of what I have to say about the world in which I live — the world in which *I* live, not the world in which railway workers live, the people about whom I've been writing plays — to try and develop my own voice. Basing work on literary conceits as in *Death Story*, or on parodies, like *Dick Deterred*, or on factual material as in the documentaries, was to a certain extent borne out of a consciousness of wanting to find something apart from myself to draw on.

Which came first, the feeling that you wanted to write a parody which would relate to those particular subjects, or a sudden clicking in the mind between the model and the contemporary relevance?

It's usually the two things coming together. Before *Death Story* I'd seen the Zeffirelli film of *Romeo and Juliet*, and walked out of the cinema shaking with fury, because I'd always been fascinated by the original play. So the first half of *Death Story* is me saying, I think the original is about this, and the second half of the play is me saying, I don't think the original is relevant. Because *Romeo and Juliet* only works if there is a strong sense not of, are they going to get away with it, but of, how on earth is the play going to kill them? And I think that's a brilliant dramatic device of Shakespeare's — that you actually are desperate, in all those melodramatic twists and turns, for it to come wrong at the end, because of what's been set up in the first half, which is about this extraordinary little girl who dreams about fucking in a charnel house, the whole connection between sex and death.

With the others, *Tedderella* started with the subject. What happened with *Dick Deterred* was that the Bush had done a revival of *Tedderella*, and asked me to do a sort of *Return of Tedderella*. I wasn't frightfully interested in that, but they'd obviously commissioned something like it, and I happened to see a paragraph in *The Times* diary about the Society of the White Boar, which was preceded by an item about Nixon, and the connecting link was another Richard who was vilified in his time. And I rang up the Bush and said, Watergate Richard the Third. And they said, wonderful, and I went back to whatever I was doing. I didn't, in fact, actually read *Richard the Third,* check whether it was going to fit, until the statutory five weeks before the play was due. In fact, it does fit, and it was mainly a mathematical task of fitting the two components together. So essentially form preceded content there.

This is just one of a range of disjunctive techniques you employ, isn't it? Like the time jumps in Destiny.

That technique in *Destiny* I've rather uglily described as 'thematic linking', which is to say that a scene is followed by one which took place seven years earlier, followed by another which took place two years before that: not because I was flashing back, in the conventional sense, but because the answer to the question Scene C has posed took place seven years before and *that* was scene D, and the answer to the question Scene D posed came two years before that, and the answer to the question Scene E posed requires us to return to the present tense. What I wanted the audience to do was actually view the play in terms of its theme, in terms of the social forces involved, not necessarily to be bothered with strict chronology. I suppose the interesting thing is why I'm so nervous about it . . .

One play which doesn't seem to fit into any of these developing techniques and patterns of work is Baby Love.

Yes. *Baby Love* is difficult to fit in. I think that was a gut play, because I was very deeply angered by the Pauline Jones 'baby-snatching' case — though I should say that the play was based on a number of cases, not just that one. I think also that at the time I was actually living the play's own ambience — that strange combination of Asians, déclassé, sub-proletarian people, and students, in that environment which is very much the centre of Bradford, with very little conventional, young working-class life within it. The character of Eileen really came out of that.

Can you say a little about your break with the General Will?

What happened was that after *Dunkirk* I got obsessed with slickness. I was fed up with seeing agitprop plays that were messy, and also I was increasingly thinking that the politics you could get across were very crude, whereas the world about us was getting more complicated. Or perhaps we were getting more complicated, and just noticing that that's the way the world had always been. And the General Will were concerned with becoming more popular, by which I don't mean with more people seeing the plays, but more popular with a capital P. And we parted company not entirely amicably, but in a reasonably civilized fashion.

I do like agitprop, and I'm fond of my agitprop plays. I'm fond of that period. There may again be a period when agitprop will have more relevance than I believe it does now. But I don't think I'll ever go back to it, because the sort of subjects that I want to deal with now won't take it. With both *Events* and *The Case of the Workers' Plane,* there were plays weaving through which the form couldn't take. There was a play about people who loved making expensive, sophisticated aeroplanes, but realized that it was a social disaster to do so. And there was a much better play in *Events,* about the conflicts between different sets of workers — the actual way, aside from the slogans, in which sets of workers allow themselves to be divided, and indeed want to be divided one from another. And both those plays weren't the plays that eventually hit the stage.

Did Operation Iskra *represent a kind of watershed in your writing?*

That's right. *Iskra* was written just before the first draft of *Destiny,* and you might compare it with, say, *The Rupert Show,* which is a play about the 'counter culture' in conflict with the host society, done in a straight, old-fashioned agitprop documentary cartoon way. Now *Iskra* clearly has *thematic* links with that. But what I did in *The Rupert Show* was to have lots of little sketches, whereas with *Iskra* I suppose the obvious key decision was to give myself the freedom of using 'faction'. I think that was a much more important decision than setting it in the future — to take real events, but to set them in time slightly off-centre. So what one might call the texture is authentic, in that I'm trying to make them talk and behave like I believed people in the Angry Brigade and the counter insurgency people did talk and behave, but to do that in a fictional way.

The other thing, which I suppose is connected with the parody instinct, was to use an existing form, in this case the thriller, in order to make a point by undermining its precepts, in very much the way that Howard Brenton and David Hare did in *Brassneck* — using that really hoary old form the saga of a family over three generations, but making the characters universally loathsome, on the one hand, and on the other hand making the relationships between the generations not domestic but to do with their different attitudes to capital accumulation. Using the form to undermine it, in short. In the same way, I believed (and still do) that part of the content of individual terrorist activity is a kind of equal and opposite mirror-image of certain aspects of capitalist ideology.

What was behind the need you were now beginning to feel for getting your plays onto a large stage?

I think it was two things. The prestige of small theatres is small, or it certainly was small. And there was a feeling that we were better than that, a natural progression. I don't think people can sit and go through the agony of writing eight hours a day if that kind of ambition isn't somewhere working away. The second point, which is much more substantial, is that Howard Brenton and David Hare and I and a number of other people wanted to write plays about subjects which required large numbers of people, and also about public subjects which did not take place in rooms but in *areas,* which it is nice to have space to represent. Because streets are larger than houses, and battlefields are larger than bedrooms. And we wanted the numbers.

In discussions about *Destiny,* which occasionally occurred during meetings that I attended to talk about the National Front, of which I've done about fifty, quite frequently somebody would ask, why did you let *Destiny* go on at the Aldwych? With its middle-class audience and so on. And the answer to that question was, because otherwise you wouldn't have invited me to speak at this meeting. Which was a slight debating trick, but I think it does contain a truth, in that *Destiny* had more effect, by virtue of being done at the Aldwych, than anything else I've written. Partly because it's better than a lot of what I've written, but partly because it became an event. And I would argue that its performance at the Aldwych had more effect than its production on television, despite the fact that it was seen by four million people on television and by twenty-two thousand at the Aldwych.

Destiny *and* Wreckers *are obviously still dependent on the documentary line, in terms of the background research that's gone into them — the minutiae of Labour Party selection procedures and so on — but at the same time the actual content and the characterization are imaginative. Do you see something in those two plays which marked a new direction?*

Yes. I think one would have to jump back slightly to include *Operation Iskra,* which, as we've discussed, worked on exactly the same principles, taking a contemporary factual phenomenon, in this case urban middle-class terrorism and counter-insurgency, but making it into 'faction', based very closely and authentically on real subject matter.

That's the line I'm now really in, and it is obviously a kind of resolution for me of ways of writing political plays which aren't allegory, which I'd had an interesting but not totally satisfactory experience of with *Death Story* and *O Fair Jerusalem;* which don't rely on playing about with theatrical conventions, like *Excuses;* and which aren't social realist in an abstract sense, like *Baby Love;* but which are plays which combine research with giving myself my own head to create characters. Having gradually convinced myself through figures like Eileen in *Baby Love* that I could actually write characters.

The first draft of *Destiny* was written just after I'd written *Operation Iskra*, and in a sense the problems of *Destiny* occur because of its five-year span. It's an agitprop structure, still, in a funny kind of way — each scene makes its own point. There is The Labour MP Who Sells Out. There is the central plot point about the supporters of fascism being betrayed by fascism, with the device of Turner's shop being taken over by Rolfe's firm. There is the meeting scene, which is one of the things that has changed very little, because it was based on an actual meeting I attended, and in one sense it's a very mechanical scene, with all the archetypes of fascism who have nothing in common beyond despair — the unemployed worker, the older worker threatened by technological change, the middle-class woman with her savings being destroyed, the polytechnic lecturer, his lower middle-class property-oriented wife, who brings in the technical worker, and so on, all being brought together by the philosophy of fascism, by the character Maxwell, who takes all their different little worries and despairs and neatly knits them together into a conspiracy theory of history — wham, bang, fascism.

The element that you couldn't get from a pamphlet discussing the class nature of fascism is the actual emotional draw — the realization of the appeal of it, and the actual connection to oneself. So I'm very pleased with *Destiny* as a play. I'm not retracting any of it, but I think if it has a major fault of which I'm aware, it's that the complexity of the characters and the complexity of the language is to a certain extent imposed on the structure, which is perhaps slightly too skeletal, slightly too meccano-like.

You've said that you now want to participate in the production process more, and certainly my own reaction, watching Mary Barnes, *was that I would have hated to direct the play without you there, because of the emphasis on quite subtle inflexions — on 'gestus', to use a Brechtian word, on the way that the lines were said by the characters to bring things out. What kind of problems do you encounter in production?*

There has been a predictable assumption by directors and actors that the writer being present and active is 'a jolly good idea', so long as that does not change the real relationships. But of course it will, in two very important ways, both arising out of the emotional deal which directors tend to do with actors, which goes something like this. A director will say, 'If you have done this line wrong today, I'm not going to tell you you've done it wrong, but by a series of manipulations I'm going to get it right at the right moment'. That sort of thing directors are trained to do: 'I will make you do something I want you to do without you thinking that you are being made to do it'.

The other half of the deal is that the actors will be treated like porcelain, for which they will, as it were, trade their right not to be manipulated. Hence, the director's classic line to the author: 'No, I can't say that, it'll upset the actors', to which one has always, under one's breath, responded, 'Nine times out of ten the actors are being paid double what I am. *I'm* upset — I think *they* are paid to be upset as well'. Like in the old Bob Hope joke: 'Upset, of course he's upset, he's a lawyer, he's paid to be upset'.

So in that sense the presence of the writer means that if the line is being done wrong, he is going to say so. If a line is being delivered in clearly the opposite way to his intention, then he is going to intervene and he is going to say so. If in a play like *Mary Barnes* there are whole scenes where the characters are not saying what they mean, then it seems to me that it's a criminal waste of the limited time available not to inform the actors of what's missing, or lead them in the direction of seeing what is going on. But this undermines the authority of the director, and it undermines the mystique of the actors. It's a very distressing process.

With The Jail Diary of Albie Sachs, *you returned to the use of existing source material. Was this your own idea, or a commission?*

The guy who owned the copyright asked me to do it. In fact the first draft of *Mary Barnes* predates *Albie Sachs,* and I'd got very interested in adaptation. There was a wonderful letter that David Hare wrote to me, about the first draft of *Destiny,* when he said, 'I know you don't think construction is very important, but this time you have Gone Too Far'. Which indeed I had. I have always had a slight inferiority complex about construction, and whatever one says about *O Fair Jerusalem,* for example, it's hardly an economical piece of work. But adaptation imposes its own economy.

I think I've always tried to solve the technical problems in a Samuel Smiles self-help fashion. I've always tried to find something in each project which will make me better as a writer. And clearly *Jail Diary* had fairly massive technical problems, the chief of which was how to represent a man being bored into submission in a way that wasn't boring. So the reason I was particularly attracted to it initially was that it was a clear subject: the whole action took place in that cell, and presented various fascinating technical problems within the strict framework. Unlike *Mary Barnes* — which was a kind of trampoline, or linear row of pegs, on which various things would hang, which would rush off down different avenues — *Jail Diary* had to be a matter of honing down, of constructing a very sculptural work, of taking what was already there — the book — as a fairly precise little block of stone, and chipping neatly away at it.

That was the technical reason I wanted to do it, and I was very pleased with the result from that point of view. The instinctive and political reason I wanted to do it was that I wanted to write a play in which the central character was a nice guy. It is such a cliché that it almost doesn't need saying, but our whole dramatic tradition has trained us very well to write plays about despair, despondency, missed opportunities, and failures. So we find it very difficult to write positively, and if one was to name one's top ten most embarrassing moments in the English theatre over the last ten years most of them would be of people trying to be optimistic and positive — you know, the end of the agitprop play when the actors having shown yet another great working-class defeat, stand with clenched fists singing a song about how it'll be all right next time, which is the moment when many people crawl under their seats, often never to come out again.

Picking up the Brechtian injunction that the theatre as part of a changing society has to participate in that change, what do you expect from your own plays? Do they reflect the reality of the situation — or in what ways do they contribute to changing it?

I used to think that they contributed to the change one hundred per cent. The function of a play like *Rent, or Caught in the Act* was to contribute to the organization of the fight back against the 1971 Housing Finance Act. I've now lost the script, which I'm a bit sad about because there are some nice moments in it which I could re-read and enjoy, but in a sense it doesn't matter, because the Act's *been* repealed, so the question no longer arises. Peter Weiss has said that when Brecht was writing in the 'thirties the choice was very clear — between fascism and communism. And that seemed to be the clear choice to thousands and millions of people throughout Europe. What's happened since has made the choices much more difficult. Of course one *is* providing theatrical ammunition, but I think the nature of that ammunition has, for me anyway, changed. It is more self-critical, in the sense of being critical of the movement of which I am part. I'd put it quantitively rather than qualitatively: the influence the theatre has is slower but deeper than I thought it was four or five years ago.

Destiny — and inevitably one keeps returning to it — has had a fairly profound influence, but, as I've said, it made a greater impact on the public imagination through theatre productions seen by about 20,000 people than in its television production seen by four million. The central point of the play being that there is no God-given reason why a national socialist movement should not arise in Britain. By virtue of becoming national socialists, people do not suddenly grow horns — indeed, it is possible for people one recognizes and sympathises with to set off on the dark and dangerous road to that ghastly and pornographic political ideology. I hope the play by treating that problem seriously got that point across, or contributed to getting it across.

I can only say that when I sit down to write a play the first question remains, and I think will always remain, what do I want to say? Which means, what do I want people who see it to think? I don't think that's the question that the archetypal 'reflective' writer asks in quite the same way. Maybe I've become more modest in my view of what the theatre can do but I don't think I've become any more modest in terms of what *I* want to do.

15
Snoo Wilson

the theatre of light, space, and time

The youngest of the writers interviewed in this volume, Snoo Wilson, like David Edgar, was at university in 1968 — although, in his own wry judgement, his 'political beliefs and opinions were lamentably slow to develop'. In so far as they are now identifiable, they seem to be sustained by a sort of anti-institutional philosophy rather than by any familiar dogmatism — a philosophy which questions, as do the plays, the conventionally-drawn boundaries of the 'exterior' and the 'interior' worlds.

It is open to debate in what proportions Snoo Wilson's abiding distrust of large-scale, establishment companies and the apparent opacity of his writing have combined to keep his plays out of the mainstream theatre. Even his commissioned work tends to end up anywhere but in its first-intended home: as he says, he gets the feeling of 'writing for one specific group of people who, as you approach them, manuscript outstretched, disappear into the mist and reform somewhere else'. Rather like the themes of a play by Snoo Wilson.

And so Wilson — another of the 'Portable playwrights' of the early-'seventies — more than most of the dramatists in this volume has largely remained a writer for the developing alternative theatre movement, its venues, and its audiences. These, though not readily classifiable by social class or political creed, have been notably more receptive than 'mainstream' theatregoers to his idiosyncratic style — which might best have been described as surreal, were it not for the inexorable logic with which its verbal and visual connections are pursued.

Whether in the early Blowjob, *apparently a skinhead thriller which dissolves into a nightmare of exploded expectations; or* The Everest Hotel, *from the mid-'seventies, where three Liverpudlian girls set out from a remand home to save the world from communism by forming a pop group at the summit of Everest; or the more recent* The Glad Hand, *in which the lost verities of the Wild West are sought by a millionaire aboard an oil tanker in the Bermuda Triangle: the tone of voice is utterly distinctive, and in some ways more truly reflective than Wilson's more overtly political contemporaries of the brainwashed logic through which the global village sustains its global village idiocies.*

As with David Edgar's prolific output, many of Snoo Wilson's two dozen or so plays have remained in some obscurity since their first productions. So when assistant editor Malcolm Hay joined Clive Barker and myself to talk with Wilson in January 1980, we were anxious to put this lesser-known work in its proper perspective. But we began, again as with David Edgar, by commenting on the unexpected orthodoxy of his upbringing as the son of a schoolteacher at Bradfield College, where Wilson himself was educated — on half fees, he explained, 'so it was a struggling *middle-class background'. We asked whether having a father as schoolteacher had had much influence upon him.*

Oh, yes, I think so. My father is well read, beside me, but very eccentric. He was the English master at Bradfield College for some time, and my mother later became headmistress at a girls' school. So the background is heavily schoolmasterly. And I did a lot of reading — *Gone with the Wind* when I was ten — and typically a kind of interiorized imagination is the result.

You went on to the University of East Anglia to read English.

It sounds very standardized, but in fact I hardly had any A-Levels. I more or less talked my way into university, which was the first kind of boost for me. Wonderful to escape school.

Did you get involved in drama there?

Yes. I did revues. I performed on the Edinburgh Festival fringe. I wrote a revue called *Girl Mad as Pigs*, and I wrote a play presented at the Student Drama Festival, called *Ella Daybellefesse's Machine*. Monomaniac stuff, lots of it very influenced by Beckett. It was an attempt to make epic theatre.

Beckettian epic theatre?

Oh yes, the sub-plots were! It was the only way I could put it together, because I had a number of scenes and so I sort of assembled them, then gave it to Jonathan Powell to direct — and he directed it with panache and misgiving. It didn't get into the finals, or whatever we wanted. But it was reasonably popular: it was quite an event in the university.

And you were there in the annus mirabilis, 1968. What was it like to be at East Anglia in 1968?

Well, it was a very rich, bourgeois university. There were, *are* a lot of cars, and it doesn't draw from a working-class-upward-mobile area, hardly at all. I think the working-class students there had a hard time. I remember the music more in 1968 than any kind of generalized political attitude on the campus. Most of the people who were involved in drama were politically very immature — I may just be projecting my own political immaturity, but I think it was true of a lot of people. I wasn't involved in anti-Vietnam War demonstrations because I was still coming out of the water, really. My political beliefs and opinions were lamentably slow to develop.

You got an upper second?

I was a schoolmaster's son — I didn't have the courage to fail in a really noisy way. I'd already decided I wasn't going to have a job, in a conventional sense, so it was only polite to behave properly for as long as possible, before letting the side down. A friend of mine, Tony Bicât, whose brother I'd been at school with a long time ago, started Portable Theatre, and it sounded a bit like the sort of things I'd been working on in university. I did my audition piece, which was my adaptation of Virginia Woolf's *Between the Acts*. This was after finals, and David Hare and Tony Bicât came down and stood around — it was at Essex University, we'd taken it there for a couple of performances, and one of the actors who was hitching didn't turn up. And so I had to propel myself to the centre of my own drama, not knowing any of the lines: the characters would shunt me around, and give me the lead-in to the next line. And subsequently I went to work with Portable Theatre — not, I hasten to add, as an actor. So, in a higgledy-piggledy way, that was how I entered the theatre, which is my real vocation and my teacher.

In retrospect, one of the fascinating things about Portable Theatre is the very different kinds of writers who emerged from it — David Hare and Howard Brenton and yourself. You obviously found some sort of common mould there within which to operate?

You could do stuff that people wouldn't bug you about. There wasn't anybody on your back. For instance, neither my *Pericles* nor *Pignight* were plays in which the others were particularly interested — they couldn't actually see the necessity for putting them on, and yet there was no kind of struggle, because there was no structure, really. There were two directors and me. If the budget allowed, you'd go out and do plays. It was hard work and quite frustrating. But you did learn about theatre audiences. You got lots of different audiences, different assumptions, and different theatres, all of which knocked the edges off your plays. You learnt about structure — that your intentions have to be realized in a specific way or not at all if they're going to get across.

Were Charles the Martyr *and* Device of Angels *done by Portable Theatre?*

Device of Angels was done by Portable. That was the first play I wrote after I left university. It's a four-hander — a science-fiction play, and just a dreadful balls-up. I was actually much happier, and came to a much more satisfactory conclusion with the kind of material I was writing for a small touring show, with *Pericles*. *Charles the Martyr* was a show I was originally going to write for Freehold, but they didn't want it in the end. The University of East Anglia Theatre Group did it as an NUS entry, and did it very badly, as I remember. It was about the failure of heroism — the title refers to the Charles the Martyr Church in Norwich, where he's treated as a martyr.

Why Pericles?

Because I think it's a lousy play. It was a bit like *Between the Acts* — if you've got a very weak classic you can get in there and cart away some of the bricks for building another structure. In the original there is a certain heroic rant to the words, which are wildly variable in quality because there were so many authors. You can treat the words as cement and restructure them round imagistic bricks. It's quite interesting. You actually follow the basic plot reasonably closely till you turn it on its head at the end. It's picaresque. Pericles simply goes to one place, then another. He doesn't accumulate psychological insights as he goes.

Were you prolific at that time? Was it a matter of actually needing to get the plays down on paper?

Well, that was why *Device of Angels* was so bad. But I didn't have the vaguest idea what to write *about*. I suppose I could have written about a lot of things, but in the end you write about what obsesses you, and in one sense, you know, I was getting rid of a lot of cultural ghosts. I think you are obliged to do that if you have my kind of background, with the family tediously quoting Shakespeare round the table, before you can make enough space to operate in your own terms.

How did Pignight *come about?*

Well, I had this deliciously nasty idea about pigs. My uncle kept a farm, and he had a piggery with two storeys. It was a farm building in a granary, and the pigs would look out of the top window. My uncle had this contract to supply a construction team who were working on a dam up the road with milk in exchange for swill. The milk would go off in the churns, to make tea and things, and the swill would come back — it was ham sandwiches very often, and the pigs would eat it. I was fascinated by these closed cycles. This was when I was very young — I was ten — and I gradually developed this . . . piggy idea. The other source for *Pignight* is in fact a publisher's logo — I can't remember which one it is, but it's a picture of the perfect servant, which is in fact a boar's head with the mouth sealed so it can't talk, the boar's head is on top and he's a man underneath. I used to see this and have nightmares about it. So I had a very big thing about pigs running for a long time, and I was able to get rid of it in *Pignight*.

It is a fairly common feature in your plays that you happily warp time in order to find a different approach to the narrative line. Pignight's *the first play in which that seems to happen.*

I think I probably learned how to do that from *Christie in Love*, which I think is a wonderful play. Also, it's part and parcel of an asyntactic version of events, because you're throwing images up on the screen, as it were, one by one, and you're not necessarily committed to following one with another. You can be *obsessive* about particular things. You can return and look at them from different angles, which is something which has always interested me. It's as if the past were a series of stills — like holograms, which you can examine from any angle. That's always interested me.

The demands on the audience are very much increased in Pignight *because of the sheer density of that play. There are so many threads and ideas running through it — not just the theme of the pigs, but the mentally retarded farmworker, the grey, political farmer in the background, the Portable playwright criminal element . . . What was it about that theme of criminality which was so fascinating?*

What was the film? *Performance.* I was very much attracted by *Performance.* There were the Krays about that time — you realized that there were all these people lurking, if not in our midst, then in somebody else's midst. There was this surrogate society, and they didn't need anybody. I think that's a good metaphor for the kind of plays which we wanted to write.

Blowjob *is in fact a much more conventionally constructed play — at least, you begin to think it will be a conventional play, but then it turns.*

I was writing the girl student in that play as a sort of anti-Laingian example of somebody who actually was mad — whom it wasn't possible to reach by *any* conventional means, even though she knew Laing's language, she knew all about the language of schizophrenia. As the Mafia say, she was just like a torpedo — she went in there unaffected by anything like social norms. But as a character she was less satisfying than Smitty, the German boy in *Pignight.* Because his fit comes again — he *has to* rehearse or replay history. His madness is a result of historically being dissociated from so many different things and being bashed around. I think the two things are not the same at all, but I find it much more satisfying to write about a closed circle than an open one. I've never been happy structurally with *Blowjob* in that sense.

Have you found that, given the anti-traditional form of many of your plays, they pose problems for the actors?

Oh, yes. Problems with motivation, and so on. I had a lot of problems with the actor playing Freud in *Vampire*, for instance, trying to work out what would motivate his character to come on. Of course, if you don't have a sense of the syntax of the play, and where it should break and become something else, that's a great difficulty. But once actors have got that, once they're prepared to go along with the basic premise, then it's fine, because they realize that the more they go with it the easier it becomes, and makes sense in itself. It needs a certain attitude. It's not too much of a problem now because actors are used to playing filmic clips, but starting off it was an enormous problem. I remember two of the actors who were in *Pericles* trying to leave after the first day's rehearsal because they said, 'The play doesn't make any sense at all'. Had to hold them to their contract. In the end they went along with it.

Were you trying to wean actors and audiences into these different kinds of expectations with The Pleasure Principle? *It's not quite such a demanding play — it does satisfy a few expectations before it lets them down again.*

It's a much more conscious attempt to cope with the different problems. This was me escaping from working on *England's Ireland*, which was really a big downer for me — I could see it not working the way I wanted it to, and I was bitterly disappointed at the lack of imaginative fire. I thought I was in a position to explain to people what I was doing. So I hoped in *The Pleasure Principle* that I was going to be able to define the middle spectrum of assumptions — about magic representation —with the partly rationalized ideology which I had developed about the kind of things I wanted to put on to make a world on stage. I'm proud of the play — it explodes assumptions.

It was written, back-to-back, as it were, with *Vampire*, and *Vampire* got on first. They're both assaults on the same thing, and on two putatively different audiences. *The Pleasure Principle* was written for the Royal Court downstairs. As it happened, the designer made a loving replica of the Royal Court downstairs in the Theatre Upstairs! The production had nice reviews. David Hare, who directed it, straightened it out a lot, stopped the limbs flailing around, and it made sense to people whose demands are usually literal. It did very well. Nobody's ever done it again. But *Vampire* was meant to be a touring show, with those assumptions of black drapes and minimal staging. In fact the last thing it is is minimal — we had a giant van to take it all around in!

Are you really talking about writing for different theatres, or different stages, or different conditions?

Different performers, I think, although they're not as dissimilar now as they seemed at the time. With *Vampire* I was writing for the Paradise Foundry performers, who were three men and three women. So I had to write a play for three men and three women, which I wanted to do at that time — write more for women, especially. So the rhetorial structures start to rearrange themselves accordingly. *The Pleasure Principle* is a joke about Freud's idea that there was a pleasure principle and a reality principle — it was about people trying to have fun. I know there are a lot of miserable buggers, and those are the types who really look seriously for fun.

You can take the first act almost as if it were a play by David Hare, and then suddenly the form breaks.

Well, they start chopping the walls down, don't they? I mean, literally: the metaphor for all the destruction of the parameters which have been initially set up. The husband is going mad, so you take down the proscenium wall. With *The Beast*, again, I thought I was building this bridge from the kind of language play which they were doing at the RSC, and in fact it was quite popular — a lot of warlocks came to see it!

Why did you want to write about that particular Satanic group?

Well, Crowley was a much misunderstood hippie before his time, and I'd become interested in him when I read his autobiography and a lot of other stuff besides. It seemed to me that his 'discoveries' about the natural world were 'magical' parallels to the kinds of discoveries about the unconscious which Freud and Jung were making. Very roughly, he is a contemporary of theirs — they are figures in a historical landscape, on the go at the same time. But Freud and Jung got kicked upstairs, and Crowley's been kicked downstairs. I was interested in rehabilitating him as a human being, so the play was intended to be a celebration of his failure as a messiah. Whereas it was widely believed that I was actually doing a *News of the World* exposé of the disgusting things which Aleister Crowley did, I was actually trying to make them explicable.

The worst problem about him was that he could never discover whether he was a magician or a gent: he always fell between two stools. So he suffered from problems of seedy gentility to the end, because that was the problem of the society from which he came. And yet I think the character has enormous dignity all the same. I'd like to see it played with dignity.

The interest in magic in The Beast *continued in* Vampire, *didn't it?*

Vampire is supposed to be like a speed-run through a hundred years of history, and it's a magical play in that sense. And yet the emphasis is not specifically on the magical — the emphasis is on how things transmute, how ideas are transmuted. And all the time, while this is happening, people's ideas about the world are changing, and other changes are going on as well because they're living in a universe which isn't totally in their grasp at any particular time. At the end of the nineteenth century people went to mediums and things: they really were up against this brick wall, and they were going to bang a hole in it and stick their heads through and everything was going to be *explained*.

The structure of that play is three acts set roughly fifty years apart, each of which reinterprets the concept of vampirism for its specific age. Did it actually come to you in quite such a neatly compartmentalized fashion?

It came all of a piece, actually, and I'll never know how I found out so much about Welsh vicarages! There are bits in that play which are hasty and imagistic — but there are other things which go very deep in me, like the whole concern with the First World War. But I wasn't able to write about it at length because I was concerned with creating a roller-coaster rather than making something which explored a particular situation. I wasn't interested in the situations themselves, I was interested in the assumptions about the situations which could be seen, as it were, through a series of different sieves, changing all the time. This element of flux is what discomfits people, because they want a firm base. The only firm base is the narrative line, which doesn't stop.

Wasn't Soul of the White Ant *written as a substitute third act for* Vampire?

Yes, that was my act of conscience for South Africa. Although you can't see the effects, it was a play for which I paid a researcher to get books for me to read up about South Africa. None of it appeared in the play, but it gave me enough confidence to write about another country.

Of course they never did it in South Africa. Dusty Hughes, who had been theatre editor at *Time Out*, and had planned a film version of *Pignight* with me, had gone to the Bush Theatre, and was looking for plays. So I rewrote it for him. It's very nice that South Africans say it's accurate, but probably I tend to write about the kind of human beings that are the same everywhere. You make assumptions about human beings, and then if you have a little bit of an ear for the language, you can cobble yourself into the world they live in for the space of the action. In fact, there are details that are definitely wrong — for instance, a town as small as the one they're meant to be living in wouldn't have its own newspaper. But that's not the main thrust of the thing, which was to write about how people are co-existing with a very old culture, and the strains which they're undergoing.

You're not afraid to tread a fairly dangerous formal and structural minefield, yet you feel the political one is too dangerous to enter into?

I would rather approach it from a structural point of view. By restructuring the semiology of people's political awareness, you can get to an understanding of how they got to that particular point. If you then want to involve yourself in a judgement on them. . . well, *Blowjob* does make assumptions that somehow bits of society can be cut off in watertight compartments. You can't get in, the overall impression is of things which are polymorphous, rather than of people's generalized ideas about culture, which is of a stem which things cling to, and which has got a top.

Can you say a little bit about the use of songs and music in the plays? Songs erupt occasionally, and particularly in The Everest Hotel — *was that simply to utilize the talents of the people concerned?*

No, they had to teach themselves how to pluck guitars and so on. I've always been interested in that point in musicals when people grab the microphone and you suddenly hear the crashing of gears and the thing gets into a different dimension. *The Everest Hotel* is so off-hand you can sort of fall off into a song at any time. So you benefit sometimes from free association, when the play is destructuralized in that sense.

But in fact you use music relatively infrequently.

Yes, it's mostly recorded stuff. Except for *England, England*. That is about the Kray twins, one's mad and the other's sane, or rather one gets madder, and they bust their way into influence and power and are taken away. It was unacceptable as a musical to large numbers of people, who stayed away in droves. Musicals are expensive, and people don't want to come and see musicals about the Krays, unless they say the things that they want to hear before they come in. It was done at the Jeannetta Cochrane as a Bush Theatre production, but if it had been done at the Bush we would have been better off, actually.

The Bush is the theatre that you've had most connection with, apart from Portable?

Well, I've been very lucky to have a good working relationship with Dusty Hughes. A lot of the things which happened in *Soul of the White Ant* were originally Dusty's editing ideas, which I incorporated. And when he did the stage version of *A Greenish Man,* with the little girl dancing on the table — everybody said, typical Snoo Wilson touch. In fact it was Dusty's.

Was that the only television play that actually got onto the screen?

No, there were two earlier half-hour plays. One was called *Trip to Jerusalem,* and there was a very much earlier one about a rock group audition called *Swamp Music.*

The early plays you wrote for television weren't accepted. Why were those accepted?

It's very difficult, because there are millions of plays which aren't done for television and there are always 'good reasons' for them not being done. The criteria for refusal are whimsical: they're usually that the play would displease somebody. I would like to have a good working relationship with a television company which would let me do what I wanted to do and make my own mistakes, like in theatre. But unfortunately television companies are either just downright commercial, or in competition with commercial companies, and there's very little room for formal experiment, except in light comedy — which is very difficult to get into.

Wasn't Elijah Disappearing *originally written for television?*

Yes, but they wouldn't do it because the characters weren't speaking like Charlton Heston — they were speaking normally. I tried to do a rehabilitation job on Elijah, because he's very much in the back seat, whereas in Jewish hagiography he's second only to Jesus and Moses, he is definitely one of the big ones. He brought down fire from heaven, and he went up in a chariot of fire. So he's obviously the sort of figure who's been overshadowed by what's happened since, and he also suffers from depression, so I have great sympathy for him. At one stage I had to learn the Second Book of Kings off by heart, so there's a lot of Biblical stuff which came out also in *Flaming Bodies.* They are just wonderful stories, and I like making them anachronistic, I like rejigging the Bible. It doesn't work for everybody of course. People get indignant that they haven't all got the right clothes on.

The other driving force in writing the play was to try and rationalize my own ideas about the tradition of the Sorcerer's Apprentice, which you get in European popular literature and also in Castaneda. You get the magician, and you get the person who's supposed to be learning from him, it's a cultural archetype — Zen Buddhists have it as well. The master is always fencing with somebody, slapping them to teach them some kind of self-awareness which they don't possess. And this is taken off in *Elijah Disappearing* as being part of the prophetic tradition — actually, it was hard work, being a prophet, and it was even harder work to bring up your successor to run the shop when you'd left. The sheer practical demands of the situation were never touched on in the Bible at all. Elijah just walks in, literally, out of the woods and there he is! There's vast tracts of heroic narrative with huge gaps in them, and I'm interested in reinterpreting these in a psychological sense.

Take Jezebel the scarlet woman — she's a wonderful case in point. She's absolutely minimally described in the Bible except for her death, which is described in gory detail as vengeance against an unbeliever. I think this is a perfect example of a linguistic semiotic paternalist tradition squeezing out everything else because Jezebel was an unbeliever. She followed the Golden Calf and Baal, and she was a woman and she was married to Ahab, so she had the King's ear, so they had to get rid of her in this terribly spectacular way — blood! terminal menstres! — because that's really what they most fear: counsel from another direction. It's what any centralist organization fears most — another point of view.

That's the root of a lot of my politics, for what they're worth. Governments traditionally have subsumed to themselves for their delight and support the sciences and the arts and religion. Look at the fuss there was over biology, with Darwin. That's not news any more, but it shook people to their very roots. In fact it had *nothing* to do with the way the country was being run, except it cast doubt on the very institutions which people stood for. And where did they stand then?

Could you say something briefly about The Language of the Dead is Tongued with Fire, *which I find an exquisite small play . . .*

Well, I wrote it for Julie Walters, who was so good in *The Glad Hand*. It was written for a short slot — it's like a short story idea. The basis of the play was this idea of an entity, this little pellet of light, very heavy, something unexplained in conventional physics, which appears in a suburban sitting room, and they follow it down and destroy the house in the process. They pursue the inexplicable and everything comes apart. The inexplicable for the woman is the unreachable — that's to say, she wants to be reunited with her dead husband, so it's like an *Orpheus in the Underworld* with role-reversal. And she actually manages to do it in the play, and they recreate one of their very boring evenings, with her husband watching television.

People's desire to be reunited with their departed is always thought of as being on the high point of ecstasy, whereas in fact there may not be many insights to be gained if you do manage it. That's the joke about the play, because the great discovery for me, that paved the way to being able to write *Flaming Bodies*, was that it was possible to take a person — in both these cases women — and get them to take off on their own, to get them to tell their stories. Actually you can go anywhere then, if you follow your nose about what works dramatically and if you can provide enough signposts to take people with you.

My plays are full of 'thirties B-movies type signposts. The signs may be changing all the time in these plays, but they do *have* signposts. One of the things I've learnt is that you have to sign what you're doing when you're doing it, because people aren't automatically attuned to the kind of changes which are going on. They may think they're watching something else. If I've learned anything, it's been to do with scoring the script. But you can't score it too much or the magic disappears. I mean in the sense of fascination. The fun of it disappears.

You make fairly rigorous technical and scenic demands in your writing — the car coming through the window in Flaming Bodies, *for instance.*

The technical problems of *Flaming Bodies* aren't that huge. The effects are quite flamboyant, but they're not impossible. You need a stage crew of three people, which given the size of the cast isn't a lot to demand of any theatre. The rest is down to good design, and I think it's right to stretch designers because they never are stretched in the theatre. And you must try to extend people's idea of what is possible. *Flaming Bodies* went round the Royal Court — everybody there read it, and their response was not 'what an interesting play', but 'how can we get a car through the window?'Now, if that is your first response, then obviously the play has passed you by. The thing is, if the play is interesting enough to do, you can do it and the design will have its own internal coherence. The design of *Vampire* in New York was very minimal, but the acting was so good that the minimalist aspect of the design didn't actually bug anybody.

I seem to remember reading that one of the seeds for Flaming Bodies *was your seeing the recent revival of* Inadmissible Evidence *at the Royal Court?*

Yes. That is a picture of the male menopause. I like the play very much — I even wrote to John Osborne, and he replied very nicely to the letter, but he wouldn't come to see *Flaming Bodies*. Osborne, I think, is interested in judging the characters in a cultural context. He's not interested in things outside that. I've lived through so many cultural collapses, inside and outside, I'm interested in pre- or post-cultural analysis — the state of waiting for another door to open is more representative of our culture than a photo of someone passing through. After all, it's only another waiting room on the other side. We're told we're living in historic times, but there's no consensus about which ephemera are going to be shot and stuffed for the kids to be told 'this is history'.

Flaming Bodies is almost a monologue for much of the action . . .

The play practically wrote me. I'd been stewing it for some time. I started off with two people, then the main character appeared. I realized I wouldn't need anybody else but those three characters — certainly not in the dream, where everybody could play everybody else. It actually made for terrific structural integrity, only using those three people. I started off writing big plays — *Ella Daybellefesse's Machine* was a play which is about one person's world, and the contradictions of one person's world — and the conflicts involved in having three people, all with their own worlds sitting in the same room, are enormous. Conflict is the stuff of drama.

Do you feel as though you're the odd person out in your generation of playwrights?

Oh, I don't know about that. I share a lot of assumptions. That Howard Barker play, *Love of a Good Man*, I thought was great. I don't feel totally on my own, though I sometimes think I'm completely up a gum tree because I'm doing things which don't go along with a lot of common assumptions.

It seems to me that there's a consistent element running through all the plays of fantasy, being pursued with an inexorable logic time and time again. You start from a basic situation — you pursue it absolutely logically — and it ends in fantasy. It seems to have some philosophical basis in the way you see the world.

I'm saying it's not really solid. The world, that is. You have the 'interior' and the 'exterior' world, right, which everybody would agree existed, although they wouldn't necessarily agree about the boundaries of them — we exist with a foot in each camp, as cultural beings. And I was rather relieved at the end of *Flaming Bodies* that we were able to get back into normal, boring, repressive, violent, sex-and-drugs-obsessed Los Angeles, out of all the wild dream stuff. By the strength of free ethical choice. The character decides not to do it this way any more. She actually decides not to be bonkers. That's *my* dramatic fiction: I think there *are* people who can't make those decisions. But you can invent a situation where you — she — *can* make a free ethical choice. I think it's nice, that. I'm glad I've been able to write a play where people make ethical choices. People in *Glad Hand* don't make ethical choices. They just crash on.

16

Howard Barker

the small discovery of dignity

Howard Barker's Love of a Good Man *was the only play actually named by Snoo Wilson in the previous interview as making him feel not 'totally on my own'. It's certainly true that Barker, like Wilson, is a writer who rarely makes concessions to the conventional expectations of an audience — though, as it happens, his use of more 'public' themes, and the tone of urban* angst *he often captures, have enabled some of his later plays to find a sympathetic home in the RSC's Warehouse. And his most recent work,* No End of Blame — *a stage version of the play discussed in this interview under its television title,* All Bleeding — *found its way to the main stage of the Royal Court.*

If Snoo Wilson typically persuades through the insistent logic of dream, Barker as often does so through the sheer mythic force of his writing, and the energy of that succession of craggy characters who clump with curious dignity across the barren, battle-scarred landscapes of the plays. Again, though, a certain receptiveness is required: and just as Wilson hoped, forlornly, to woo an orthodox Royal Court audience with The Pleasure Principle, *so Barker, in* Stripwell, *carefully set out to write a graciously witty play for the middle-class gatherings a commission from Michael Codron appeared to assume. But, as he reflects here, 'the play was too mean for that kind of audience to be nourished'. He was 'quite glad' to have found that he couldn't work the trick.*

Thus, although Wilson and Barker are of much the same age and antecedents as Edgar and Brenton, stylistically they appear more like prophets of a theatrical generation yet to come into its own — perhaps the 'new theatre voices' of the 'eighties. Certainly, the twelve years which separated the politico-theatrical watershed of 1956 from 1968 had again ticked away by 1980, and more than one theatrical institution — including his own — was approaching that ten-year danger period of which Peter Hall had warned. But, predictably, the cuts in Arts Council funding, which affected Theatre Quarterly *among some forty other recipients in December 1980, were aimed at centres of innovation rather than established 'excellence'.*

It was in the August of 1980 that Malcolm Hay and I went down to Howard Barker's home in Brighton, and the interview which follows appeared in Theatre Quarterly's *fortieth issue — which ended, whether or not for good, our own decade of publication. We asked Howard Barker how he had begun writing plays.*

With a trio of radio plays. When I was at Sussex University I'd written three or four bad novels. University intensified my tendency to introspection, and the novel was the obvious form for me. Someone said the dialogue was the best part of these and urged me to write for radio. My first radio play was *One Afternoon on the Sixty-Third Level of the North Face of the Pyramid of Cheops the Great,* a half-hour comedy about a slaves' strike during the building of the pyramids. I was encouraged to write a couple more. These were *Henry V,* where the king says that anyone who fights with him that day shall be his brother. A common soldier takes him up on it. He calls on him in England some years afterwards and finds he's not as welcome as he expected. The other was *Herman with Millie and Mick,* a parable about the work ethic. It's been done on radio stations all over the world. They are original, clever, young man's plays.

You weren't particularly active in the theatre while you were at university?

No, not at all. I'd come from a stable working-class background — relatively prosperous and socially ambitious, with my parents who believed passionately in the idea of a 'good education' — but theatre played no part whatsoever. My school was a philistine South London grammar school, so 'O' and 'A' level texts were the only plays I was acquainted with there. But a few of us — regarded warily by teachers and the bulk of the school — used to improvise a satirical/surrealist serial every lunchtime in the back of a disused army truck. We acted characters we despised, like Dr. Barnardo, Ernest Shackleton, Kennedy, Christ, and James Bond. We had diabolical figures too, like Crippen and Hitler. We never saw ourselves as making theatre, though. So when the thing ran out of steam and died, no one thought the next thing to do would be to prepare a script. I suppose the whole flavour of what we were doing was influenced by the rising satire boom, but we were very vicious, with all the cruelty of schoolboys stuck in the particularly oppressive non-culture of a grammar school.

Then I went to university and read History. I found it a shock, a vast and alien environment peopled by baying public schoolboys. I began a process of withdrawal which made me suspicious of, and ignorant of, the politicization of 1968. This was peculiar because I had very strong political instincts. I had a fundamental Stalinist education from my father who was a shop steward, and a very developed sense of class — class conflict if not class struggle.

No One Was Saved *was the first of your plays to be staged?*

Yes. Once I'd shown *Cheek* to the Royal Court, they asked whether I had any other plays that might be suitable for a season for schools that Pam Brighton was mounting, so I gave her *No One Was Saved.* It was done for the schools programme but the run was extended because it was so successful.

Was the play a direct response to seeing Edward Bond's Saved?

I'd gone to *Saved* on the strength of a review we'd read saying that this was life in south London epitomized. We just didn't think that that was so — we didn't understand much about what Bond was trying to do with the language of the play. That was why I wrote *Cheek*, and also why I took up the gang of youths from *Saved* and used them in *No One Was Saved*.

What relationship did the play have to the John Lennon song Eleanor Rigby?

That was fundamental. I was groping blindly towards some description of the parasitic relationship between art and experience. The song had a rare concern with despair and defeat — very unlike a modern pop song — but I was always suspicious of the Beatles, and Lennon in particular: all the financial manipulation and posturing with maharishis struck me firmly then as an indictment of the 'sixties. So I created a fantasy in which Lennon had actually known this girl Eleanor Rigby, who was not an old woman as I thought the song implied, and served her up as song material.

It's very clearly a despairing play — what comes over is a lack of hope. You don't allow one small gesture of optimism.

That ties in with *Saved* again. When Bond and others claimed that the end of *Saved* was optimistic because of the action of mending the chair in the last scene, I never found the argument very convincing. The image of hope is dwarfed by having been given so much evidence against it. So I wasn't able or prepared to make a similar gesture in my play. The whole question of pessimism in my plays comes down to that, really — my inability to manufacture optimism out of situations that are amazingly dark.

Your characters do have a capacity to be fairly thoroughly defeated in one way or another. Laurie, in Cheek, *is the next in line . . .*

Yes. *Cheek* is a very personal play, almost an autobiographical play. It's as near to naturalism as I've got, although the language is clearly stretched. I regarded what happens to Laurie as a fair interpretation of experience, certainly of the lives of the people I knew in the bit of south London that I lived in. Some of the characters in that play are people I knew.

Right from the start you seem not to have had any problems with creating a dramatic structure, with organizing material into scenes.

It's extraordinary you should say that. I was thrown out of a very successful agency for failing to understand the laws of structure, whatever they may be. And Michael Billington is under the impression I can't do it, either. In fact I do it well, and have got a good deal of pleasure from arranging quite complex plots, which is one aspect of it at least.

Where does the idea for a play come from?

I tend to start a play from an idea about a character rather than about an event. That's certainly characteristic of the earlier plays, and even of a play such as *The Hang of the Gaol*. I also know what tensions will exist in a play, what the general situations will be. But the motive force is almost always a character. Sometimes I may carry around an idea of a character for a long while and never find a situation or a place for him. With *The Hang of the Gaol*, for instance, I'd had the character of Jardine in my head for a long time, but I had no particular use for him. Then I read about the fire at Chelmsford Prison and I saw a link.

How directly were you involved with the productions of the early plays?

Nothing like as closely as I wanted to be. By which I don't mean I was excluded. I was for a long time bedazzled and bewildered. There was the grotesque problem of seeing theatre as other people's property. It made me feel very alienated. And there was this very particular style and regime at the Royal Court which was unwelcoming. You were dealt the impression that it was a great privilege being there. I didn't know what the writer's function at rehearsals was, so I sat very quietly at the back and watched while Bill Gaskill directed the play and was thrilled by it in the event. But I very rarely spoke to the actors. It was a painful time for me, shame and pride coming in quick succession.

How consciously were you using the early plays to express particular viewpoints?

They express particular viewpoints, but without complexity. I placed the characters in *Edward, the Final Days* squarely in their social context, but only as subjects of lampoon, because I hated them and was offended by them. I am still deeply offended by society, and still hate as much, but the habit is no longer iconoclastic, as it was automatically then. It is a habit that is only now beginning to recede in my work, partly because I recognize the value of iconoclasm and feel a powerful reflex for it. It occurs in *The Love of a Good Man*, well and healthily, but in an entirely richer context. Plays like *Edward*, *Skipper*, or *Reach for the Sky*, spring from an uncontrolled antagonism. They are a heaving out of the pain of an oppressed English youth. In that period I was further from any feeling of involvement with my characters than at any time before or since. I began to feel that being involved with my characters at all was a weakness.

What was your own political thinking at the time?

I am never certain of the nature of my political thinking. It is easy to say you are a revolutionary socialist, but it is stale with cliché and a certain vanity. I knew that then, as now, I believed revolution necessary but unlikely. That tension is at the hub of my work.

You were never associated with any group, such as Portable Theatre, although some of your early plays — Alpha Alpha, *for example* — *seem very similar to the kind of work that Portable was producing.*

That's true. I was never even part of their group authorships. I don't know much about Portable's origins, but I'd imagine the impulses behind their work were very similar to mine. At one time I'd perhaps have liked the chance to work with them: I envied their solidarity, they had an armour. Knowing myself better now, I don't think it would have been possible for me. But the connections are unavoidable, because of a common subject matter and ideological base. But they were ahead of me, putting their theatre together long before I wrote a play.

There's an ambiguity in your early plays between the social context and the psychological context — particularly the theme of parental domination.

Yes. This must be why I am not a good political writer. There is a persistent upsurge of the personal into what superficially appears to be a didactic exercise, an eruption of private will and shameful motive. The parent-child relationship is strong in *Claw, That Good,* and *Edward,* too. In *Claw* there is a struggle for possession of Noel's soul, but it is actually social values that initiate the psychology. The mother's contempt for her husband, her loathing for his sexuality, is almost entirely because of his social failure, his inability to deliver her from the misery of a poor life. Eddie's Toryism, and sensitivity to disgust, is produced by his father's insistence on the general squalor of the human animal, which litters contraceptives on his tiny lawn. It is not unjust to see Toryism as a manifestation of life-hatred. And Rhoda's politics in *That Good* are wrong-radical, the outcome of a personal disgust. She is persistently mocking her mother's sexuality, and desperate for sensation. So, yes, all the political positions are mediated by psychology but not dictated by it.

Sexual relationships in your plays tend to be governed by selfishness and opportunism.

Yes, but also by social malformation. The weakening and distortion of sexuality and the mutilation of passion is identified socially. In *Claw,* Noel's desire for Angie is heightened, not lessened, by his discovery of her origins. They share a conspiratorial passion. But she is the victim of her own material circumstances. I am saying that class is the enemy of freedom in every respect, not least sexually. It's true that any potentially vivid sexual relationship is distorted by a social relationship which frustrates or murders it. At its worst, the sexual pleasure comes from this degradation. Nattress in *Birth on a Hard Shoulder* can only enjoy sex through degradation, like Gadsby in *Alpha Alpha.* Rhoda's sexual response to Godber is anything but spontaneous, is almost an act of social defiance. Some of the characters, rather than endure this deformation, make a sort of withdrawal — Hilary in *Birth* refuses to discriminate, and Jane in *Hang of the Gaol* simply retires.

How easy has it been to exist as a full-time writer?

I'm one of the few younger dramatists to survive through film writing, I think. *No One Was Saved* was filmed as *Made* with Carol White, a disastrous and painful experience which exposed to me the commercial degradation of the industry here, as far as the studios are concerned. I then scripted *Aces High*, whose theme reveals in comic clarity the absurdity of producer-power in an artistic enterprise. It involved converting *Journey's End* into a flying film. Of course all the power that play possessed — and it's not a play I like — was instantly dissipated, and you were left with a lot of public schoolboys flying over Surrey.

What of television?

The more seriously I've taken writing for television the less success I've had. And I've written well for it now, as the readings at the RSC have shown. This is a very painful irony. My first was *Cows* in 1972, a domestic story, very much an exercise in the existing Play for Today convention, I believed. I then wrote *The Chauffeur and the Lady,* and *Mutinies,* two half-hour studies in resentment. These were not much liked by the authorities there. Then *Prowling Offensive* was blue-pencilled. I submitted to this, in the wrong belief that it was better to say something than nothing, but even then they were out to ditch it. It was made and then abandoned, so the series it was meant to be a part of went out one short. I have become *persona non grata* in television. The terrible scandal of the drama department is not known to the public. There is good work there, in the bottom of steel cabinets.

Between the early satirical plays and Stripwell *and* Claw *there's a gap of a couple of years. Does that also reflect a time when you weren't writing?*

No. There have never been gaps when I wasn't writing. Looking back, it might have been better if there had been. I have to keep on working through until I've exhausted a certain kind of play, before I'm in a position to develop in some other direction — unlike some writers, who may not write a play for a couple of years and then produce one which isn't obviously connected with their previous work. I knew when I'd written *Claw* — it was written before *Stripwell* — that I'd made a definite advance, largely because of the third act, which I regarded as a triumph. It was almost a new form for me: in prose, with very long speeches — even longer to begin with than they are in the final text.

In that third act you also seem to be offering an interpretation of the action in a way that you deny to audiences in your earlier plays.

Yes. There is a withdrawal from the action on my part, too: it is less insistent. Nothing in the act relies on the shared assumptions that I have expected audiences to respond to in other acts. It was the beginning of a confidence to remove myself from a common ground. I dislike a play in which the dramatist overstates his intentions, making matters easy for his audience. It produces this rather unhealthy expectation that we should all know what it's about by the interval. To continually undermine the expected is the only way to really alter people's perceptions. Act three of *Claw* does this superbly, but other plays also attempt to defy an audience, to force it to struggle a little. This tension is what costs me a lot of support — people must have it all in their hands, but the effects of my work are always underneath, always tending to dissolve associations. *Love of a Good Man* perpetually dislocates.

Are Stripwell *and* Claw *companion pieces?*

I always think of them as mutually antagonistic. When Michael Codron first commissioned *Stripwell*, I deliberately chose to write a play for middle-class audiences. I wanted to get a play into the West End. I thought I could represent that familiar middle-class drawing-room milieu effectively enough to be successful in those terms. But the problems of the bourgeois individual were not problems I felt very strongly about. What I wrote was an attempt at a middle-class tragedy, and consequently it had all those values that sustain that kind of a play — a sweeping humanitarianism, elegant wit, a familiar situation. It involved tremendous self discipline. Some of the moments, I thought, were effective. I produced what I thought were a lot of elegant lines which would go down well in the West End. They didn't. Essentially, I suppose, the play was too mean for that kind of audience to be nourished by. I can't do a Simon Gray. I'm quite glad to have found that I can't.

In contrast, I was very concerned at one stage that *Claw* was too nakedly agitprop, that it might look crude in that respect — the way in which the father always holds the holy grail of political truth before him, and is proved right by the conclusion of the play. I was worried that that would look clumsy. There's nothing worse for an audience than knowing you can more or less predict how the relationships in a play will operate. With *Claw*, I not only think that you can't deduce what the ending will be, I don't even think you can deduce the second act on the evidence of the first. In act one, it looks as if the play will be a 7:84-ish tale of a working-class youth discovering the guts of society. The second act is very different, closer to *Stripwell* in its drawing-room elegance.

Do you feel there is an identifiable audience for which you are writing?

At one time I would have said that there was — the young radical audience. When I wrote *Edward, the Final Days,* I believed there was a young, united, euphoric audience hostile to Heath and Toryism, optimistic about the prospect of a Labour government under Harold Wilson. I knew who I was talking to, and we spoke the same language — especially since satire is a very easy language to use and understand, because there is little ambiguity involved. But as my work has become more complex, the appropriate responses to political issues have also become more blurred. We've seen the collapse of Labour as a viable source of change in our society, and I've reflected that in my work. You can't rely on that shared optimism any longer. I find now that I don't get very much support from critics on the Left.

So I'm no longer sure where my audience comes from. I do have a following, I'm aware of that, but who they are I'm not sure. It comes down to how well you articulate the political sense of your time. Because my work is not cohesively political, but I capture the bewilderment which is the common condition now. The fact that things are not tied down and easily explicable in my work is a virtue in that respect. The tension in the plays often comes from knowing what I don't like, what offends my sensibilities, but at the same time not being able to pose an alternative. I don't find that a weakness. I don't know that dramatists can pose alternatives.

There are character types which recur in your plays, even to the extent of some of them reappearing, like the two undertakers Hacker and Clout in Credentials of a Sympathizer *and* The Love of a Good Man.

Yes. In that case it was because *Credentials of a Sympathizer* was never produced, and an interesting relationship wasn't going to be used. The old Gocher figure in *Fair Slaughter* is a character from *Heroes of Labour*. I sometimes go back to characters if I feel that I haven't exhausted their possibilities. Sometimes a character with a very small role in one play will feature quite largely in another. And clearly there are other characters who are very similar to one another: you could link Jarrow in *Stripwell,* for example, with the sold-out Labour politician in *The Hang of the Gaol* — that kind of malleable Labour politician who is adept at exploiting opportunities, but in terror of change.

What about McPhee in That Good between Us?

McPhee is a rootless individual with vast resources of untapped humanity. His survival is not the ground for optimism in the play. Survival is never enough for that. But he has achieved certain insights, and we know he will go on surviving, if only because he is never the victim of an idea. All the other characters are governed by thorough notions. All McPhee has is a passion for contact, and this overcomes persistent betrayal. I think that is good going as optimism goes.

Have you been influenced by any other writers?

I have liked plays rather than writers. I have terrific respect for Charles Wood's *Dingo*. It's an important, seminal play, and he is a great master of language, a very underrated talent. I like Arden's *Musgrave,* some of Brecht. Shakespeare, of course. I say of course because you gauge his power from even a slight acquaintanceship. I hadn't seen *Hamlet* until this year. I was shocked at its structural weakness. I love him for the contempt he had for structure, formality. And of course, the work of my peers. As a body, it's very impressive — the break with naturalism, the re-annexation of ground lost in the theatre during its bourgeois period, the struggle towards new forms and language, the moral power. We have done a great deal, and will do more. Otherwise the influences have been from novels. I read Dickens and Hardy regularly, for example.

The chronological shifts from past to present that you have used in your more recent plays seem to go together with a search for some sense of historical development in the way that people have become disillusioned with society. Was Fair Slaughter *the first time that you used that technique?*

Yes. I used it extensively, too, in the television play *All Bleeding* and in the stage version of that. There are great problems in it, because such a long passage of time dissipates the degree of emotional commitment characters can expect. There's something in the unities. But history is a vastly important factor in my plays. It broods over most of my work, it lurks in the back of the characters' minds, and is a persistent justification for action. The right-wing characters invoke it continually (Fricker in *Loud Boy*, Nattress in *Birth on a Hard Shoulder*) and the left fret about its judgement (Stagg in *Hang*, Orbison in *That Good*). I'm very concerned about Europe, about its pain and its destiny. It's massively contradictory, full of agony, bent on suicide. In England the last thirty years have been years of defeat. Only recently have I come to believe in the possibility of overcoming.

What of Heaven?

I'd been interested for some time in the subject of those 'traitors' who, if they'd remained in this country instead of defecting, would have become leading figures of the establishment. That spectacle of the massive move to the left by upper-class figures in the 'twenties and 'thirties is something I find very powerful. In some ways their treason was ambiguous, in that there's no doubt that all of them might have expected to come back to England as members of some socialist commonwealth — which didn't happen. At the same time, although they were communists, they subscribed to many ruling-class attitudes. In Philby's book *My Secret War*, when he's explaining why he became a spy, he says that he was offered the chance to join the most elite corps in the world — the KGB. How could he refuse? That is the voice of a ruling-class Englishman, locating where power lies and capturing it. Then there are also the people who remained here, like Tom Driberg, who maintained a classic communist position but didn't really find any way of using it in our society. *Heaven* was about those two options: either to remain here, in the Labour Party, and become a gossip columnist, or to become an outright traitor.

Do you hope that the audience will sympathize with your characters?

I want my characters to earn the love of an audience. That is why I don't like

Stripwell, it's far too easy to like him. It's a bourgeois habit to insist on immediate identity, and left writers do it too. They place all their wit and sympathy with their hero, who becomes a strenuous voice of reason, knocking all the right targets. It's hard to like Noel Biledew, McPhee, Hacker, Erica, Downchild, but, because it's hard, they lodge the better.

With Fricker, though, in The Loud Boy's Life, *I never felt that he would be successful in gaining national power.*

I find Fricker — and Enoch Powell, on whom he is based, and all those people who over-reach — very interesting. He's placed in a context where he's made to look horrendous because of his colleagues, because of the company he keeps — all those obnoxious social types who cast a large shadow over him. He despises them and at the same time controls them with a malicious elegance.

In all the plays of mine that deal with English society — *The Loud Boy's Life, The Hang of the Gaol, That Good Between Us*, the play I'm writing about Tom Driberg — I've always hoped to create a complex picture, to cover as wide a scope, as many classes of people, as possible. I have the feeling that this play about Driberg will be the last of those plays. I think I've done a good job of describing our society. I can't go on doing it much longer.

In the television play All Bleeding *the character of the East European cartoonist presumably reflects that ambivalent feeling you described, which involves wanting to preserve the best of the British national identity?*

The character Bela misconceives what British freedom is all about. After a life in Europe, England in the 'thirties was rightly regarded as a haven of liberty, and only a fool disregards these freedoms now. It is the institutional life of England which is so fundamentally rotten, and that's why parliamentary change has been so grotesquely irrelevant. But the really defensible — the traditional culture of liberty — is vital. What Bela does in the stage version of the play is to insist on blame — and the worst aspect of humanism is its rejection of blame, the idea we are all guilty. A wicked, paralyzing posture.

Have you felt — or do you feel now — any particular attachment to any of the theatres where you've worked?

I've been on the move a lot — from the Royal Court to the Open Space and then on to The Warehouse. In many ways my work is probably more characteristic of the Warehouse style than anyone else's. The actors at the RSC mean a lot to me, and they know how to use my language very effectively. I can write on a scale that I like to write on. I hoped to graduate to the Aldwych — to have a second shot, after *Stripwell*, at filling a big house. After *The Love of a Good Man* I was confident that I was popular enough as a writer to manage that.

Do you write with a certain actor-audience relationship in mind?

Not often. I write with actors clearly in mind, and think about possible situations for presenting them. I have enjoyed working with Ian McDiarmid and conceived *Downchild* for him. Some actors I've had a long and stimulating history of working with. The great Roger Sloman, for example. I feel tremendous warmth for people who do my work well, go away and say I must do a part for him or her. Actually I am enthusiastic for myself, because they have done my work so well, and am re-inspired by them. Jill Baker did this in *The Loud Boy,* so did Donald Sumpter. But I could list so many brilliant performances in my work. I am a performance writer. Look at McDiarmid in *That Good,* or Pat Stewart in the same play, Clive Merrison in *Loud Boy,* Fulton McKay in *Hang of the Gaol.*

What particular demands do your plays make on actors?

A readiness to tackle quite difficult linguistic problems, and a vast amount of energy. The plays are in high gear all the time, there is little room to lean back. I probably don't get on with actors who work on psychology. Actors have to feel a 'type' quickly, and elaborate on that. Of course, comic ability, but not acting comic. It has always been good working with RSC actors, but it was interesting watching Max Wall in *Fair Slaughter,* too. Here was an actor with no formal training and little grasp of the play's ideology. But he grasped the dialogue naturally — it was completely truthful for him. He said lines in a way no trained actor would have come across. And I'm no naturalistic dialogue writer.

An actor can play the part quite successfully without necessarily agreeing with what you're saying?

There's a lot of lip-service paid to the idea of an actor *completely* comprehending a text. Naturally I would prefer that. But I don't think it's necessary. I have worked mainly with young actors, most of whom share my convictions. Actors more than anyone else in the theatre tend to like my work.

Do you feel frustrated that you haven't broken through to big stage productions?

It is rather frustrating after some ten years. I'd feel it more, though, if I weren't conscious of a very clear development in my work. The venues for large company plays are shrinking. The Warehouse, for example, doesn't appear to be that confident about its continuing existence as a venue for new plays. Perhaps dramatists will have to adjust to this situation — unless, that is, they're in favour at the National Theatre. The play I'm writing now only has nine characters.

I am disconcerted about the critical hostility I sense towards my work. I do feel that people I might have relied on for support a few years ago no longer supply it with the same readiness. Critics like Michael Billington or Irving

Wardle — that range of middlebrow critic — now seem to be actively hostile towards my work. But I'm not hostile towards the critics: there is a good role for them. I had a lot of respect for Harold Hobson: he was an enthusiast who would celebrate something new and interesting even when he didn't fully understand it. Every new generation of writers, every new form of theatre, requires a new theatre critic to write about it. Outside the pages of *Theatre Quarterly* and *Time Out,* the mainstream critics seem not to know how to deal with what's happened in the past ten years. Consequently they live a truly parasitic existence, in that they're discouraging public interest rather than arousing it.

How would you describe your own position now, after ten years writing?

Downchild is my final play on English society and politics. I hope I've made a significant contribution in describing a society and a time. I think, taken as a body, my 'English' plays amount to an indictment and a compulsive collection of writing.

But of course I cannot and do not want to go on doing this. I want to say my final piece on the Wilson era, which I hated — to nail that. After this, I sense a change of direction. I do not feel safe, partly because of the welter of critical hostility. I certainly don't intend to aim for more 'maturity', 'fair-mindedness' or any other of the weary baggage of critical humanism. I've never been interested in fair-mindedness, it's death in drama.

Ten years is a long time, but I have changed, I have got better. Morally, I am moving nearer to a sense of overcoming. But I develop slowly, over many plays. I feel, too, a move away from the 'populist' figures who have dominated my work, characters like Gocher in *Fair Slaughter,* Hacker in *That Good,* towards more intellectual heroes. I also feel the stirrings of some change in form, which cannot be thrust on a play, but comes out of failures. Every play is a failure on which you aim to build. If the form cannot contain your intention, you must break it. Finally, in retrospect, I am not happy with what I've done. I never am. I rejoice in the performance, but worry because I sense I have not written the play I thought.

Have you been happy with the designs for productions of your plays?

I've not always had the designs that I wanted. In some cases the flavour of the text has been interpreted much too literally. That has sometimes created an aura of melancholy and gloom which the actors have had to struggle to work against. One of the reasons why I despise setting scenes in rooms is because it always seems to produce a set of clichéd images on stage. I like props — I'm not that keen on sets.

Did reading history at university in any way provide you with tools for your writing?

It made me refuse the obvious in the political play, made me cautious, even suspicious, especially of crude political solutions. It's also given me a profound sense of European suffering. Anyone who knows something of Russia in this century is bound to be both deeply moved by suffering and ferocious at the cold war propaganda we are subjected to. History makes you angry.

In the past your work was often linked with that of Howard Brenton. Do you see any similarities?

I found it interesting to talk to him recently about the question of the optimism of the will and the pessimism of the intellect. I think that Howard is much more inclined now to invoke the former. The fact that he is and I'm not is perhaps because he's a better socialist than I am. Those areas that we have in common can be traced back to our both having been satirists in the 'sixties: the attack on establishment individuals, the anger at being in a society which is declining. In my appreciation of history, some societies have declined even though the forces did exist within them that could have regenerated them. In our society now the progressive forces exist, the analysis of the problems exists, but for historical reasons it is difficult to assemble the opposition. That's why I'm a pessimist in political terms. Brenton has the same fury.

Your characters are full of despair, or apathy, or ready to compromise at the drop of a hat.

Not at all. That is a description of the political people, the office-holders, the Staggs, Clapcotts, and so on. They are compromisers, but others are not: McPhee, Old Biledew, Gocher, even Fricker, cling desperately to their truth. Erica, Finney in *Birth on a Hard Shoulder*, are deeply principled. What I do rarely show is the bold, confident projection of left-wing ideology, flashed at an audience in the expectation of instant support. There are no guerillas in my plays. There are the expedient and the resisters, and always a tremendous presence of pain, even in the eventual capitulation. Jardine in *Hang* cheats at the end, but is a great sufferer. What I celebrate is energy and the small discovery of dignity. I think that is socialist. From confronting the pessimism comes the will to change. I think if my work does anything it forces a changed perception, even reluctantly. And it does this by refusing the expectation at every turn.

Index